"SERIOUSLY, NOW..."

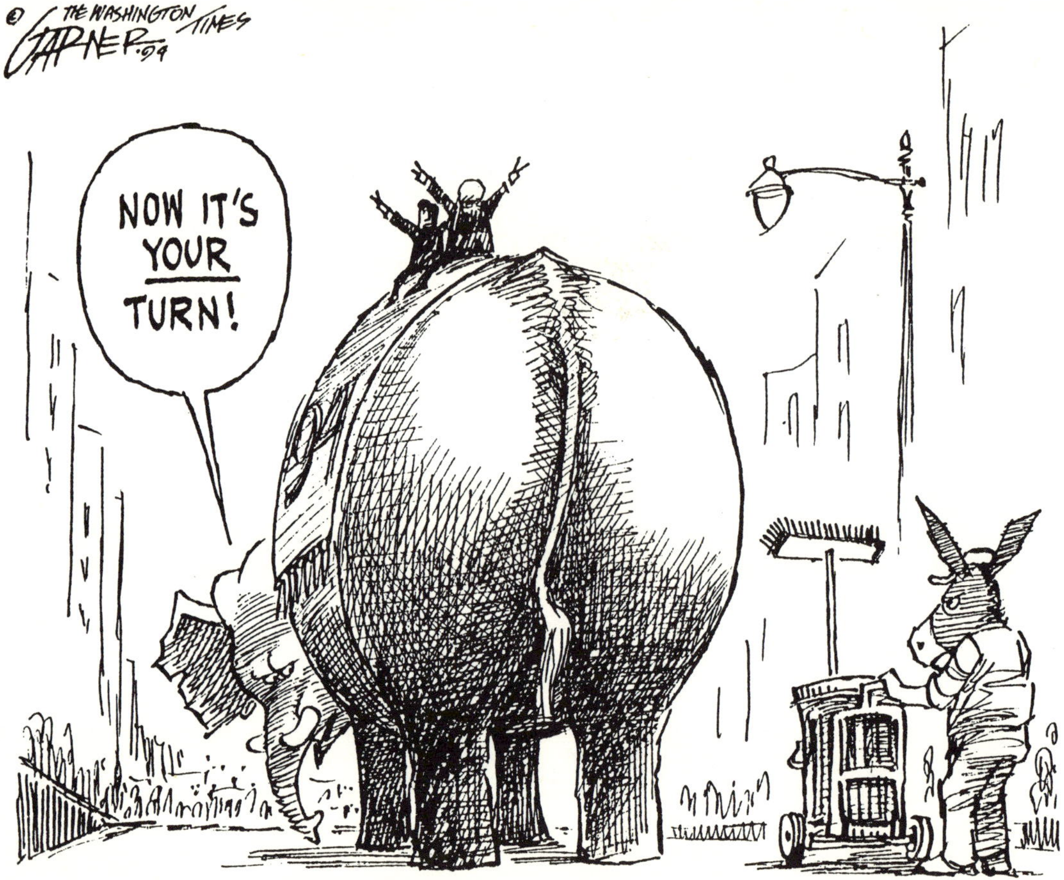
© THE WASHINGTON TIMES
GARNER '94
NOW IT'S YOUR TURN!

"SERIOUSLY, NOW..."

Bill Garner

Foreword by Tod Lindberg

Paul, my dear friend – Here's your very own book, just in case Lulu throws hers away for being too far right for her taste.
— Bill

PELICAN PUBLISHING COMPANY
Gretna 1995

Copyright © 1995
By *The Washington Times*
All rights reserved

To Patty

Thanks to my mentor, Gib Crockett; to the following editors: Newbold Noyes, the late Michael Grehl, the late Anne Crutcher, Woody West, Tony Snow, Tod Lindberg; and a very special thanks to Smith Hempstone, whose help and encouragement got me started on this wild and happy journey

Cartoons reprinted by arrangement with The Washington Times

The word "Pelican" and the depiction of a pelican are trademarks of Pelican Publishing Company, Inc., and are registered in the U.S. Patent and Trademark Office.

Manufactured in the United States of America
Published by Pelican Publishing Company, Inc.
1101 Monroe Street, Gretna, Louisiana 70053

Contents

Foreword 6
Bush 9
Congress 15
The Economy 23
'92 Election 29
The Moscow/Berlin Connection 43
Clinton 51
Hillary 63
Whitewater 71
Foreign Affairs 77
The Media 97
The Military 105
D.C. 111
OJ 117
Sports 123
'94 Election 131
. . . and Other Issues 139

Foreword

It's a long story, the story of the time we published a Bill Garner caricature of the two of us, Bill and Tod, on the editorial page of *The Washington Times*. It was my idea, I'll admit, and if you want to think the worst of me for the sheer vanity of commissioning a cartoon depicting myself and publishing it on my page in the newspaper, I can't blame you. But like sleazy Hollywood starlets who say they only do full frontal nudity and numerous sex scenes when those are essential to the plot, I have an explanation.

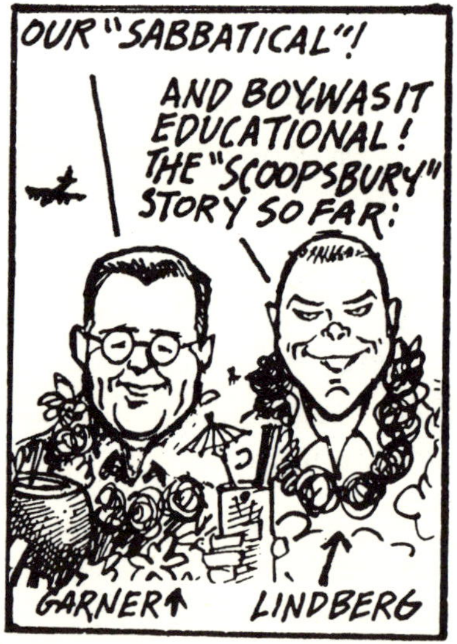

OUR "SABBATICAL"!
AND BOY, WAS IT EDUCATIONAL! THE "SCOOPSBURY" STORY SO FAR:
GARNER
LINDBERG

We were doing this parody series of an Extremely Famous comic-strip artist who specializes in political topics. Extremely Famous has a record of taking extensive time off from the strip every now and again. Extremely Famous also has a record of calling his long vacations "sabbaticals." Very fancy term, that. So when a long-scheduled vacation of Bill's was going to interrupt our series midway through for a week, we decided we'd just run a little line in the paper the week Bill was gone announcing that we were "on sabbatical." And when he got back, that was when we'd run the caricature of our very own selves as we recapped "the story so far."

In other words, I didn't really have a choice. I had to commission a cartoon of myself. It was essential to the plot.

So off Bill went to draw. And back came Bill with the 'toon. My first reaction was poker-faced shock.

"Ouch!" said I to myself. "I do not look like that. I do not in any way resemble this smirking, corpulent, semi-Oriental weenie of Bill Garner's imaginings." But, of course, I do. It's all there, right in my very own face—or your face—just waiting for some wise-guy cartoonist like Bill Garner to tease it out.

You may wonder what the real Bill Garner looks like. The answer is that he actually does look like that drawing of himself. My friend and former colleague Richard Starr took a look at that 'toon of Bill and me and said he didn't believe he'd ever seen such a kind Garner rendering of the subject of a Garner cartoon as this very drawing that Bill Garner had just done of himself.

This is not to say that there is a self-serious bone in Bill's body. He's a kid on a trike with a slingshot and a peashooter—always has been, always will be. He told me how old he is once, but I forget. A lot older than he looks or acts, this is certain. In the winter, when the grandkids are around and there's snow, he likes to hook up the sled to the back of his four-wheel drive and take them for a ride. He'd be just as happy riding in the sled, of course, but that will have to wait until the grandkids are old enough to drive.

I often find him leaning against the waist-high rail of the mezzanine of *The Times,* which overlooks the hundred and some desks of the newsroom below and, beyond that, through a two-story glass wall, the stunningly beautiful National Arboretum. Sometimes Bill's got a distant expression on his face. The big smile always comes up the second he sees you and calls, "Hey, chief," in that fabulous Texas voice I can only describe as a rapid-fire drawl. But I don't think his fleeting distant look is a product of staring mesmerized at the trees. Oh, no. That look means, I think, that with all the good humor in the world, Bill Garner is about to skewer someone.

As my friend Richard said to me the day he saw the caricature, "I never noticed before that you look a little bit Chinese."

Now, of course, Bill has drawn me exactly once (that I know of—oh, mercy, what if there are more somewhere?) whereas he has drawn, say, Bill Clinton and George Bush doing silly things hundreds of times apiece. And yet I feel a bond even with presidents and potentates, for I, too, have felt the sting of the India ink on the nub of the pen in the hand of the master.

And he was being *nice* to me.

TOD LINDBERG
Editorial-Page Editor,
The Washington Times

Bush

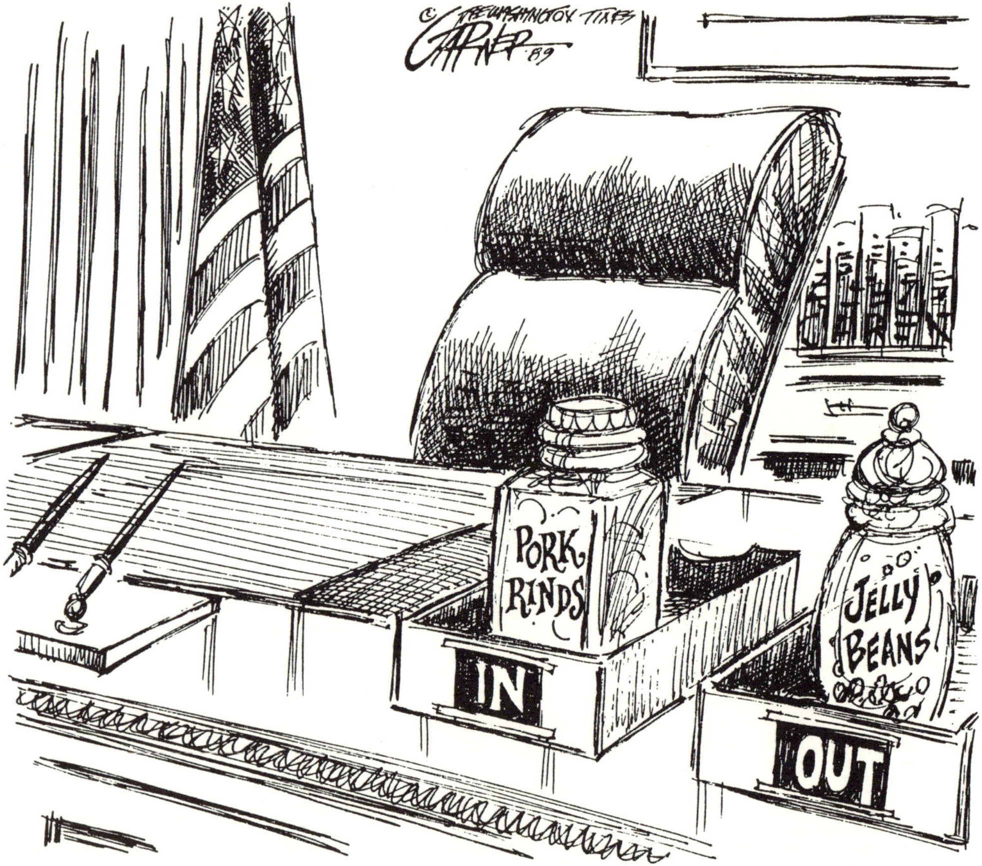
© THE WASHINGTON TIMES
GARNER '89
PORK RINDS
IN
JELLY BEANS
OUT

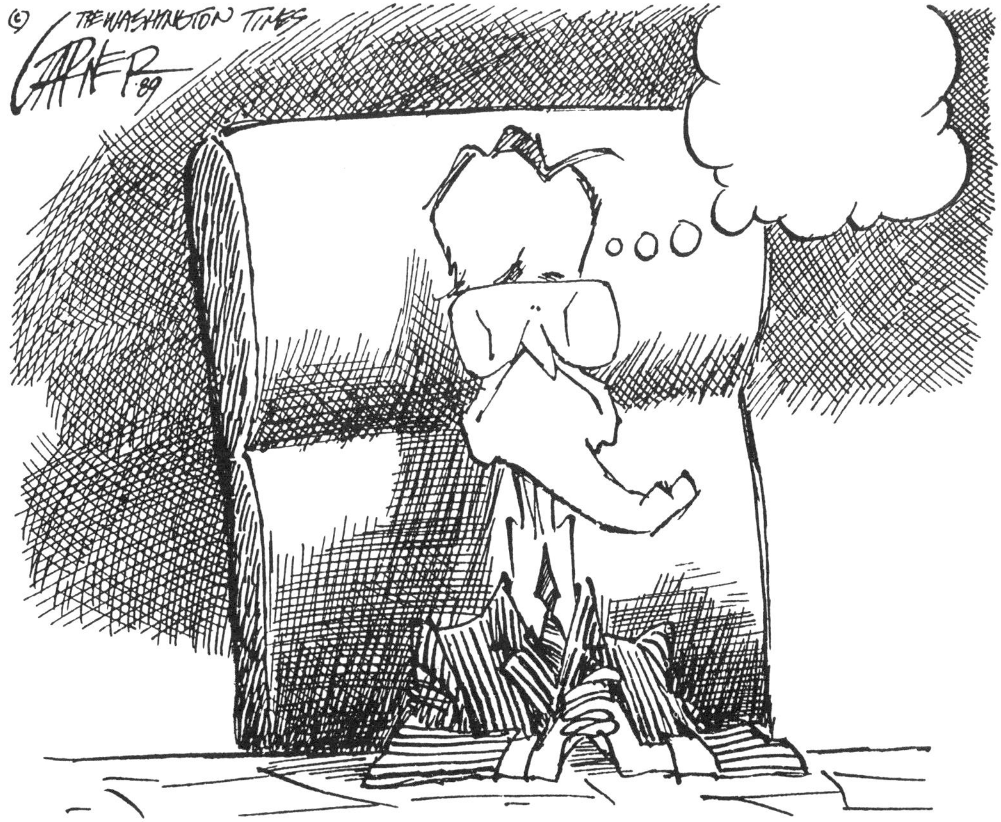
© THE WASHINGTON TIMES

THE PRESIDENT'S LATEST TAX POLICY

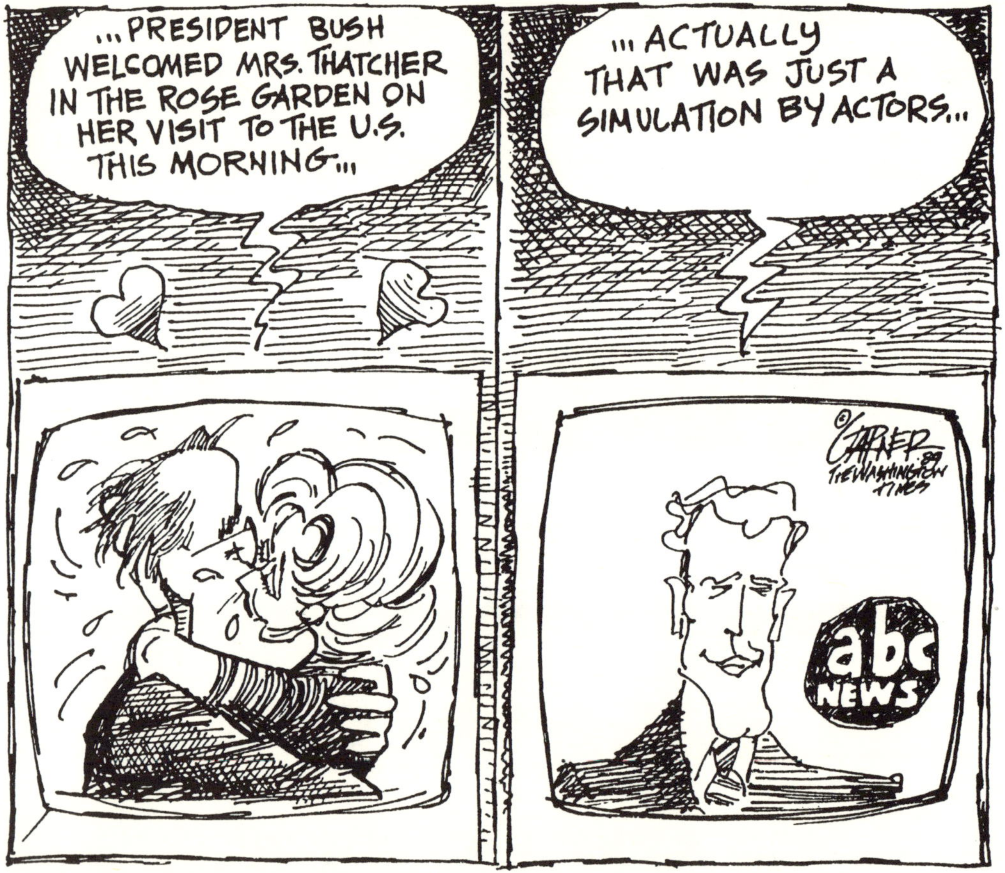

...PRESIDENT BUSH WELCOMED MRS. THATCHER IN THE ROSE GARDEN ON HER VISIT TO THE U.S. THIS MORNING...
...ACTUALLY THAT WAS JUST A SIMULATION BY ACTORS...
© GARNER '89 THE WASHINGTON TIMES
abc NEWS

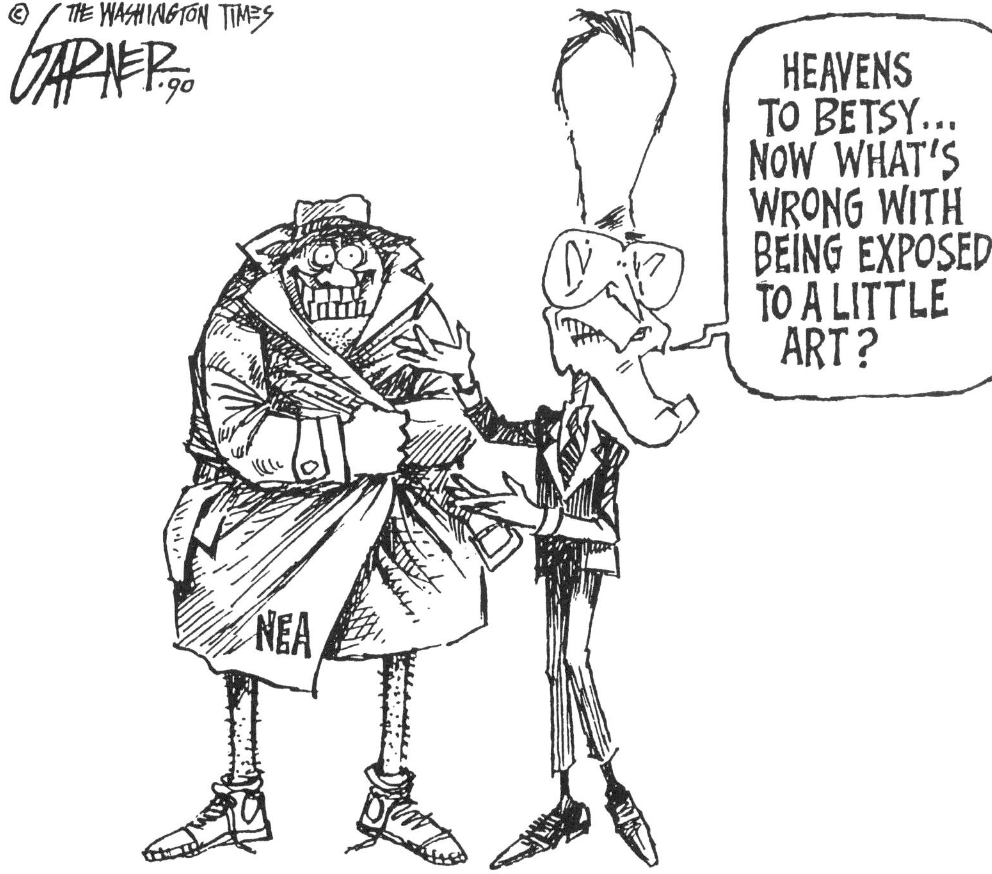
© THE WASHINGTON TIMES
GARNER '90
HEAVENS TO BETSY... NOW WHAT'S WRONG WITH BEING EXPOSED TO A LITTLE ART?
NEA

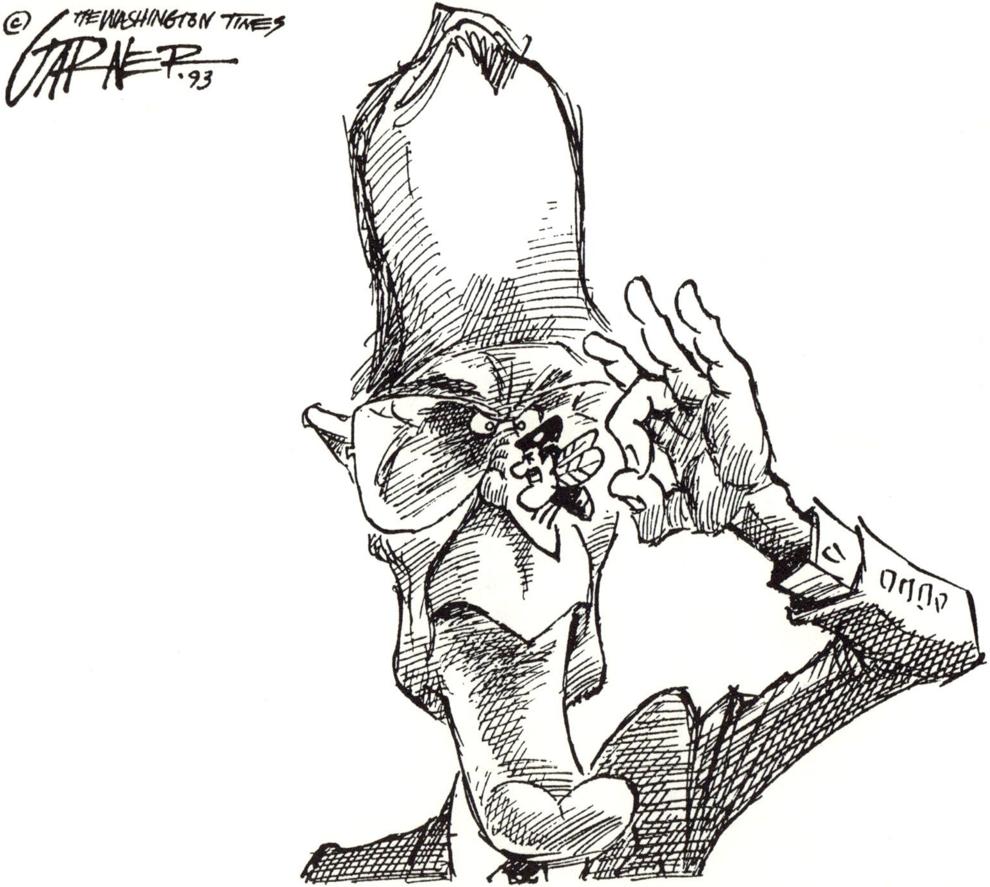
© THE WASHINGTON TIMES
GARNER '93

Congress

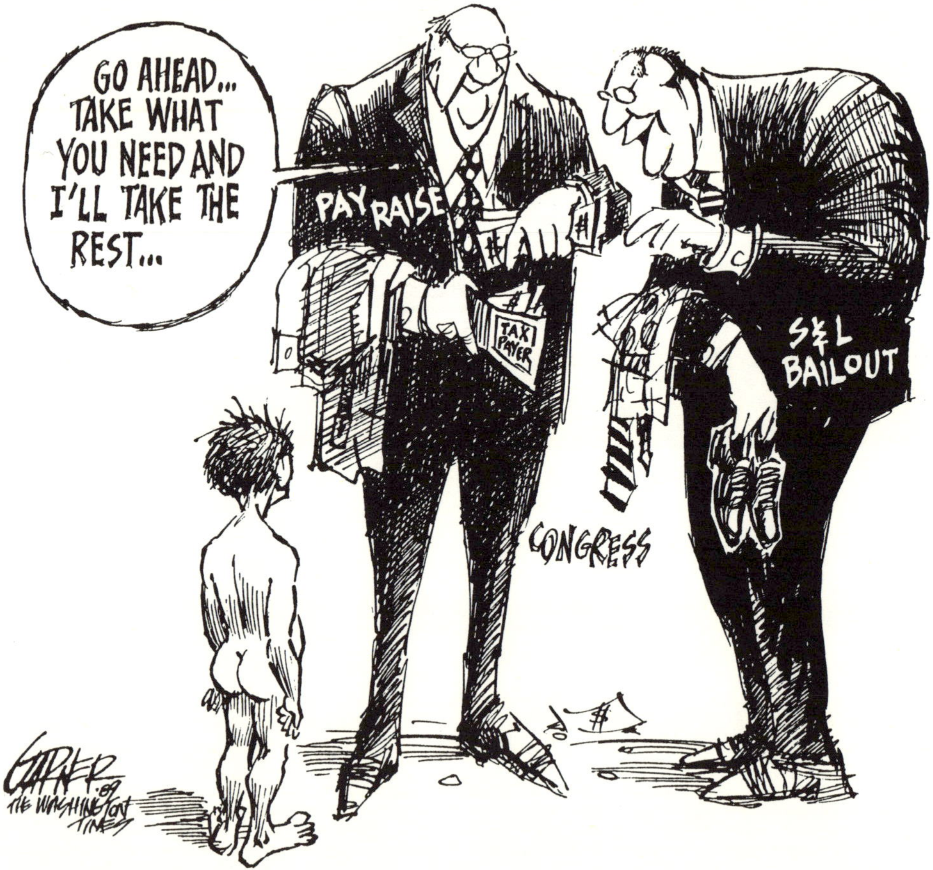
GO AHEAD... TAKE WHAT YOU NEED AND I'LL TAKE THE REST...
PAY RAISE
TAXPAYER
S&L BAILOUT
CONGRESS

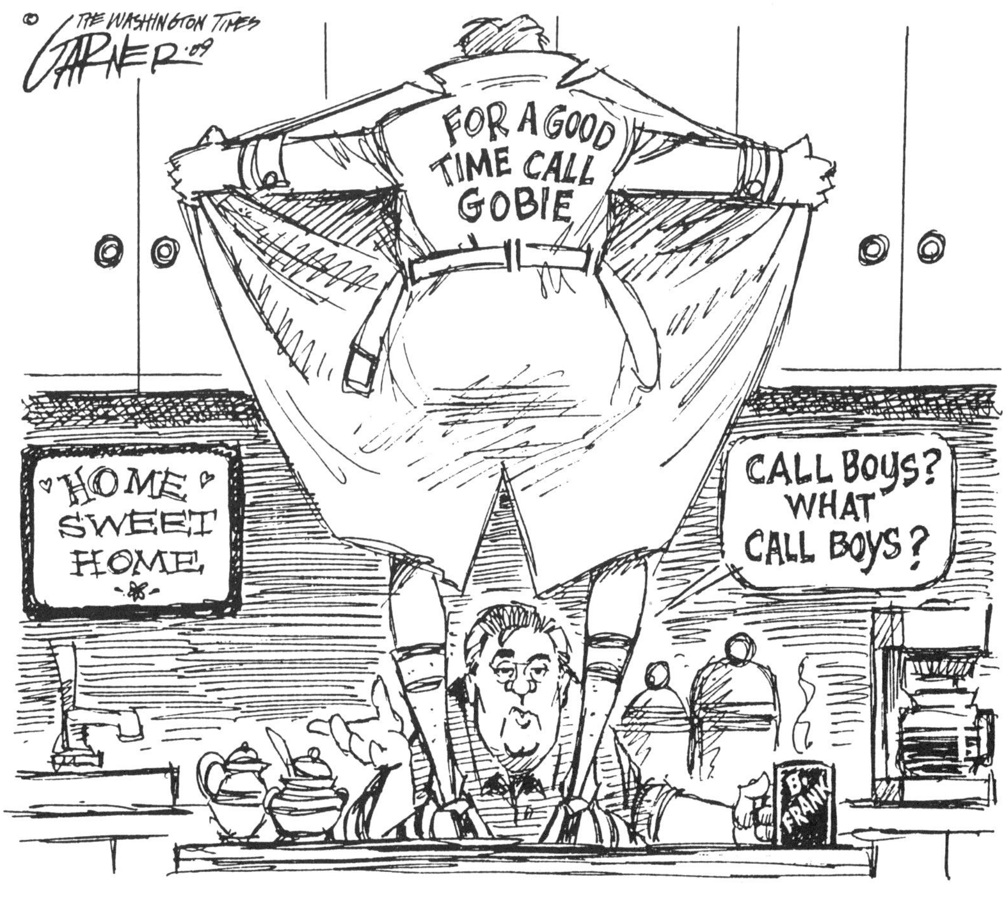
© THE WASHINGTON TIMES
GARNER '09
FOR A GOOD TIME CALL GOBIE
HOME SWEET HOME
CALL BOYS? WHAT CALL BOYS?
B. FRANK

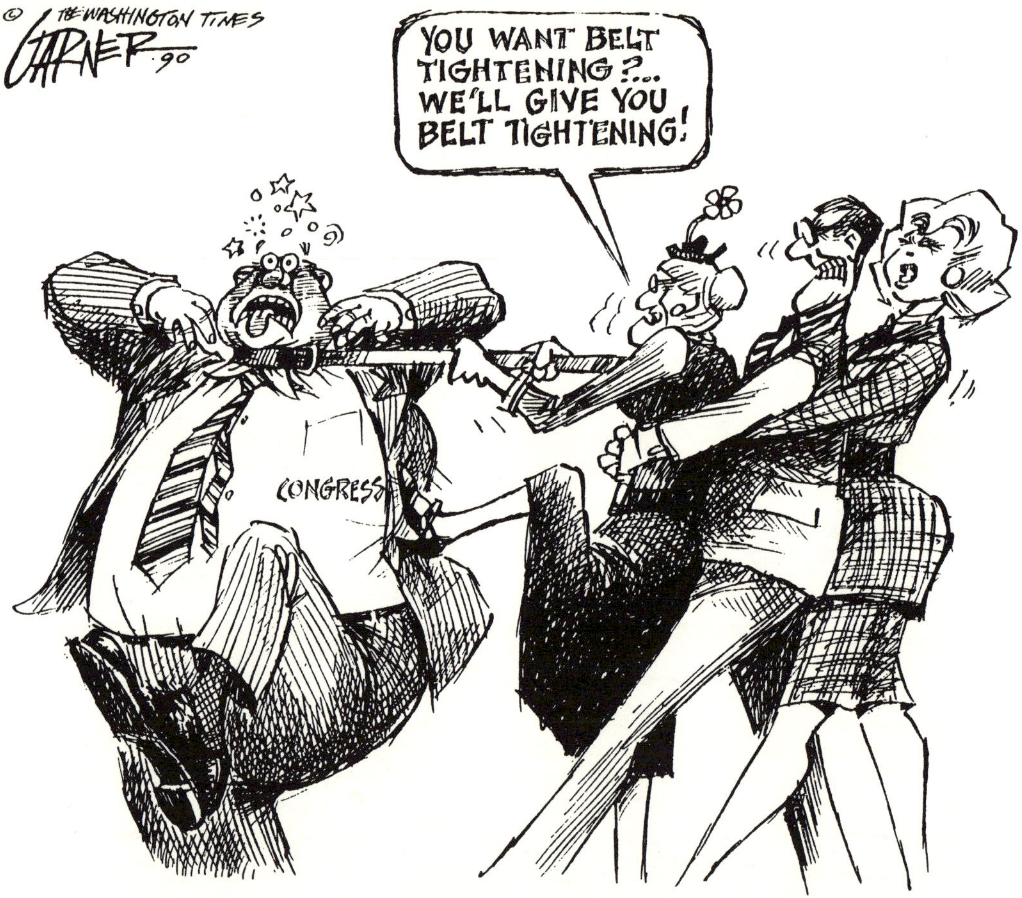
© THE WASHINGTON TIMES
GARNER '90
YOU WANT BELT TIGHTENING?... WE'LL GIVE YOU BELT TIGHTENING!
CONGRESS

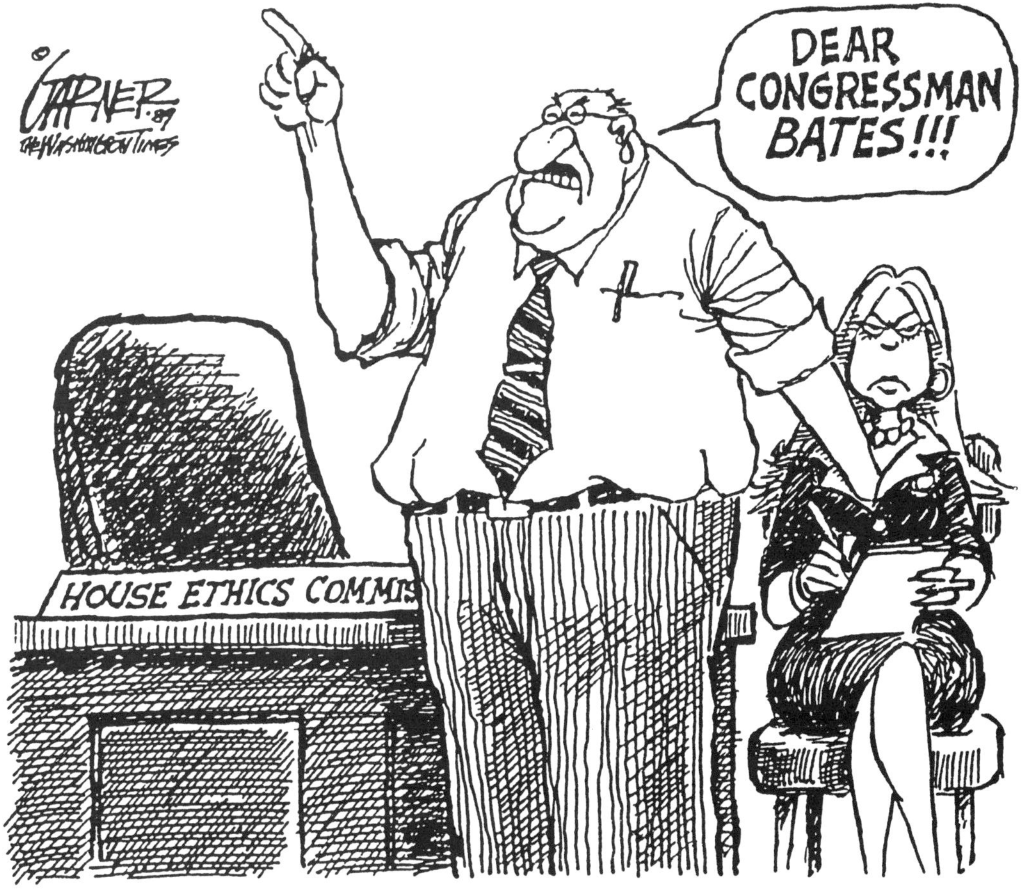
DEAR CONGRESSMAN BATES!!!
HOUSE ETHICS COMMIS

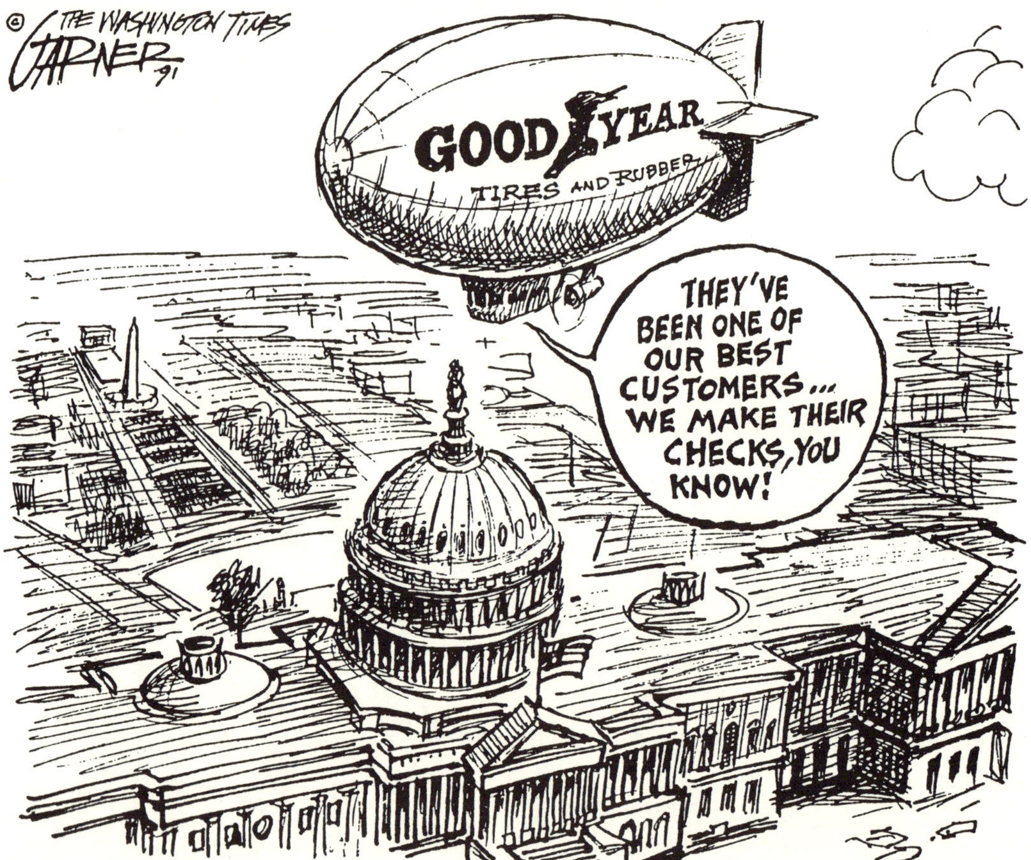
© THE WASHINGTON TIMES
GARNER '91
GOOD YEAR
TIRES AND RUBBER
THEY'VE BEEN ONE OF OUR BEST CUSTOMERS... WE MAKE THEIR CHECKS, YOU KNOW!

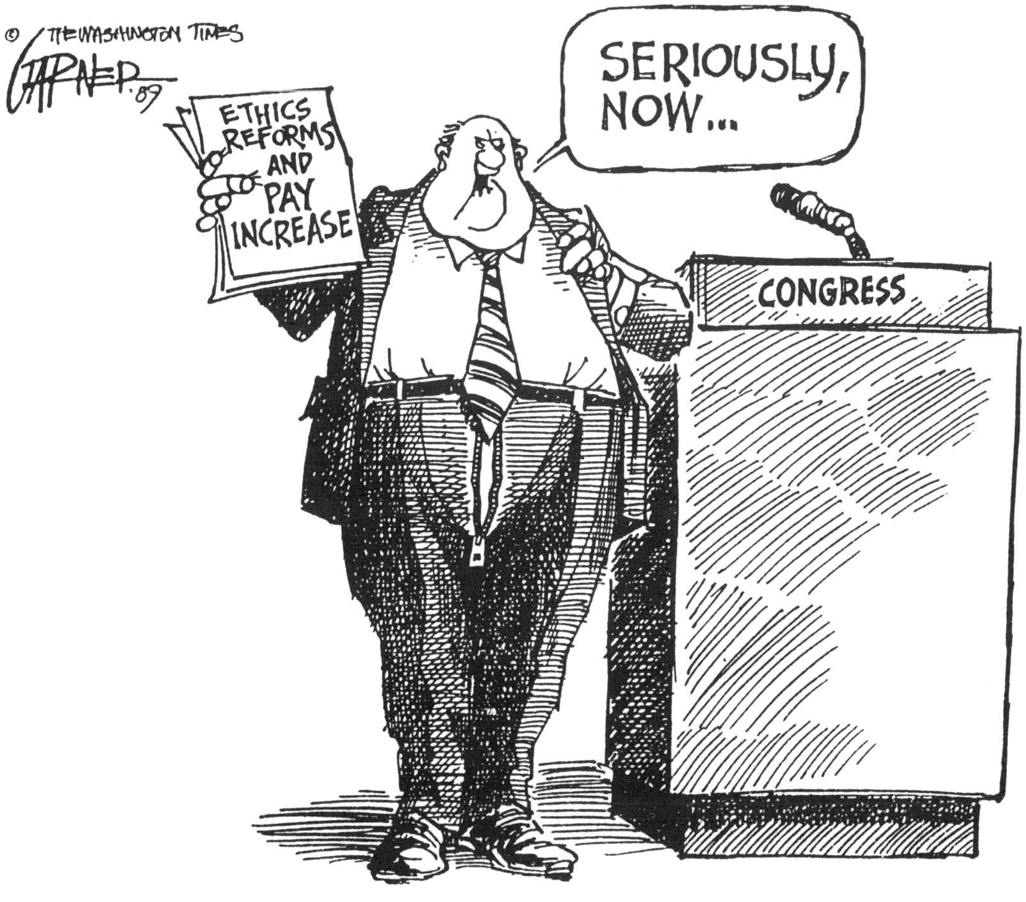
© THE WASHINGTON TIMES
GARNER '89
ETHICS REFORMS AND PAY INCREASE
SERIOUSLY, NOW...
CONGRESS

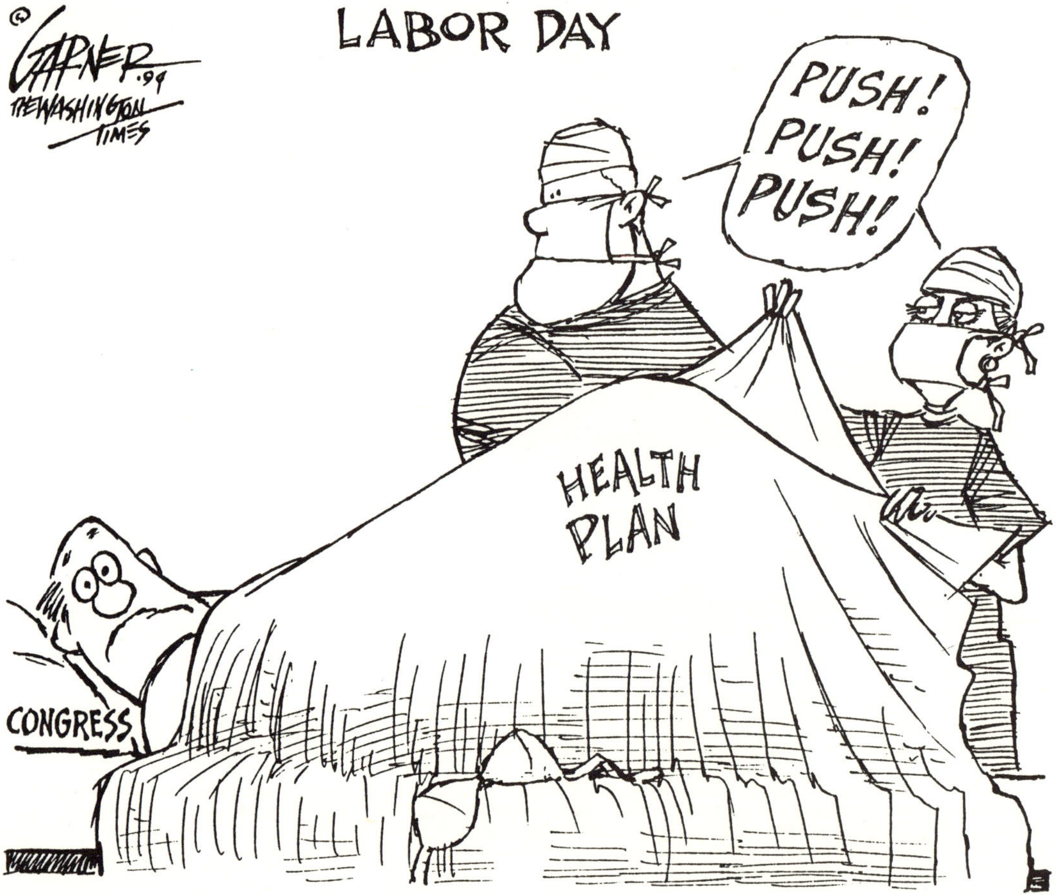
LABOR DAY
© GARNER '94 THE WASHINGTON TIMES
PUSH! PUSH! PUSH!
HEALTH PLAN
CONGRESS

The Economy

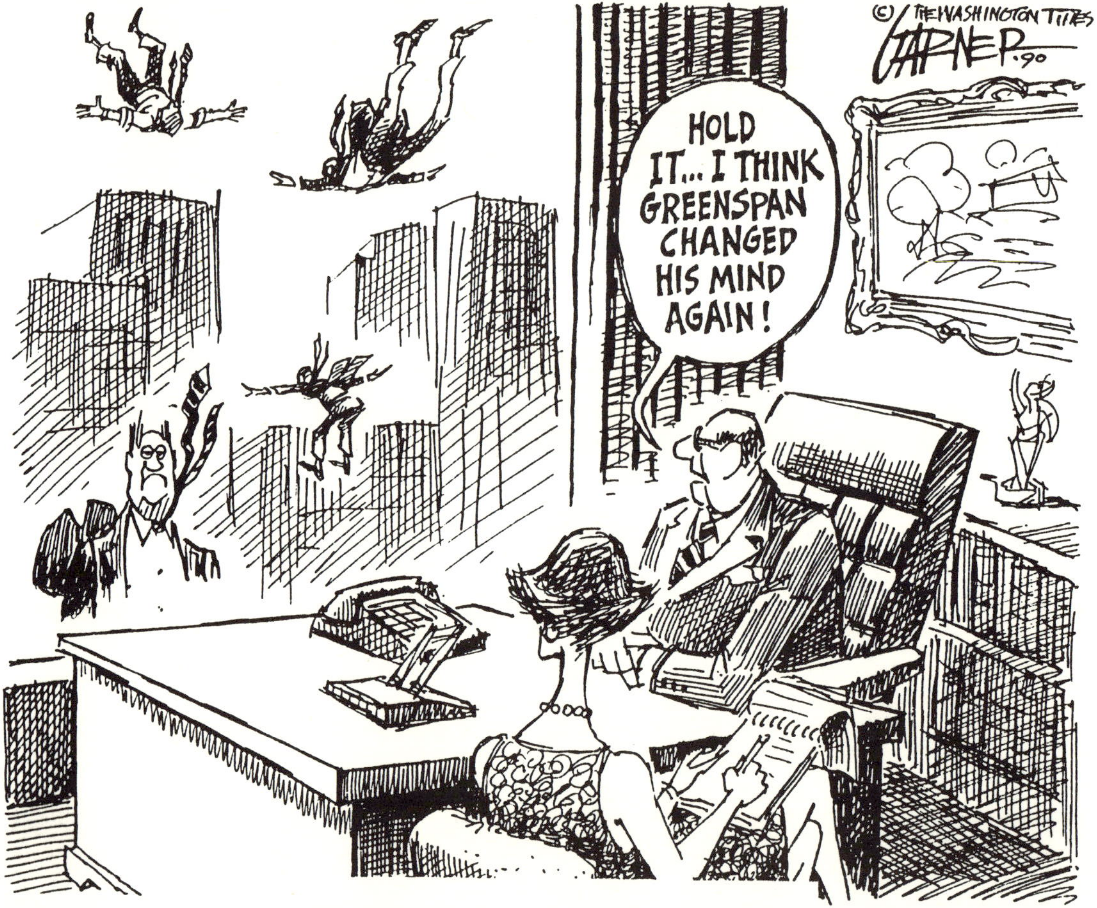
© THE WASHINGTON TIMES
GARNER '90
HOLD IT... I THINK GREENSPAN CHANGED HIS MIND AGAIN!

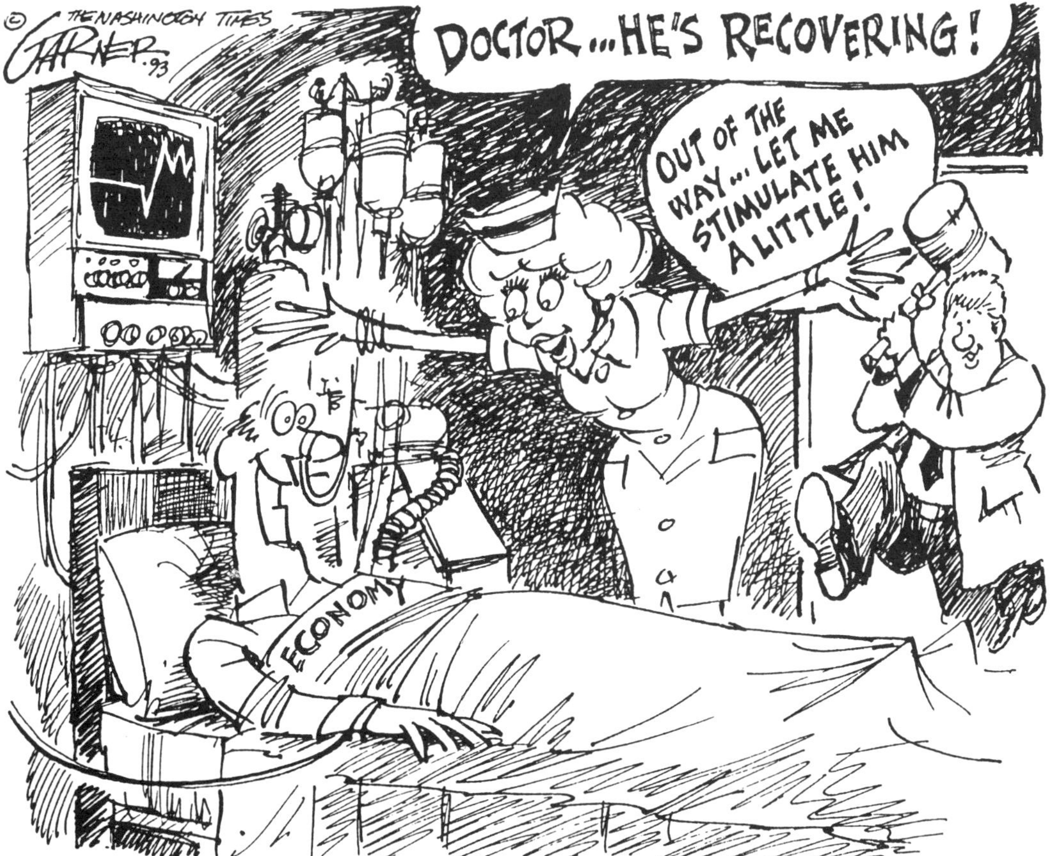
© THE WASHINGTON TIMES
GARNER '93
DOCTOR...HE'S RECOVERING!
OUT OF THE WAY... LET ME STIMULATE HIM A LITTLE!
ECONOMY

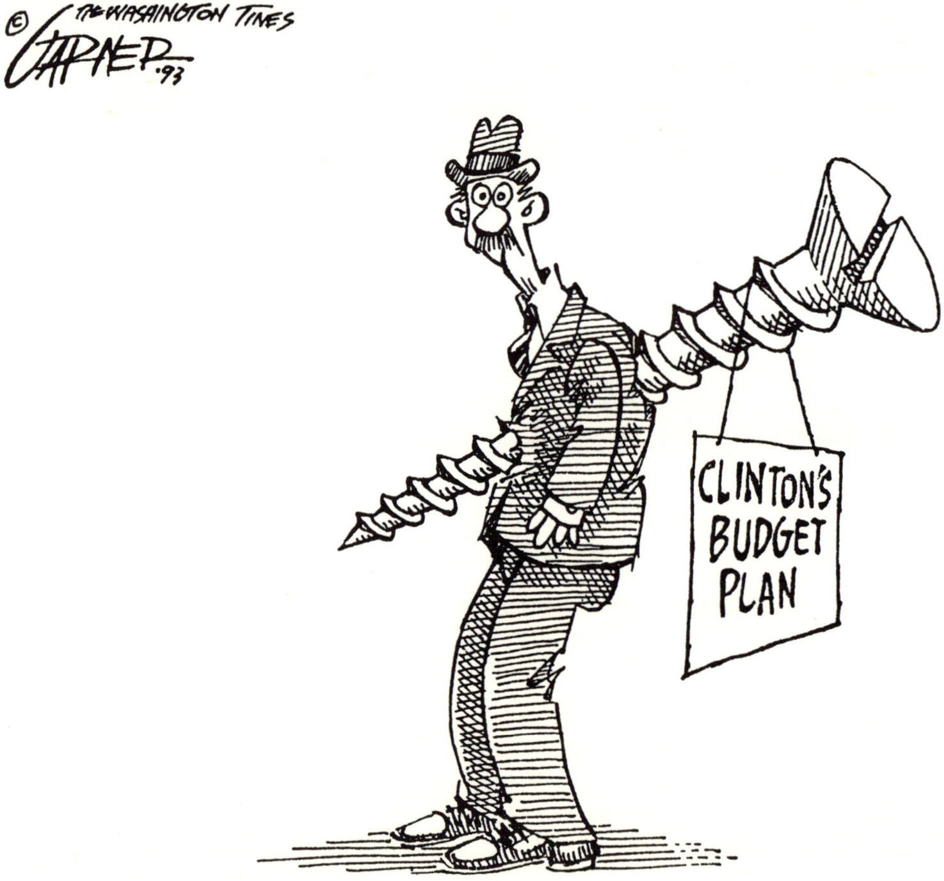
© THE WASHINGTON TIMES
GARNER '93
CLINTON'S BUDGET PLAN

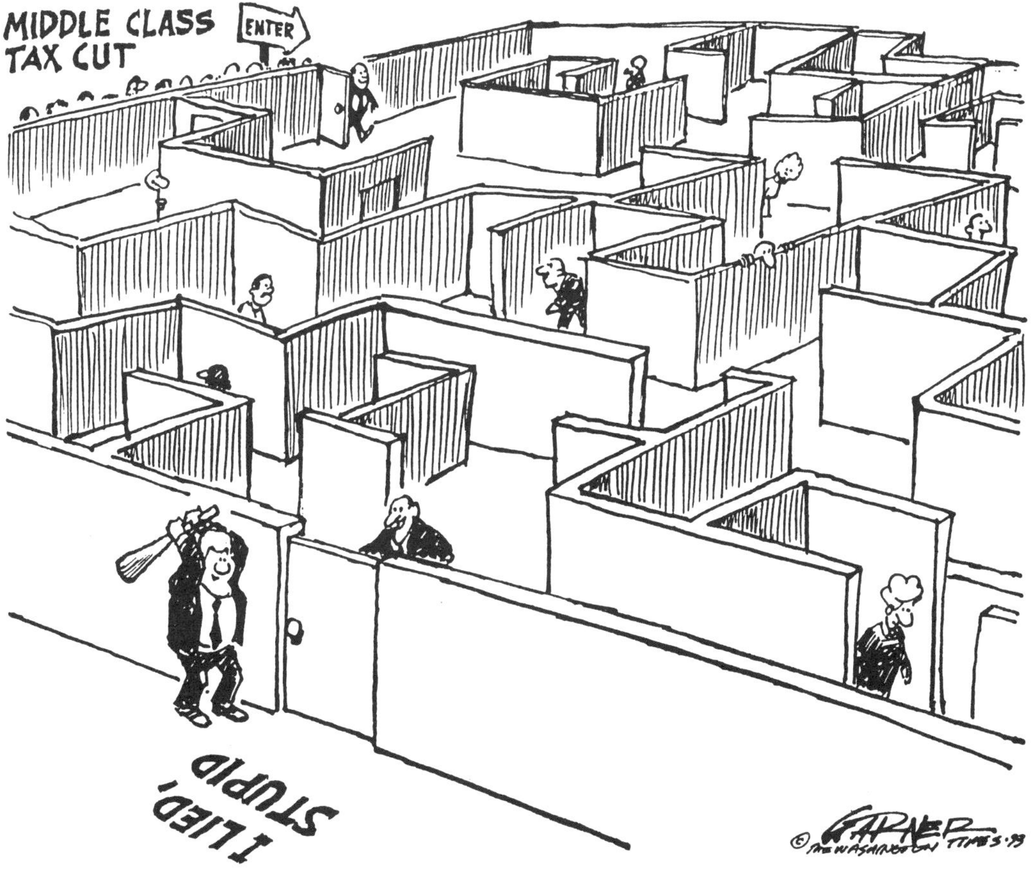
MIDDLE CLASS
TAX CUT
ENTER
I LIED,
STUPID
GARNER
© The Washington Times '93

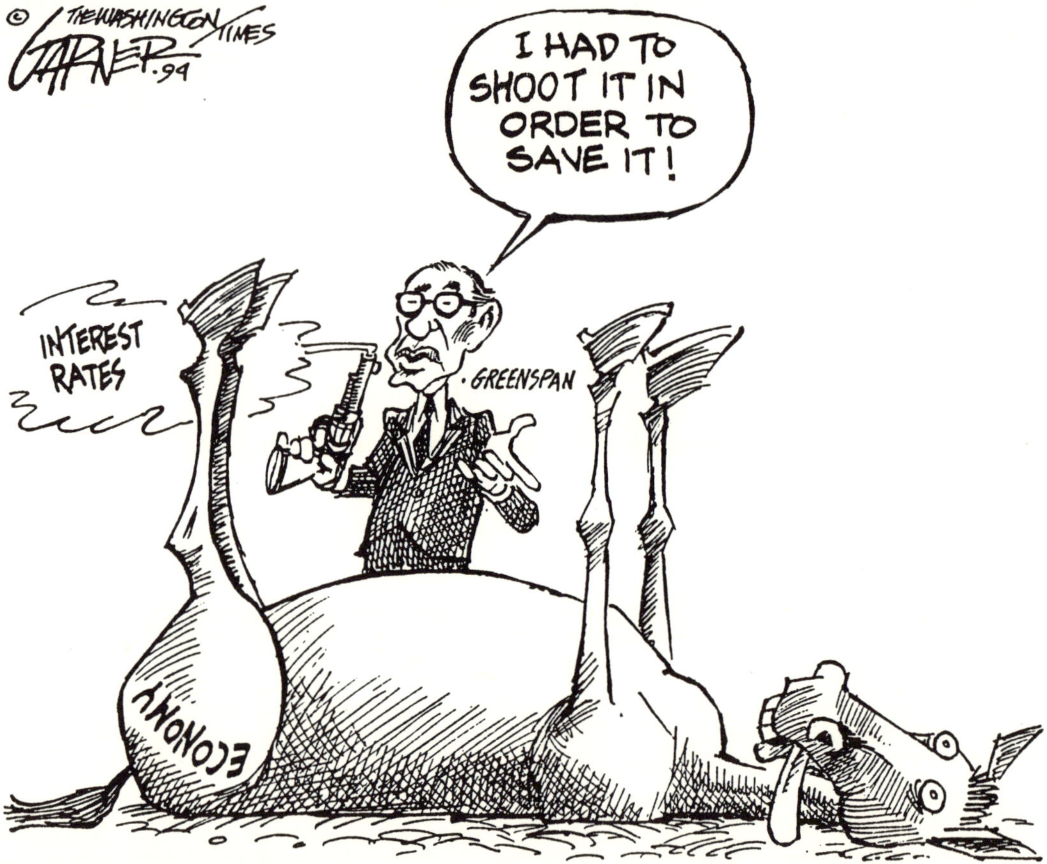

© THE WASHINGTON TIMES
GARNER '94
I HAD TO SHOOT IT IN ORDER TO SAVE IT!
INTEREST RATES
GREENSPAN
ECONOMY

'92 Election

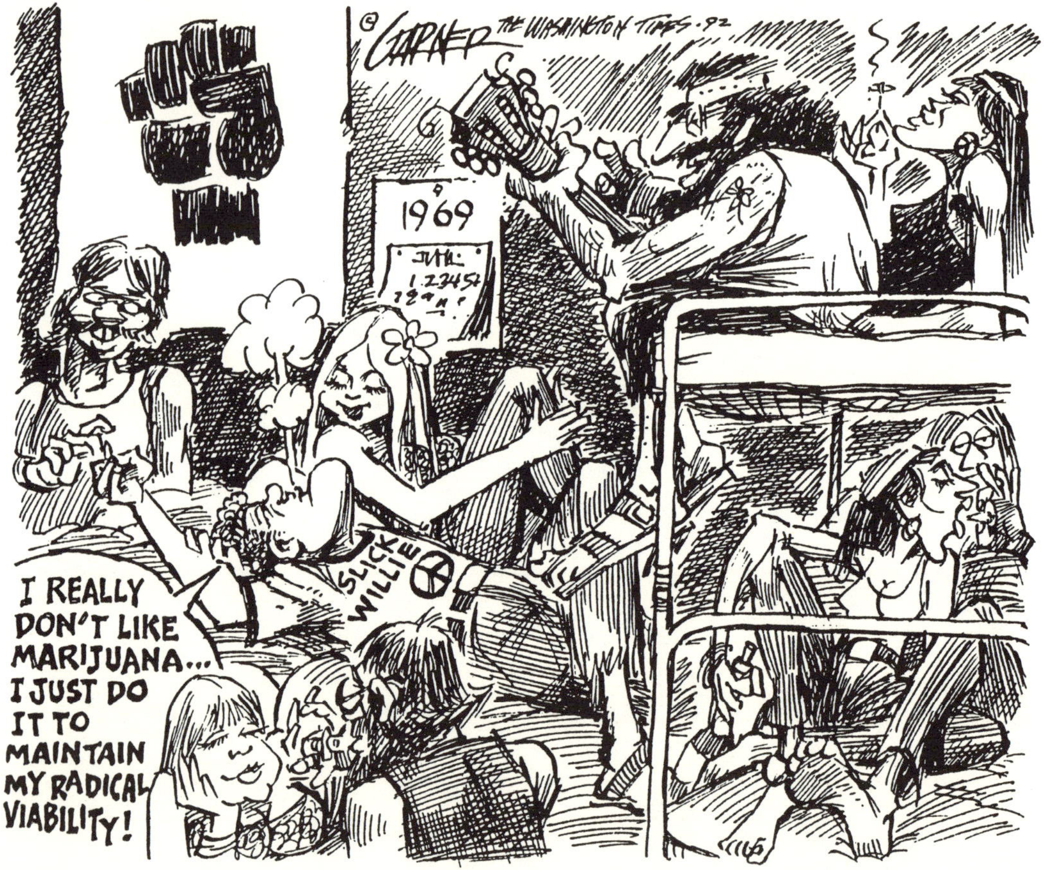
© GARNER THE WASHINGTON TIMES '92
1969
SLICK WILLIE
I REALLY DON'T LIKE MARIJUANA... I JUST DO IT TO MAINTAIN MY RADICAL VIABILITY!

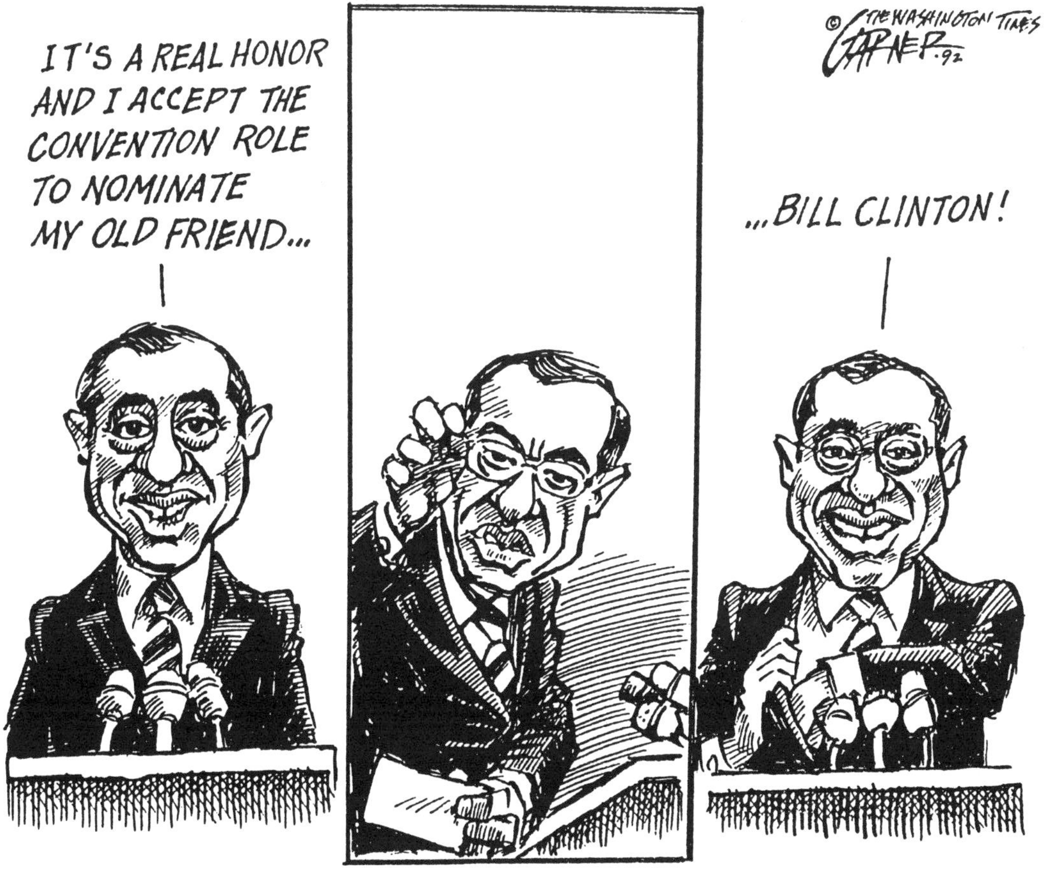
IT'S A REAL HONOR AND I ACCEPT THE CONVENTION ROLE TO NOMINATE MY OLD FRIEND...
...BILL CLINTON!
© THE WASHINGTON TIMES
GARNER '92

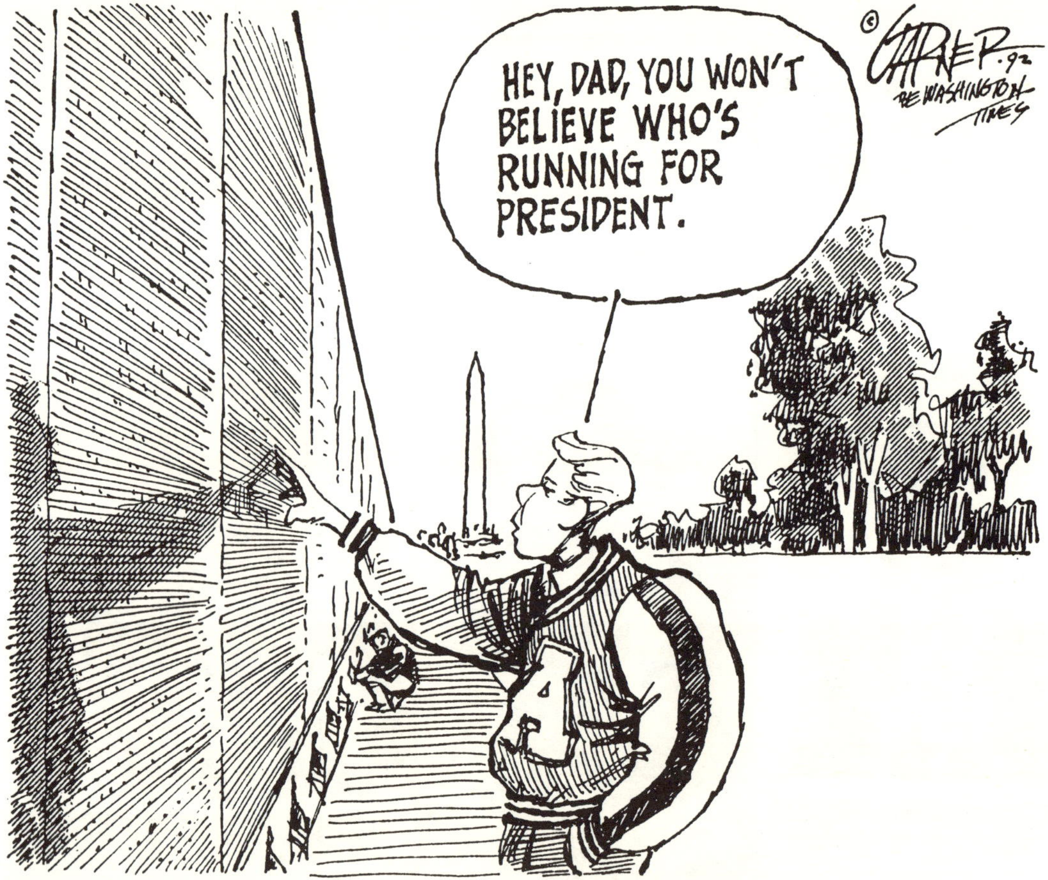
HEY, DAD, YOU WON'T BELIEVE WHO'S RUNNING FOR PRESIDENT.
© GARNER .92
THE WASHINGTON TIMES

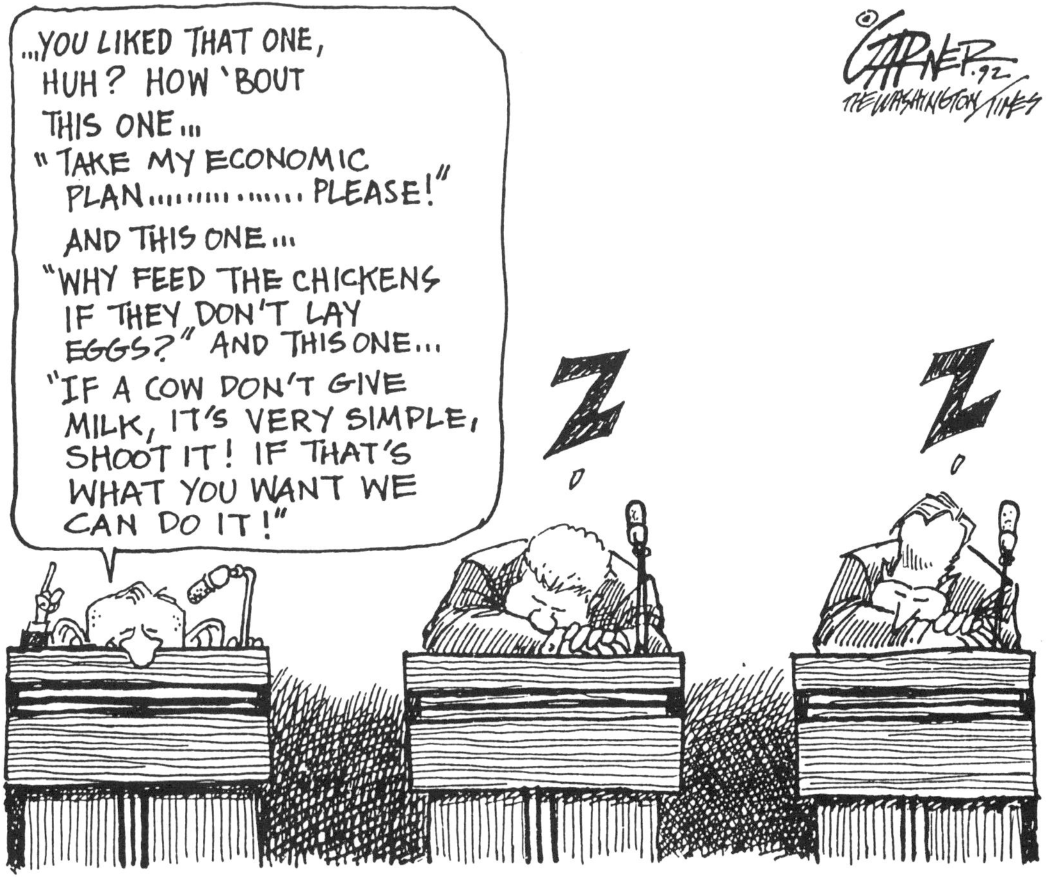
...YOU LIKED THAT ONE, HUH? HOW 'BOUT THIS ONE... "TAKE MY ECONOMIC PLAN.................. PLEASE!" AND THIS ONE... "WHY FEED THE CHICKENS IF THEY DON'T LAY EGGS?" AND THIS ONE... "IF A COW DON'T GIVE MILK, IT'S VERY SIMPLE, SHOOT IT! IF THAT'S WHAT YOU WANT WE CAN DO IT!"
Z
Z
© GARNER '92 THE WASHINGTON TIMES

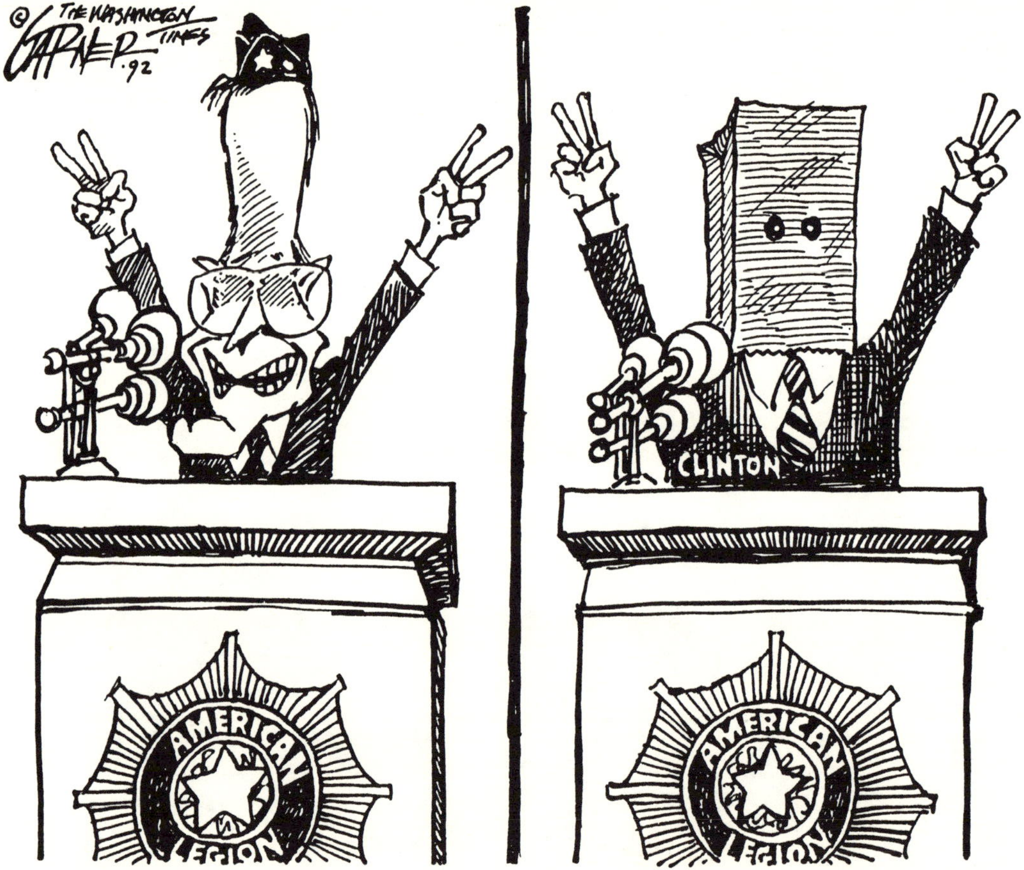
© THE WASHINGTON TIMES
GARNER '92
AMERICAN LEGION
CLINTON
AMERICAN LEGION

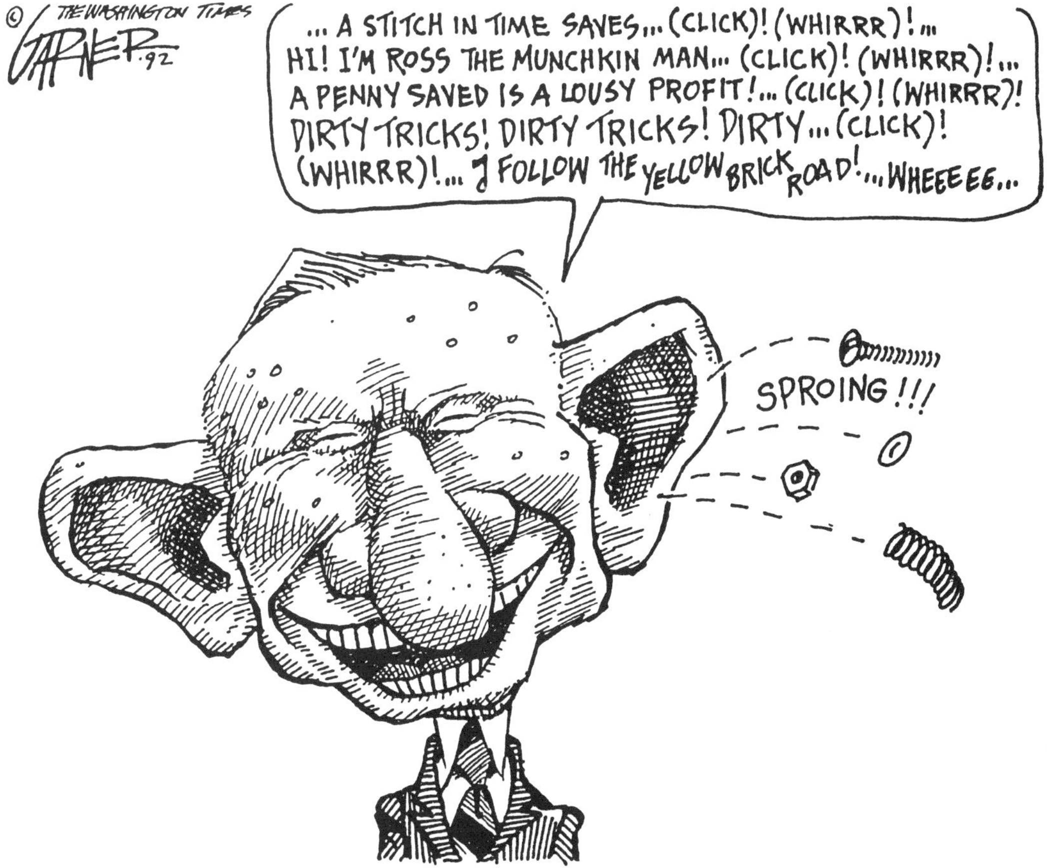
© THE WASHINGTON TIMES
GARNER '92
... A STITCH IN TIME SAVES... (CLICK)! (WHIRRR)!... HI! I'M ROSS THE MUNCHKIN MAN... (CLICK)! (WHIRRR)!... A PENNY SAVED IS A LOUSY PROFIT!... (CLICK)! (WHIRRR)! DIRTY TRICKS! DIRTY TRICKS! DIRTY... (CLICK)! (WHIRRR)!... ♪ FOLLOW THE YELLOW BRICK ROAD!... WHEEEEE...
SPROING!!!

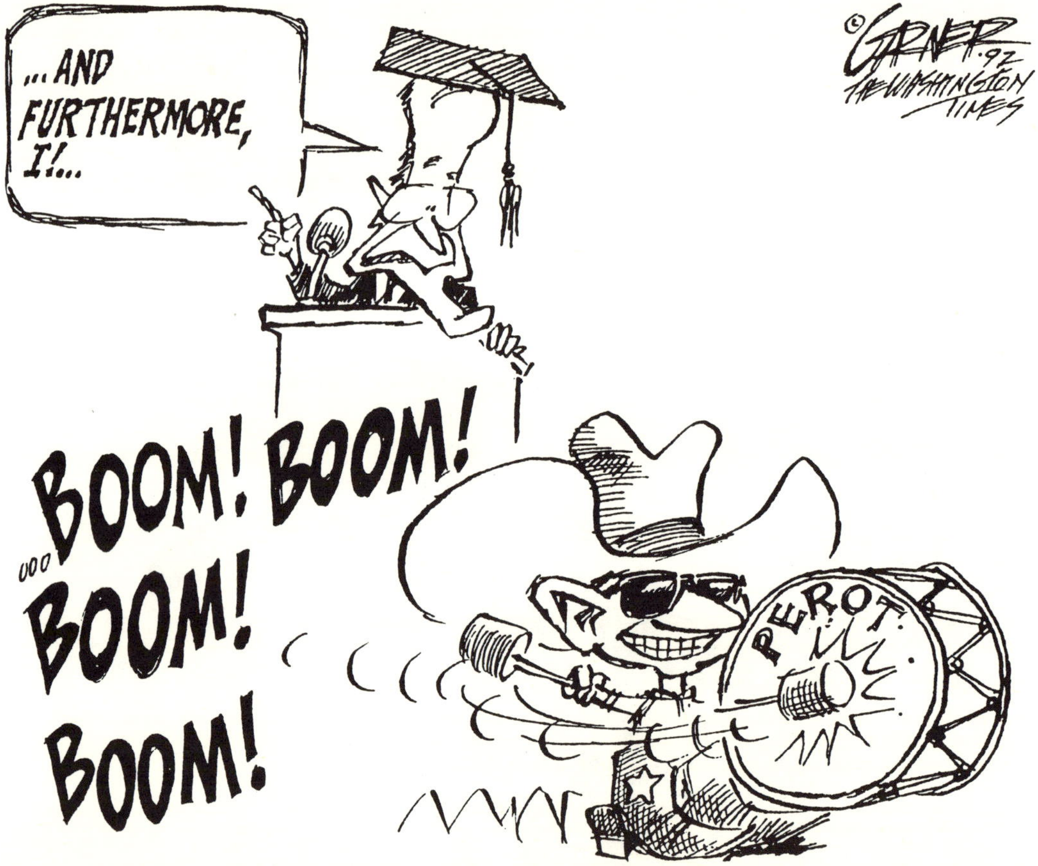

...AND FURTHERMORE, I!...
...BOOM! BOOM! BOOM! BOOM!
PEROT
© GARNER '92 THE WASHINGTON TIMES

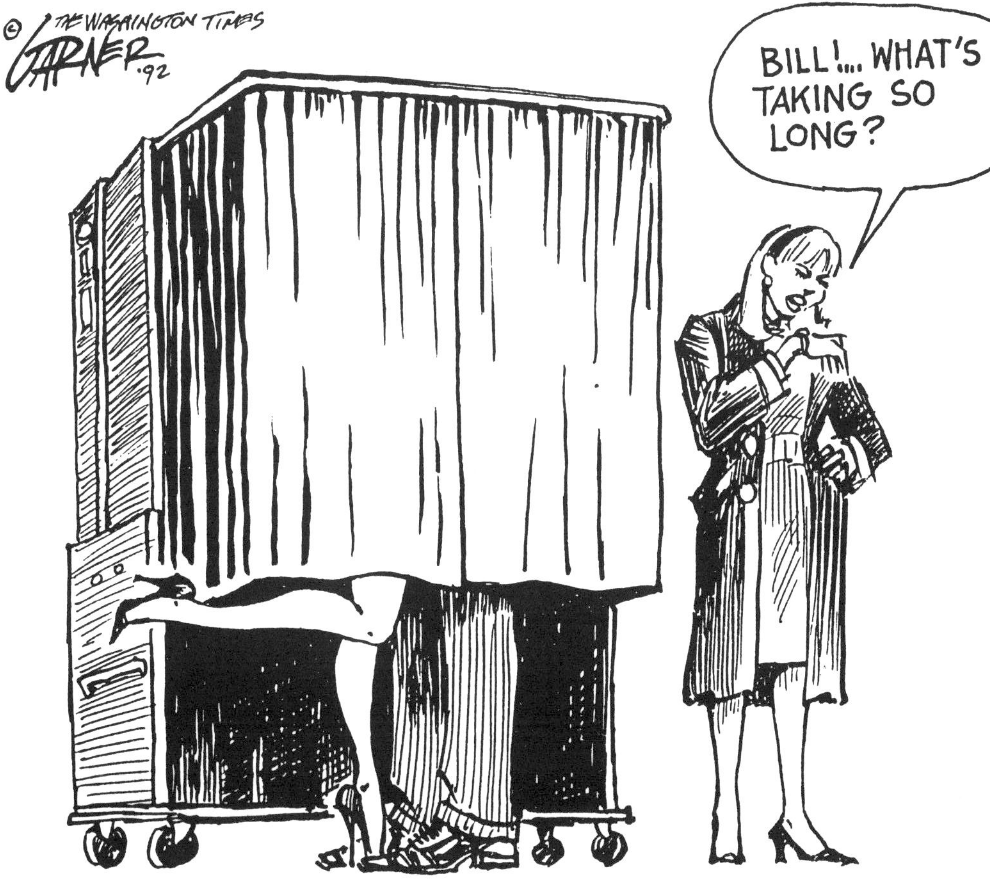
© THE WASHINGTON TIMES
GARNER '92
BILL!... WHAT'S TAKING SO LONG?

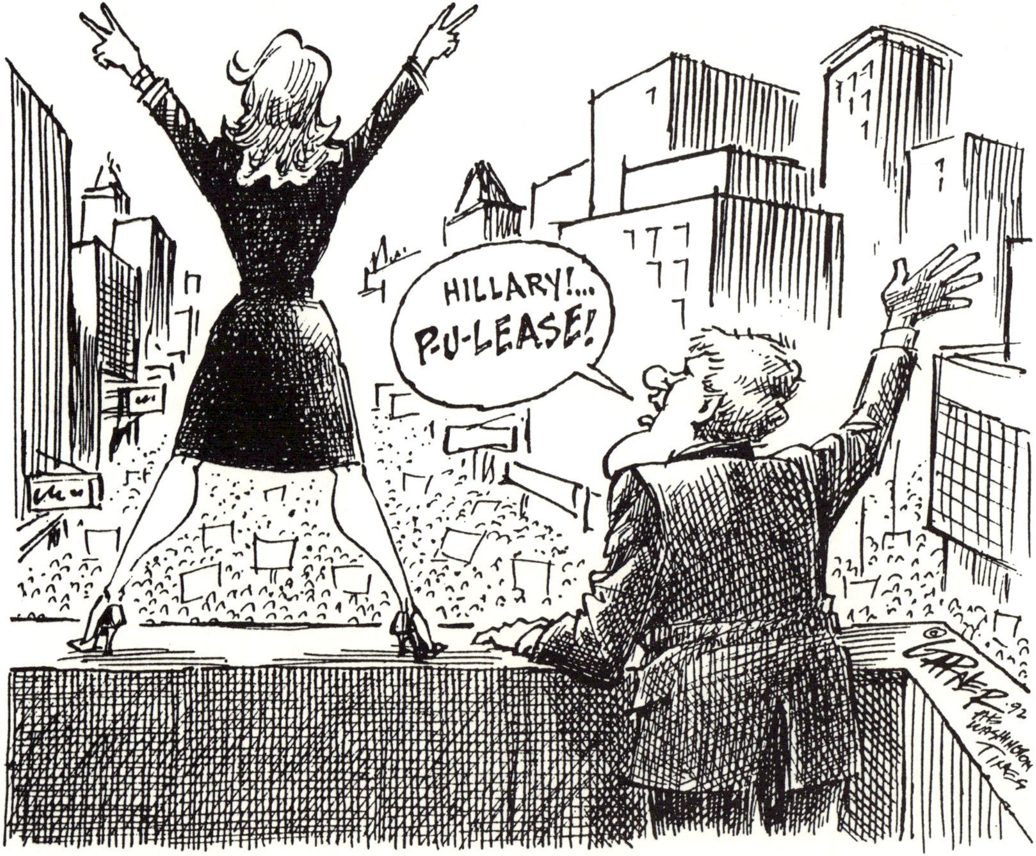
HILLARY!... P-U-LEASE!
© GARNER '92 THE WASHINGTON TIMES

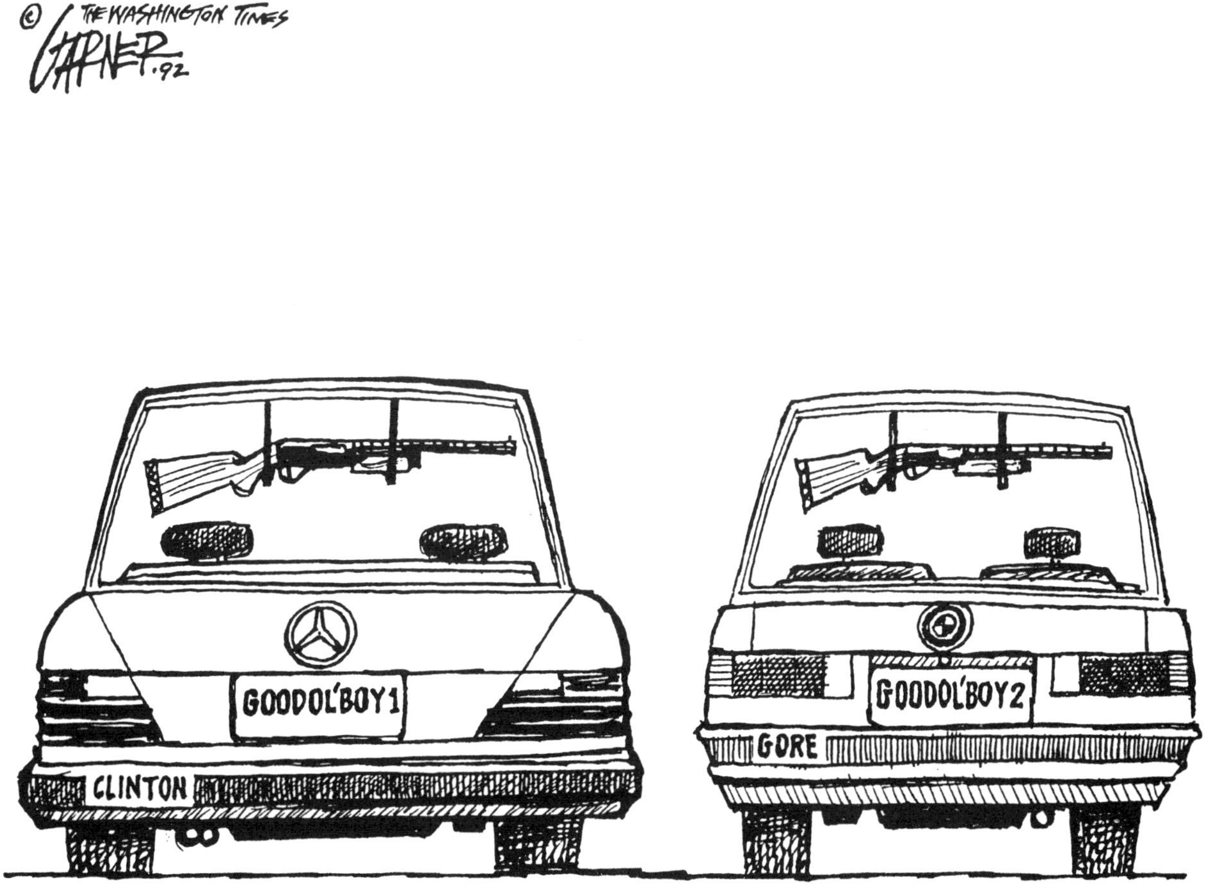
© THE WASHINGTON TIMES
GARNER '92
GOODOL'BOY1
CLINTON
GOODOL'BOY2
GORE

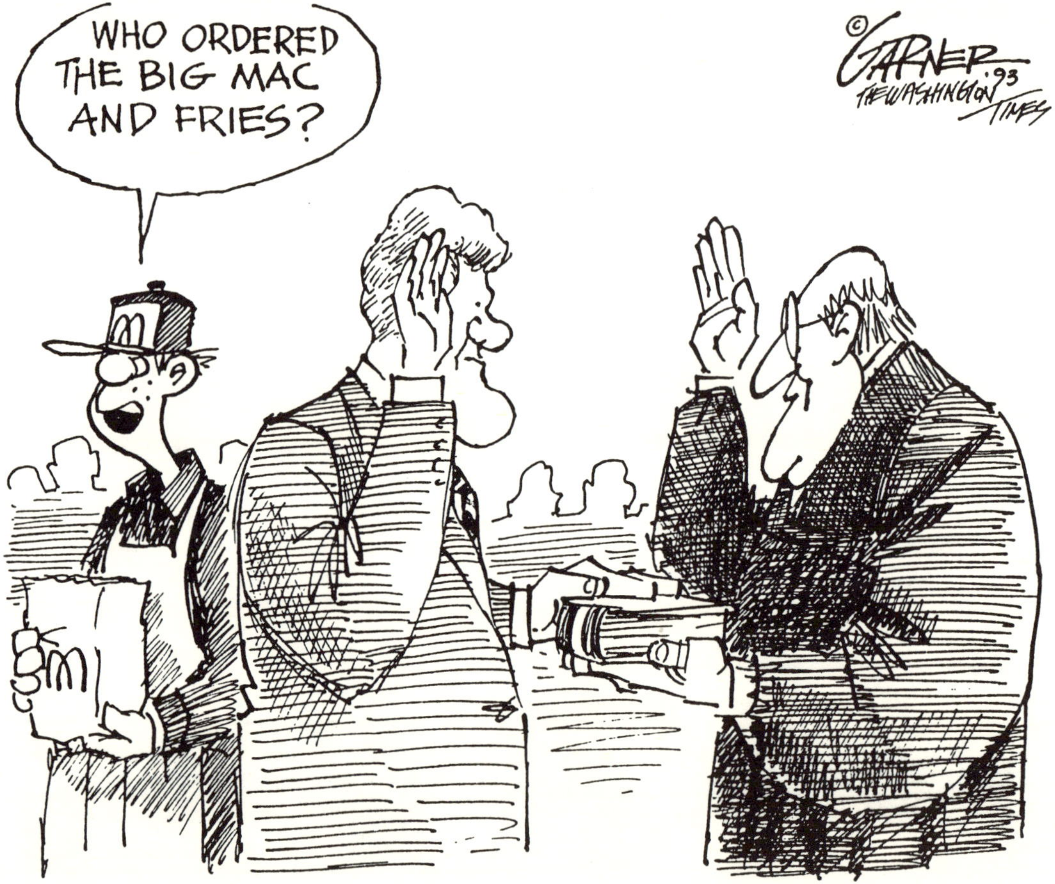
WHO ORDERED THE BIG MAC AND FRIES?
© GARNER '93 THE WASHINGTON TIMES

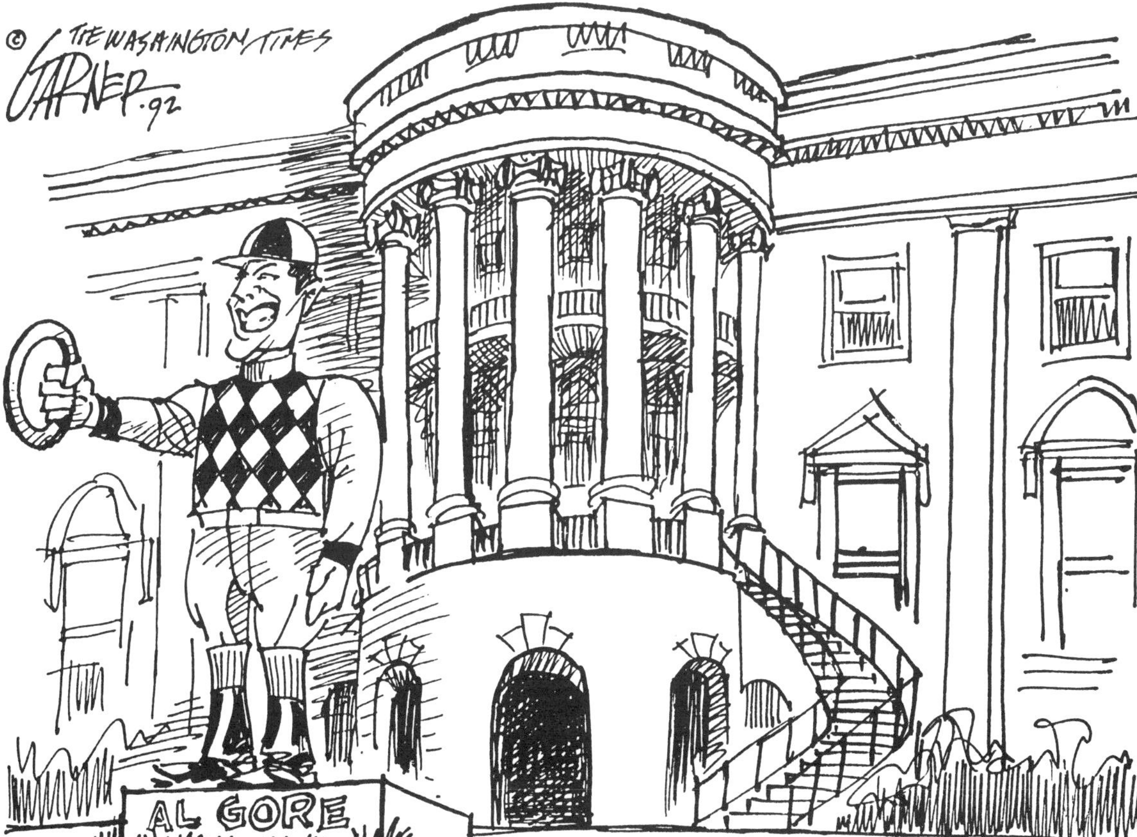
© THE WASHINGTON TIMES
GARNER '92
AL GORE

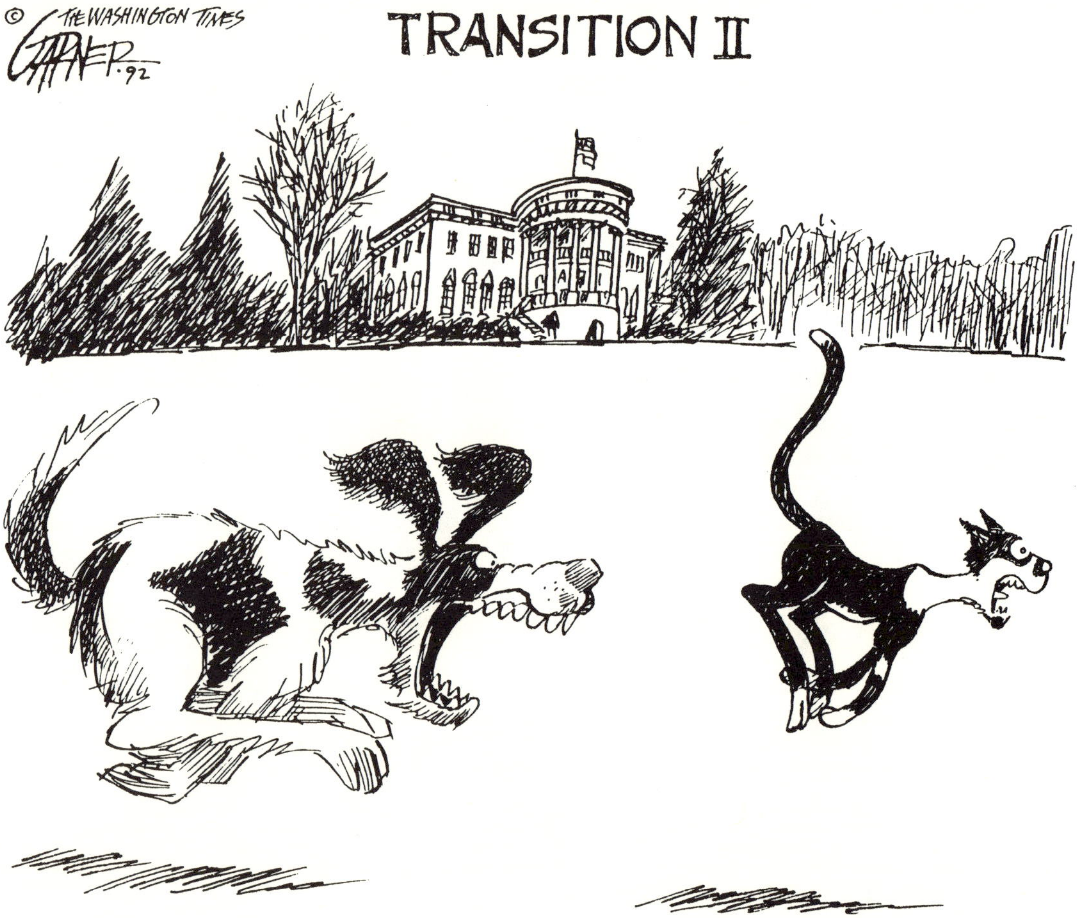
TRANSITION II
© THE WASHINGTON TIMES
GARNER '92

The Moscow/Berlin Connection

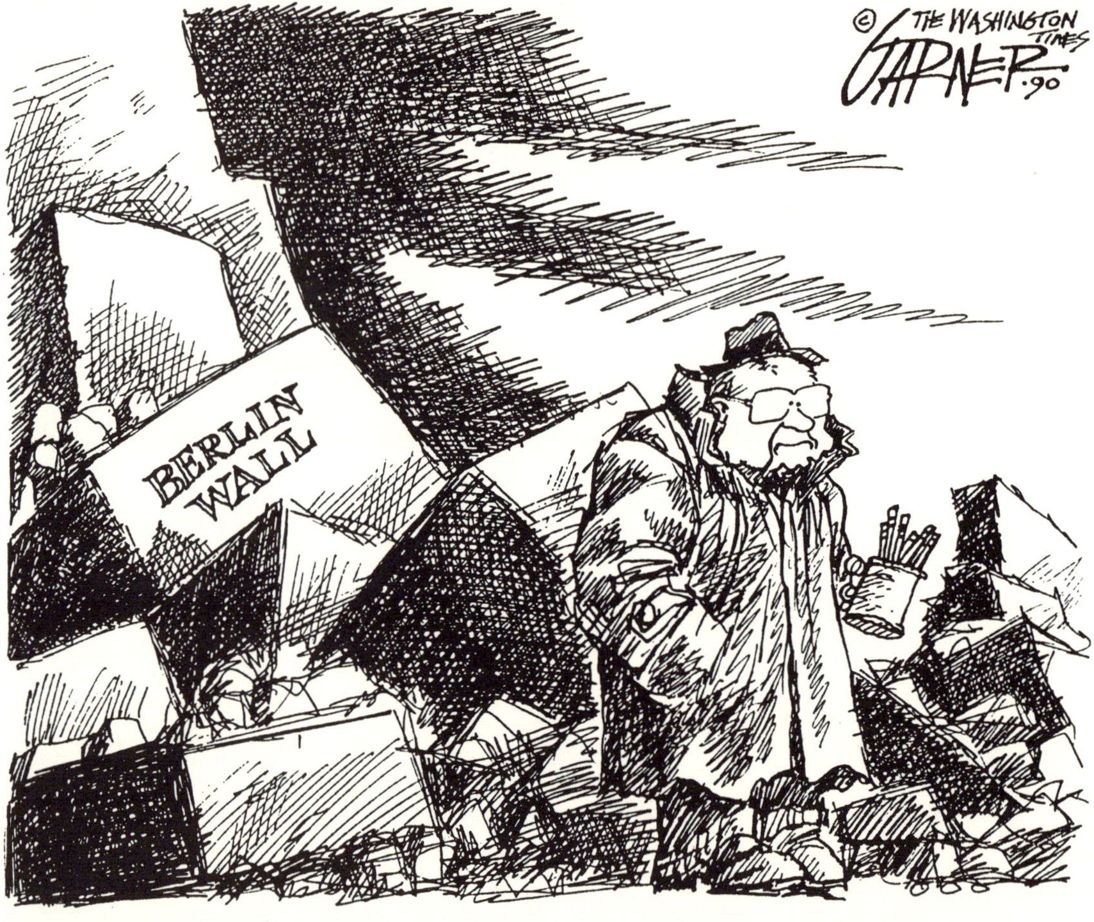
© THE WASHINGTON TIMES
GARNER '90
BERLIN WALL

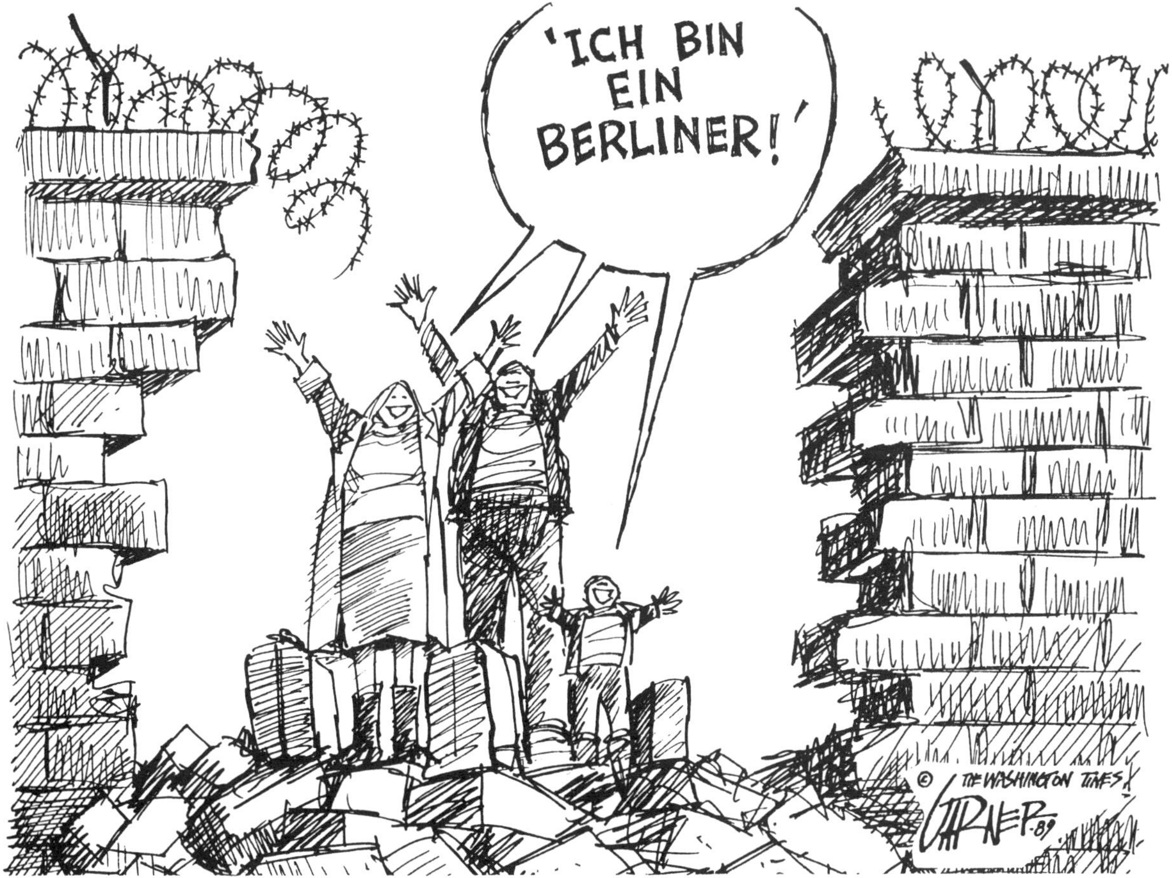
'ICH BIN EIN BERLINER!'
© THE WASHINGTON TIMES

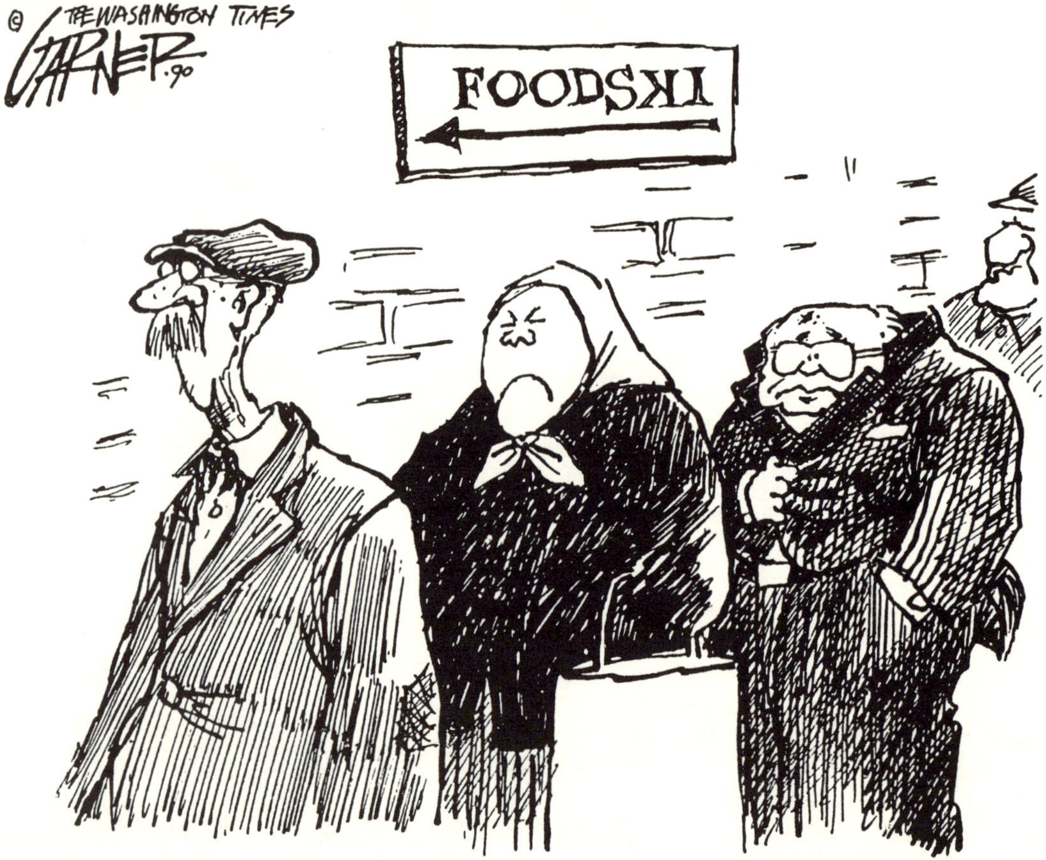
© THE WASHINGTON TIMES
GARNER '90
FOODSKI

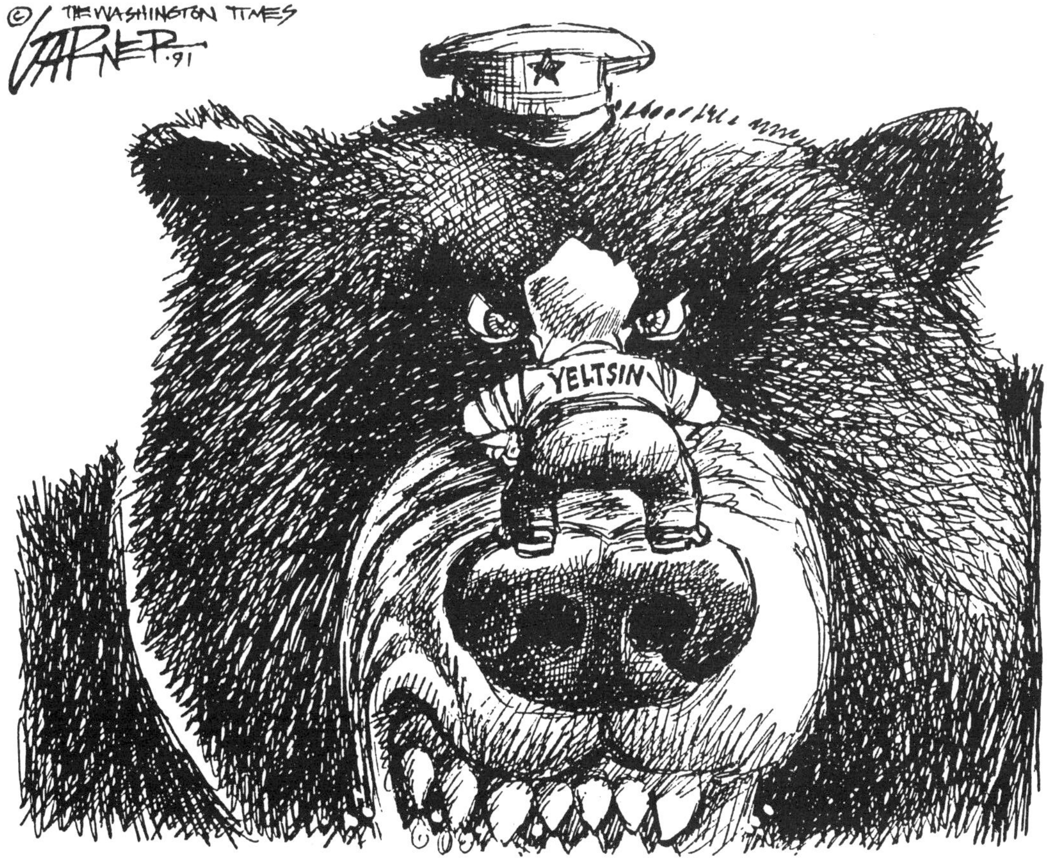
© THE WASHINGTON TIMES
GARNER '91
YELTSIN

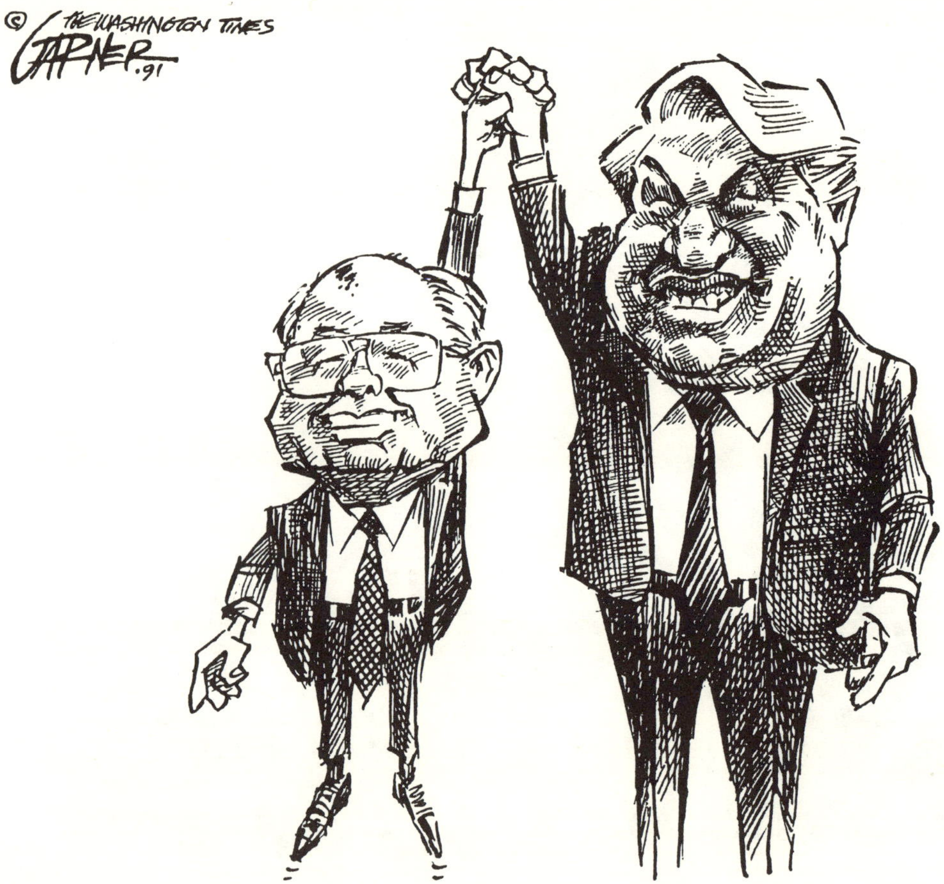
© THE WASHINGTON TIMES
GARNER '91

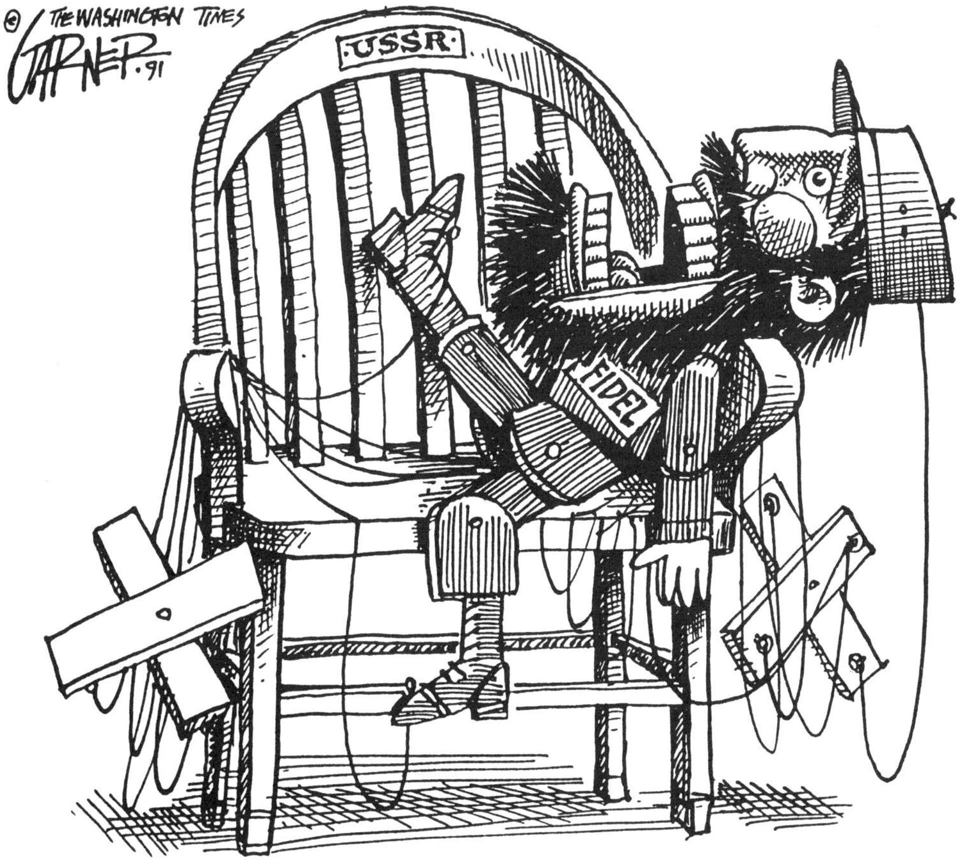
© THE WASHINGTON TIMES
GARNER '91
USSR
FIDEL

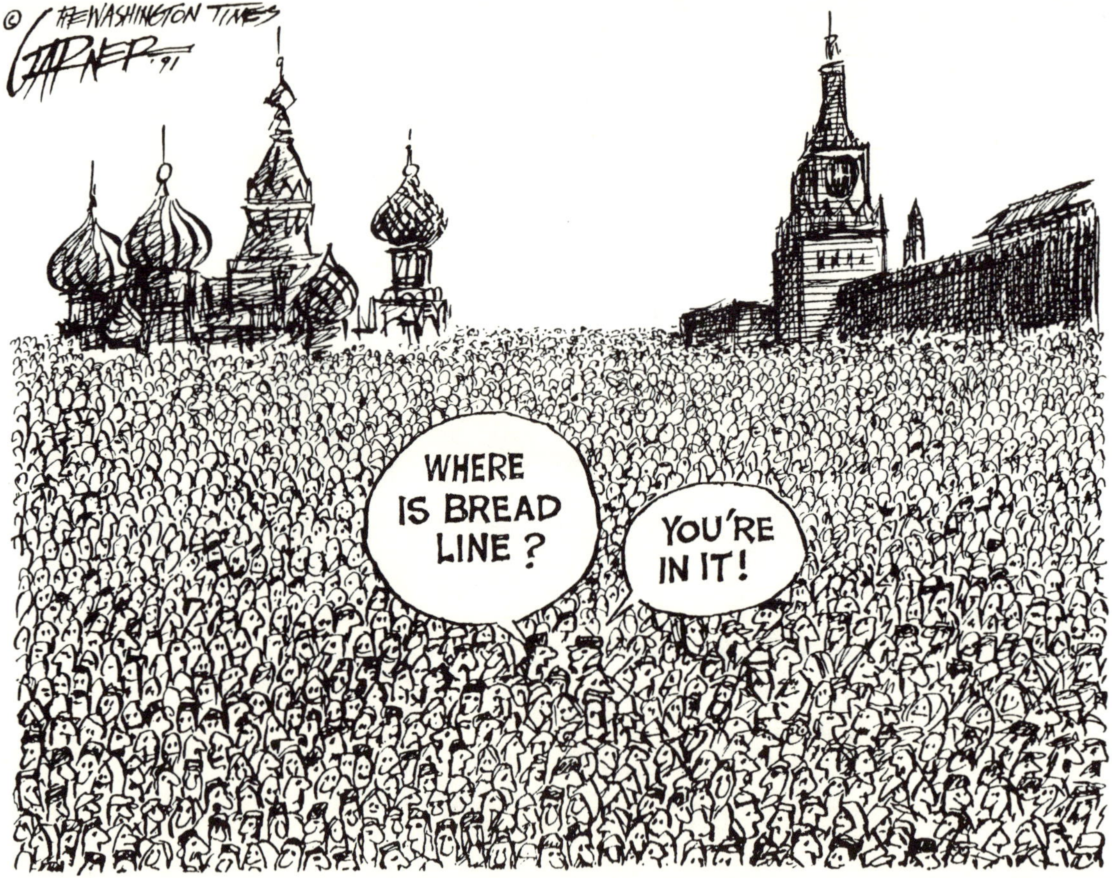
© THE WASHINGTON TIMES
GARNER '91
WHERE IS BREAD LINE?
YOU'RE IN IT!

Clinton

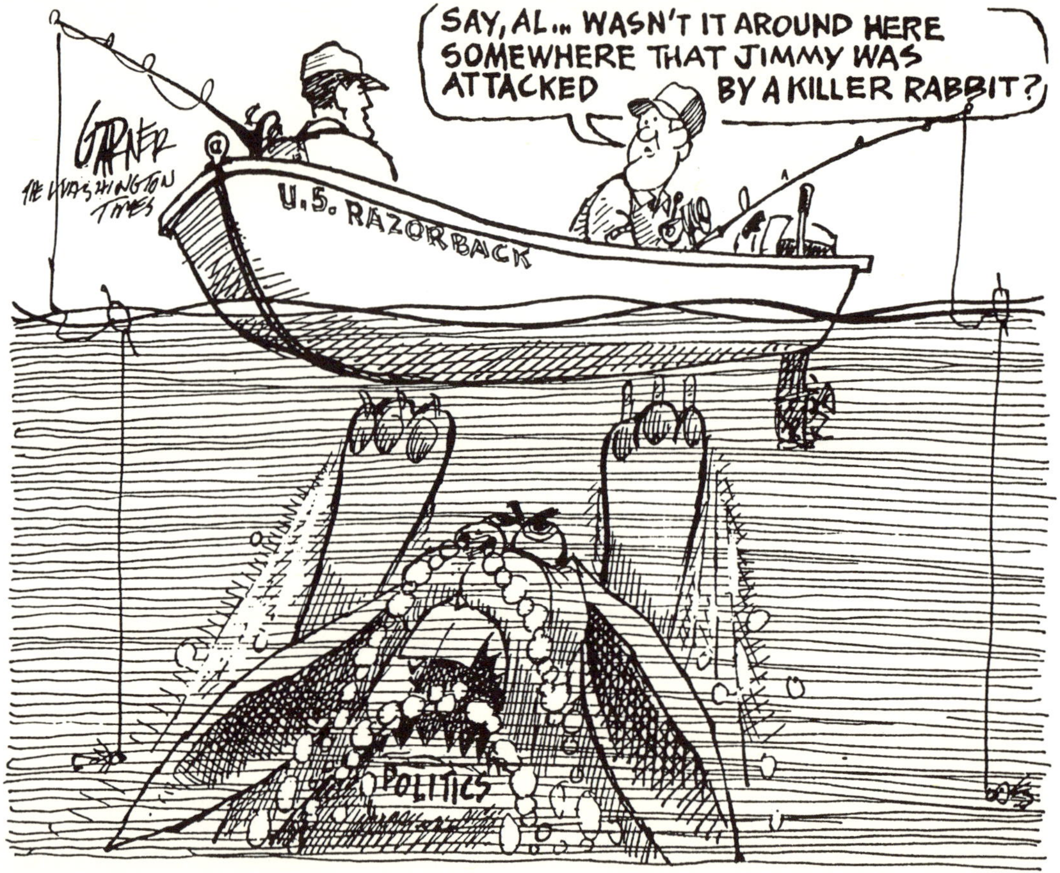
SAY, AL... WASN'T IT AROUND HERE SOMEWHERE THAT JIMMY WAS ATTACKED BY A KILLER RABBIT?
GARNER
THE WASHINGTON TIMES
U.S. RAZORBACK
POLITICS

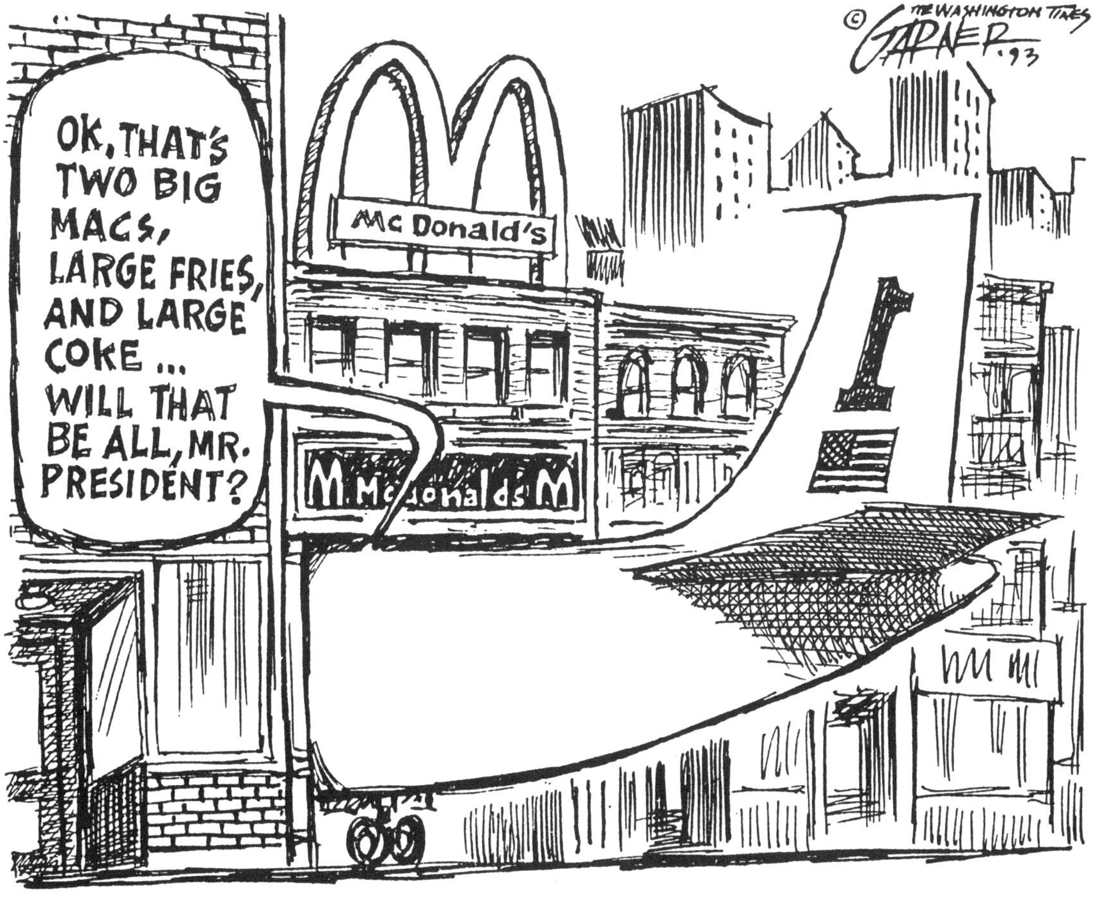
OK, THAT'S TWO BIG MACS, LARGE FRIES, AND LARGE COKE ... WILL THAT BE ALL, MR. PRESIDENT?
McDonald's
McDonald's
© THE WASHINGTON TIMES GARNER '93

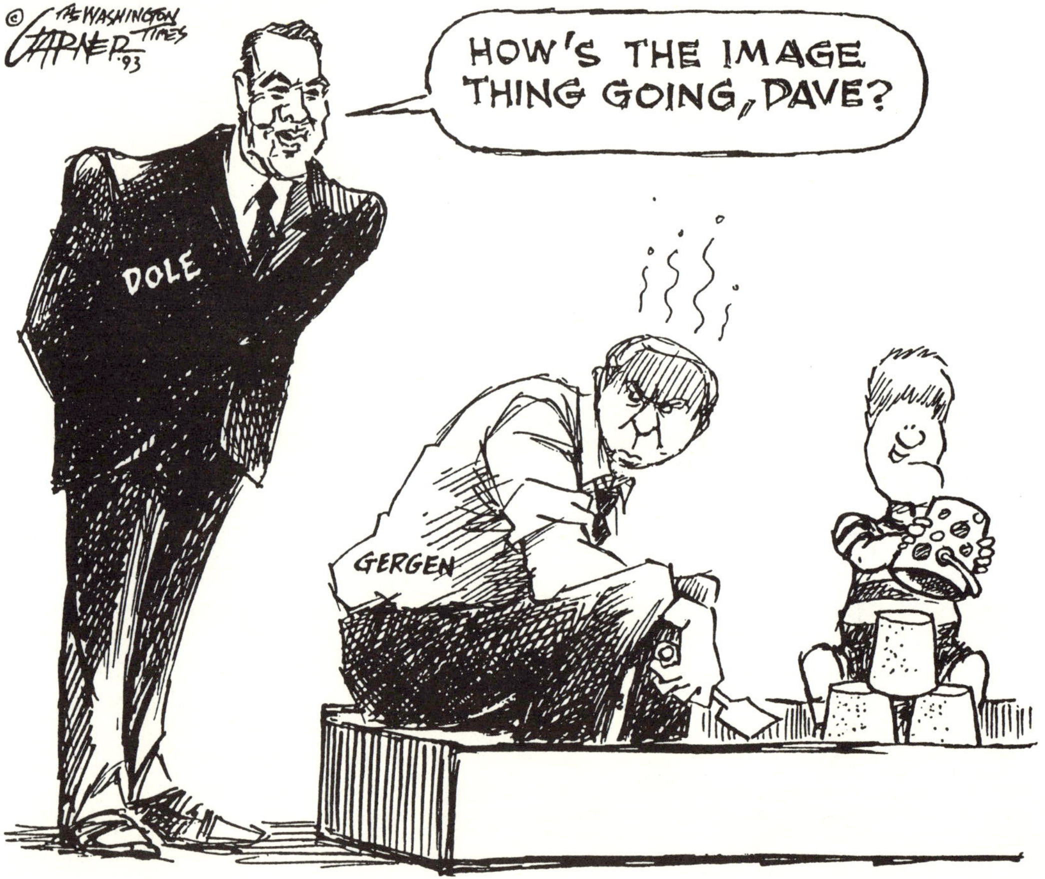
© THE WASHINGTON TIMES
GARNER '93
HOW'S THE IMAGE THING GOING, DAVE?
DOLE
GERGEN

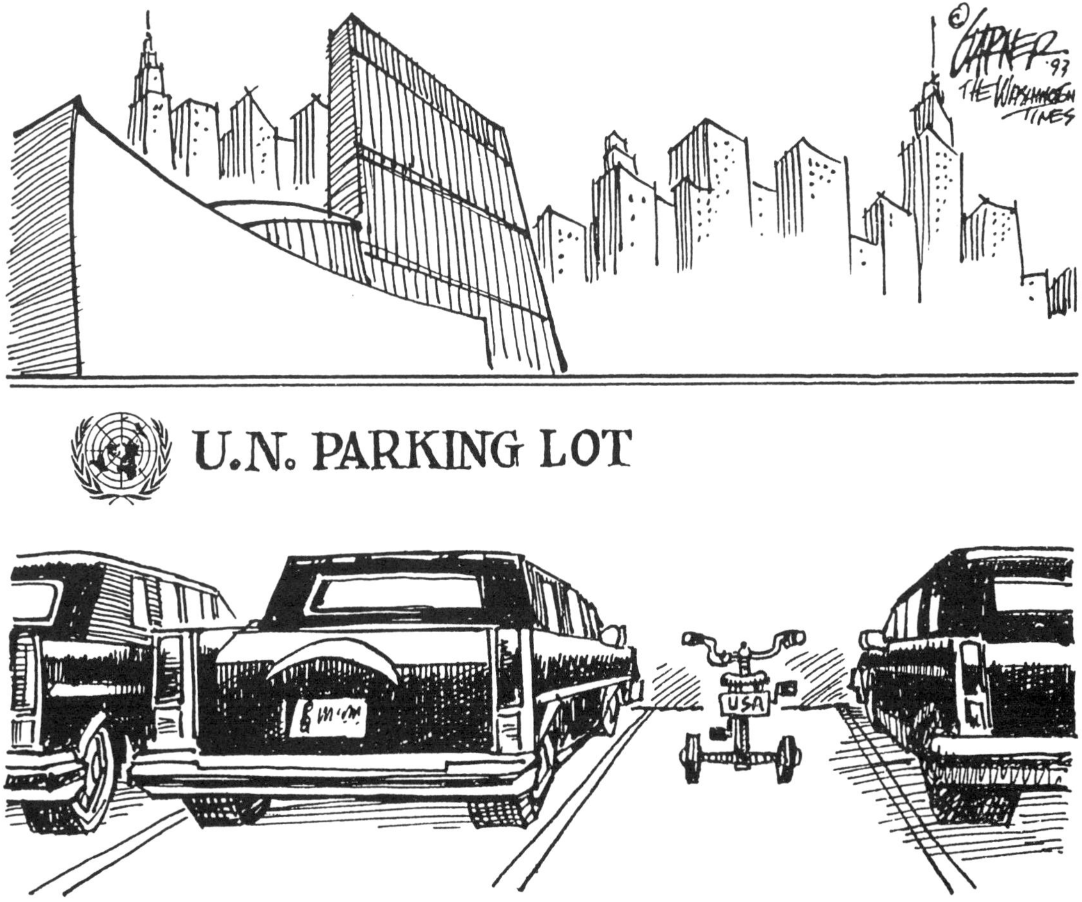
U.N. PARKING LOT
USA

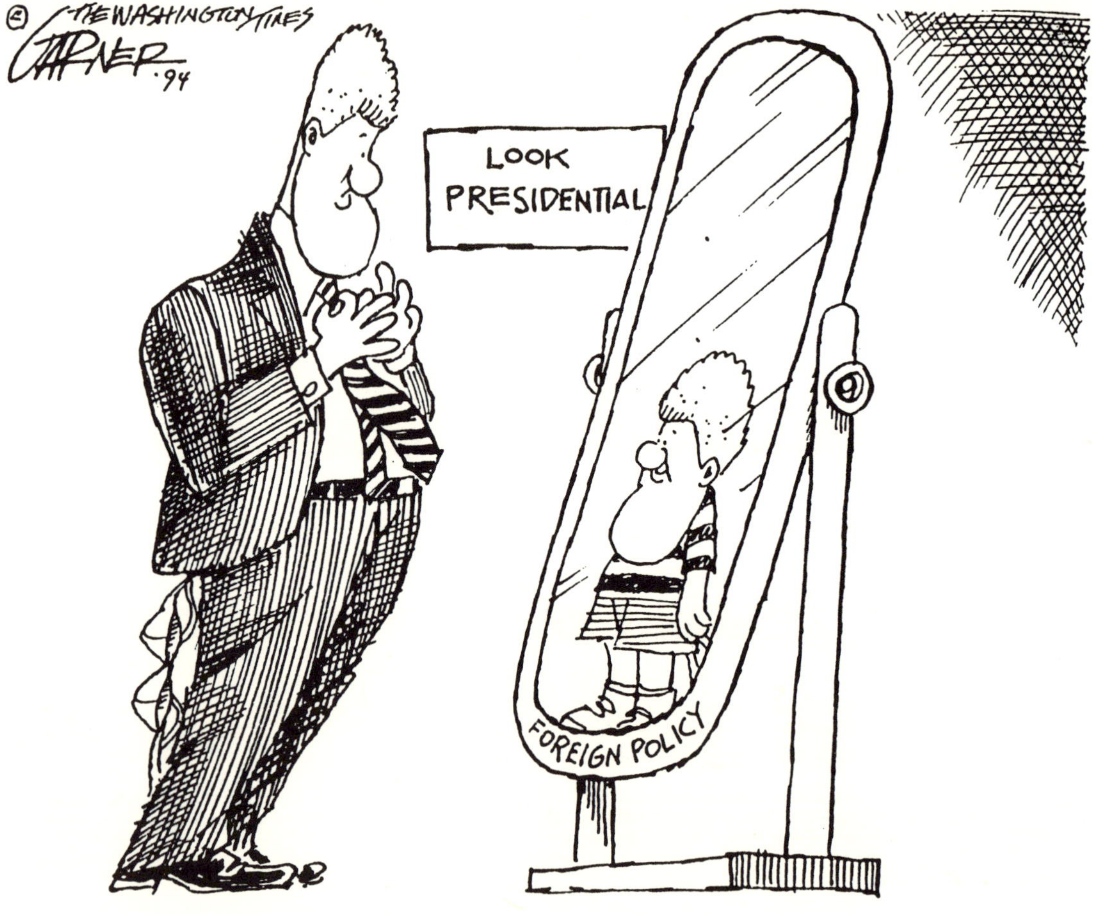
© THE WASHINGTON TIMES
GARNER '94
LOOK PRESIDENTIAL
FOREIGN POLICY

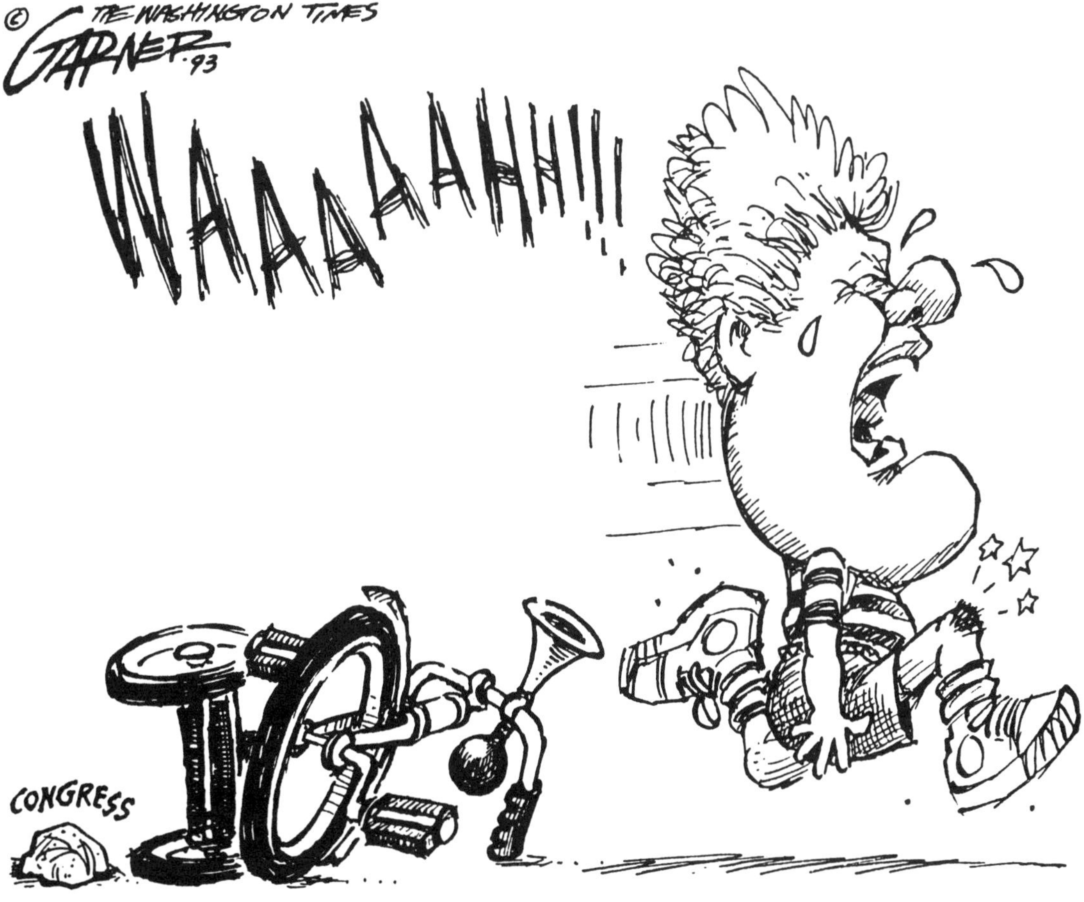
© THE WASHINGTON TIMES
GARNER '93
WAAAAAHH!!!
CONGRESS

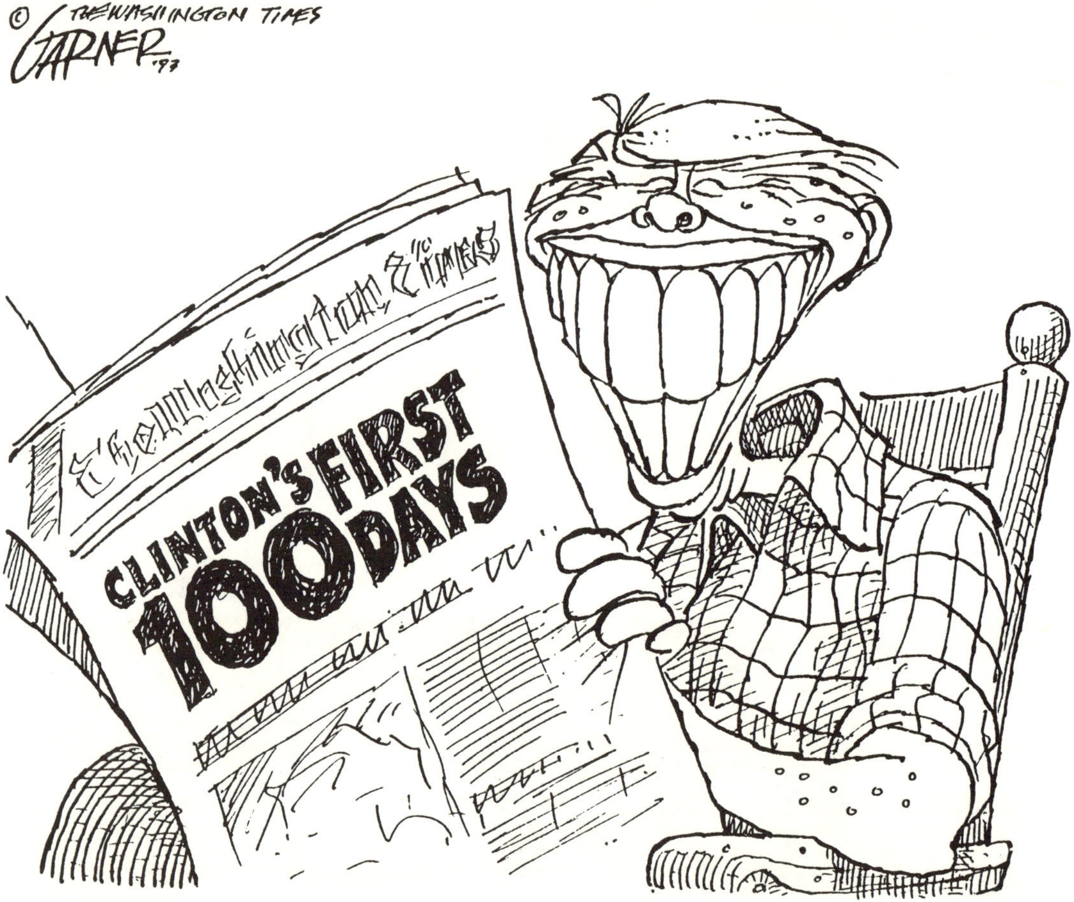
© THE WASHINGTON TIMES
GARNER '93
CLINTON'S FIRST 100 DAYS

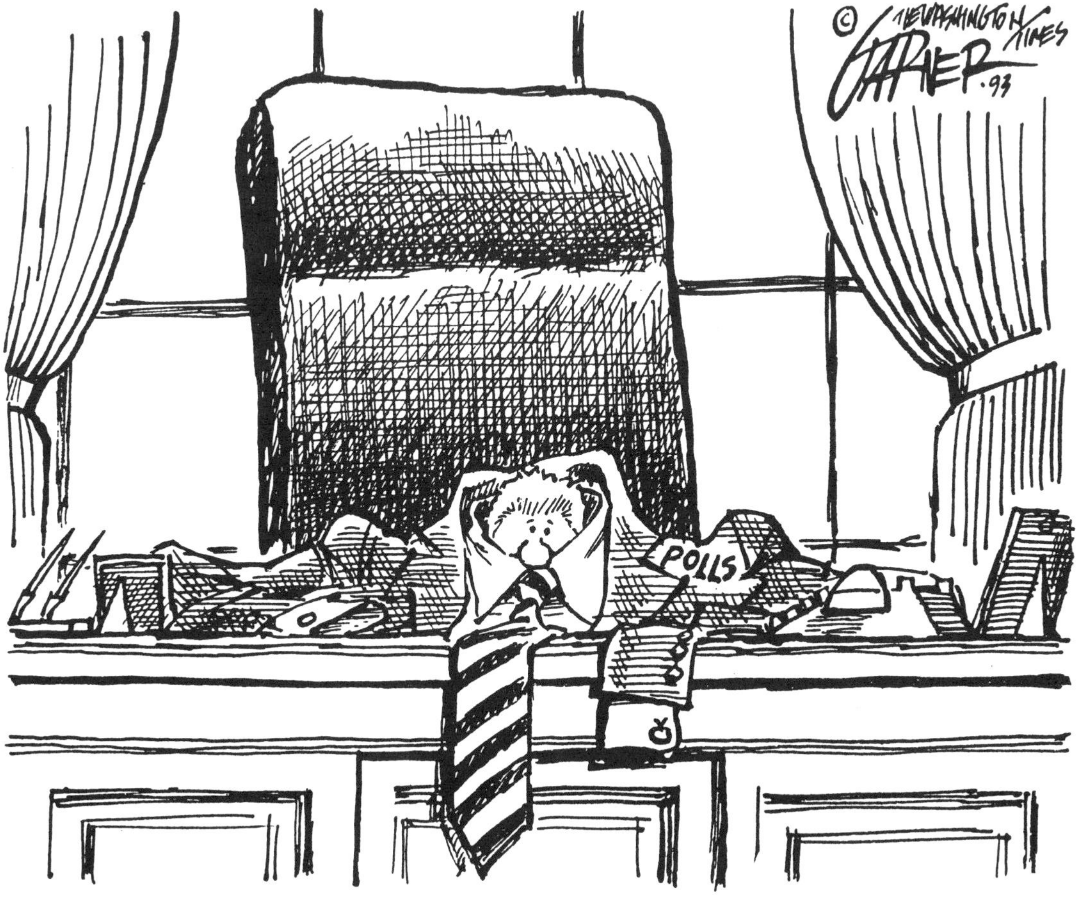
© THE WASHINGTON TIMES
GARNER ·93
POLLS

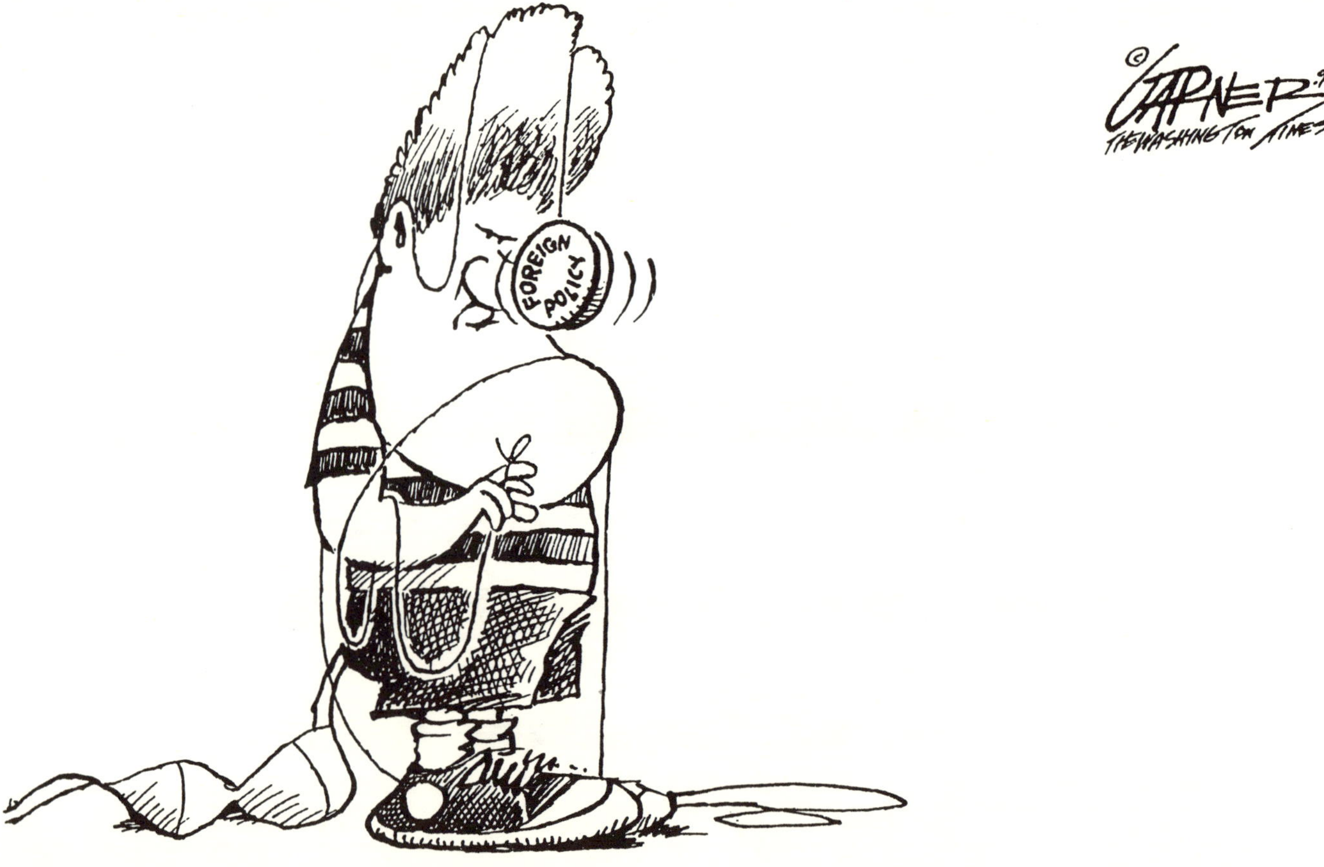
FOREIGN POLICY
© GARNER '94
THE WASHINGTON TIMES

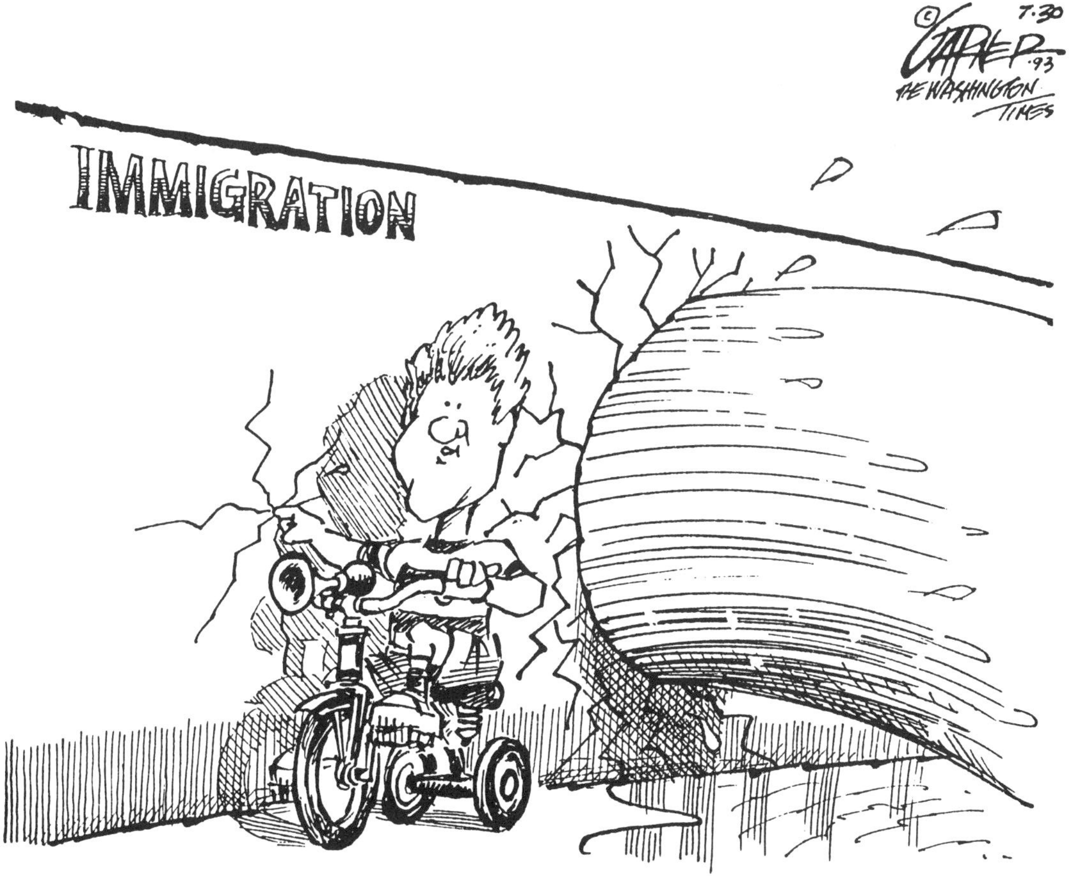
IMMIGRATION
© GARNER 7-30 '93 THE WASHINGTON TIMES

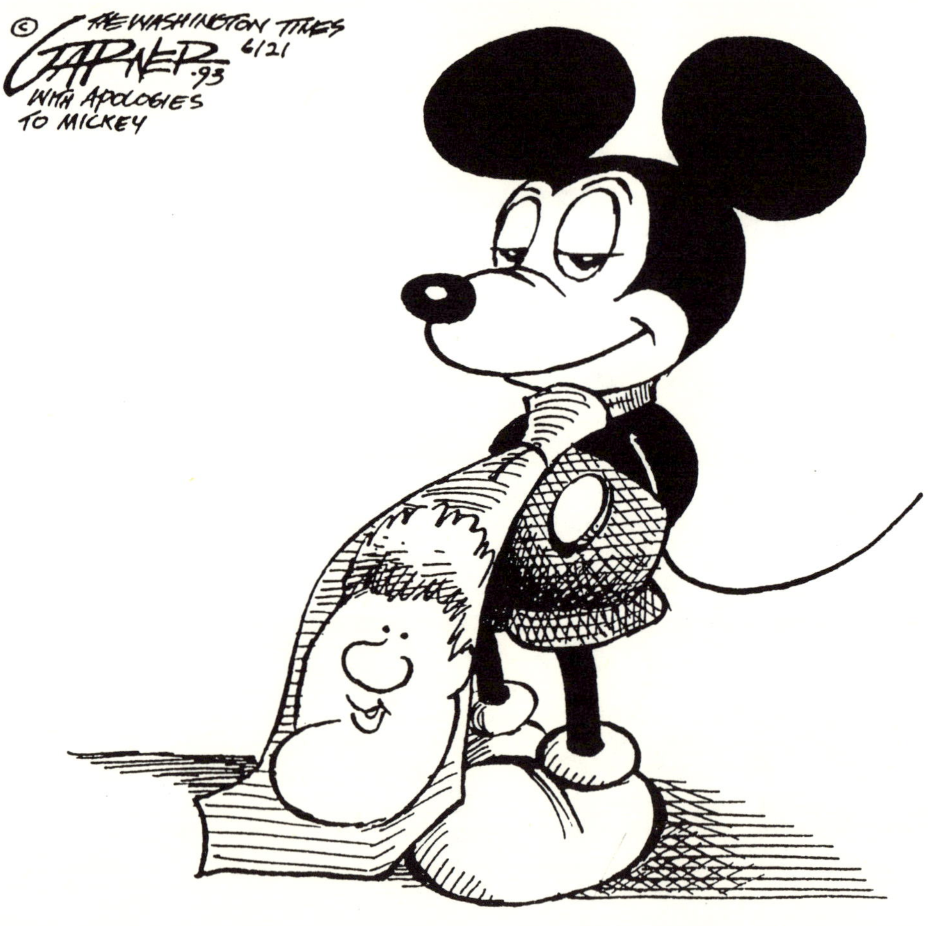
© THE WASHINGTON TIMES
6/21
GARNER
.93
WITH APOLOGIES
TO MICKEY

Hillary

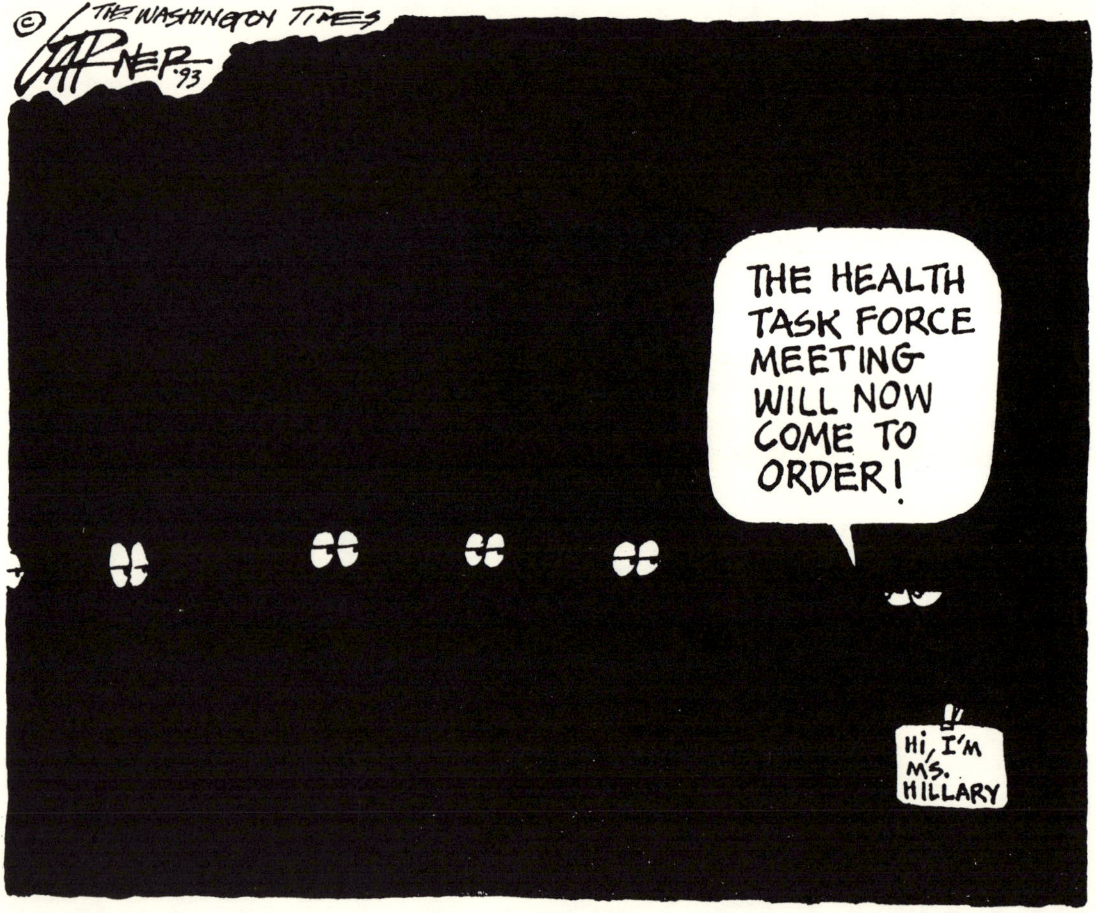
© THE WASHINGTON TIMES
GARNER '93
THE HEALTH TASK FORCE MEETING WILL NOW COME TO ORDER!
HI, I'M MS. HILLARY

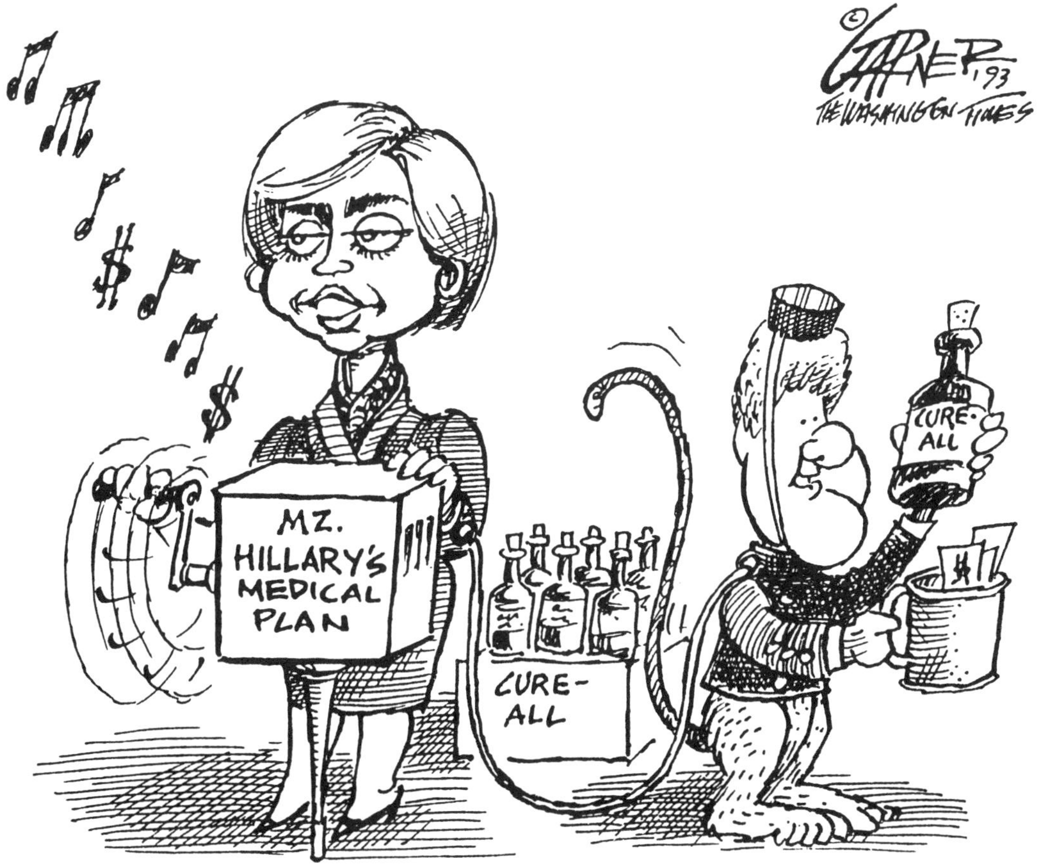
© Garner '93
The Washington Times
MZ. HILLARY'S MEDICAL PLAN
CURE-ALL
CURE-ALL

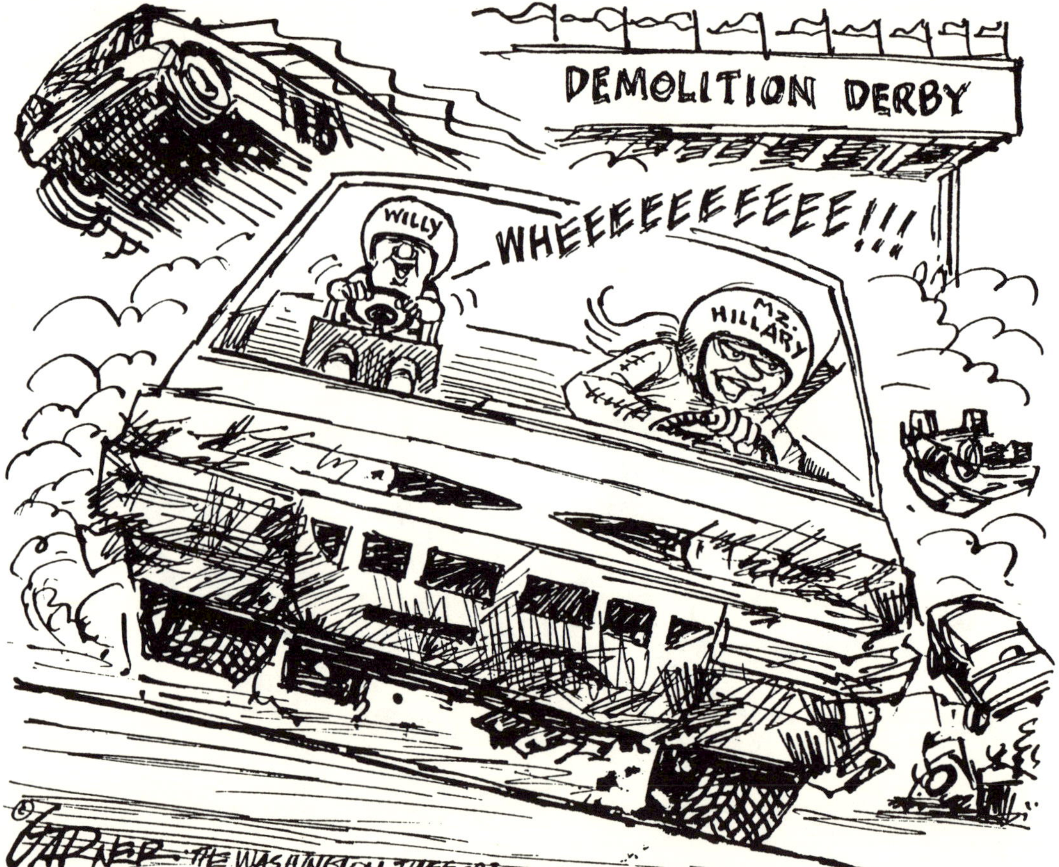
DEMOLITION DERBY
WILLY
WHEEEEEEEEEE!!!
MZ. HILLARY
© GARNER THE WASHINGTON TIMES '93

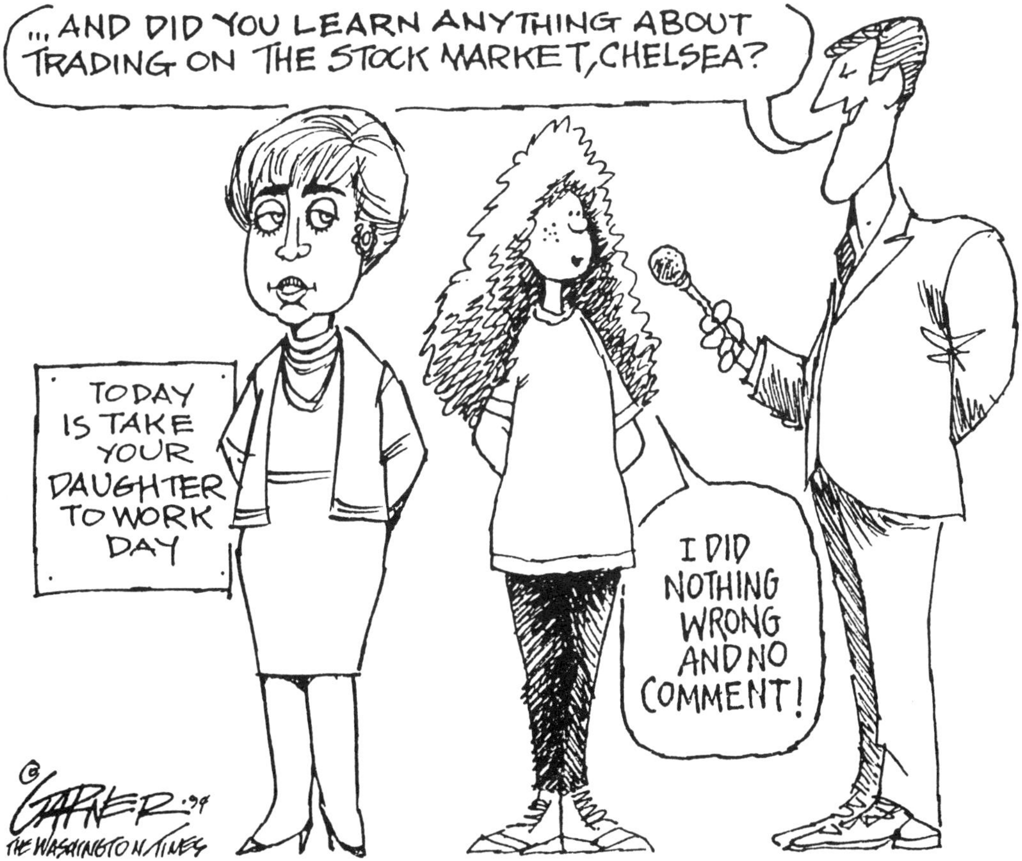

...AND DID YOU LEARN ANYTHING ABOUT TRADING ON THE STOCK MARKET, CHELSEA?
TODAY IS TAKE YOUR DAUGHTER TO WORK DAY
I DID NOTHING WRONG AND NO COMMENT!
© GARNER '94 THE WASHINGTON TIMES

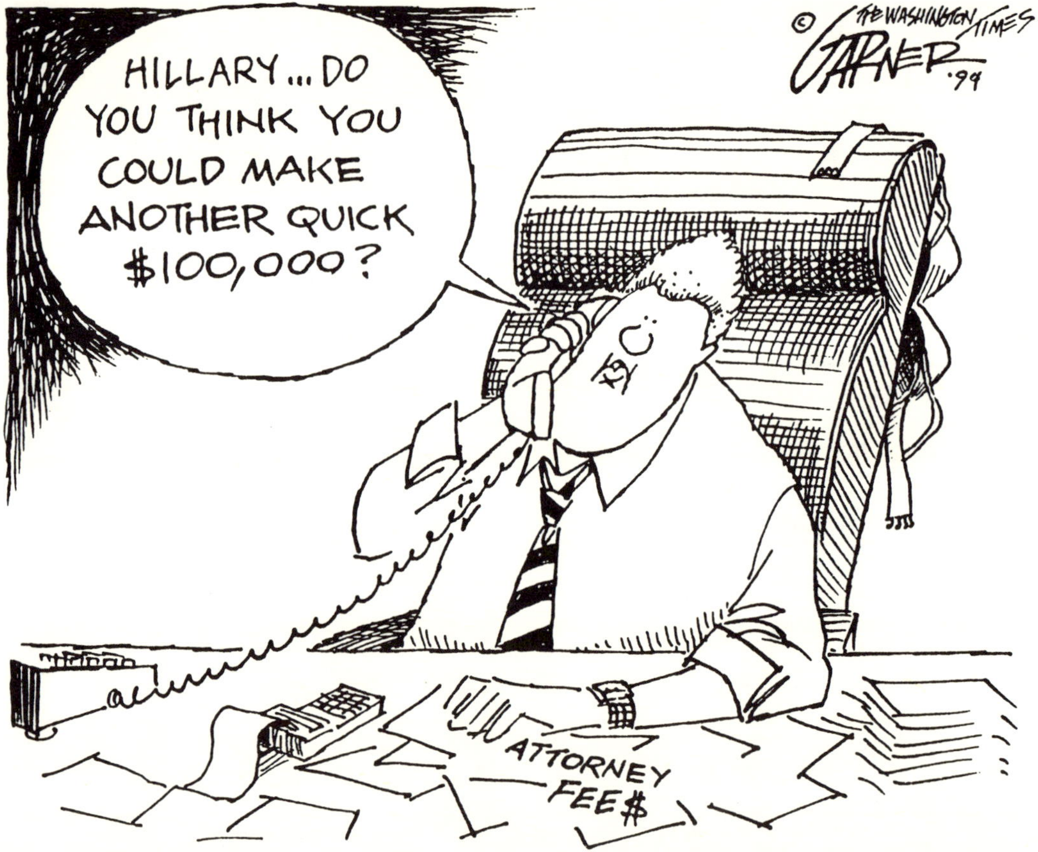
© THE WASHINGTON TIMES GARNER '94
HILLARY... DO YOU THINK YOU COULD MAKE ANOTHER QUICK $100,000?
ATTORNEY FEE$

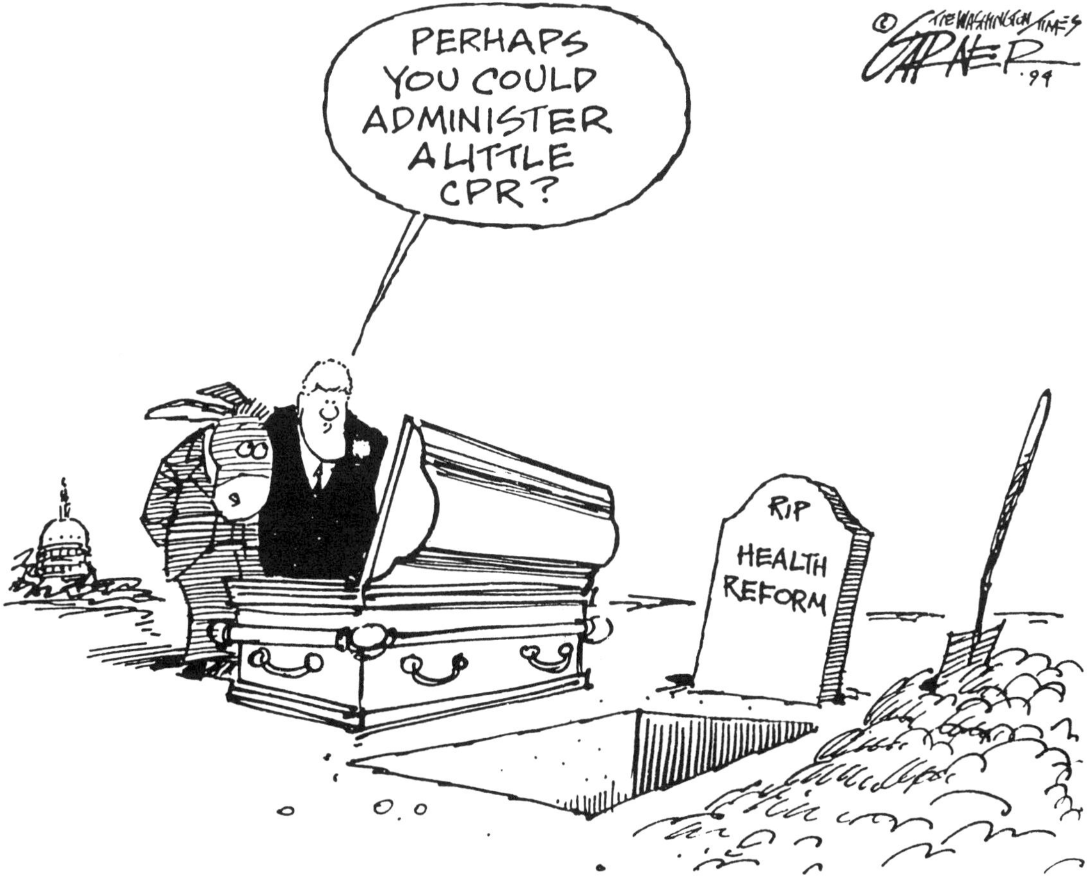
PERHAPS YOU COULD ADMINISTER A LITTLE CPR?
RIP
HEALTH REFORM

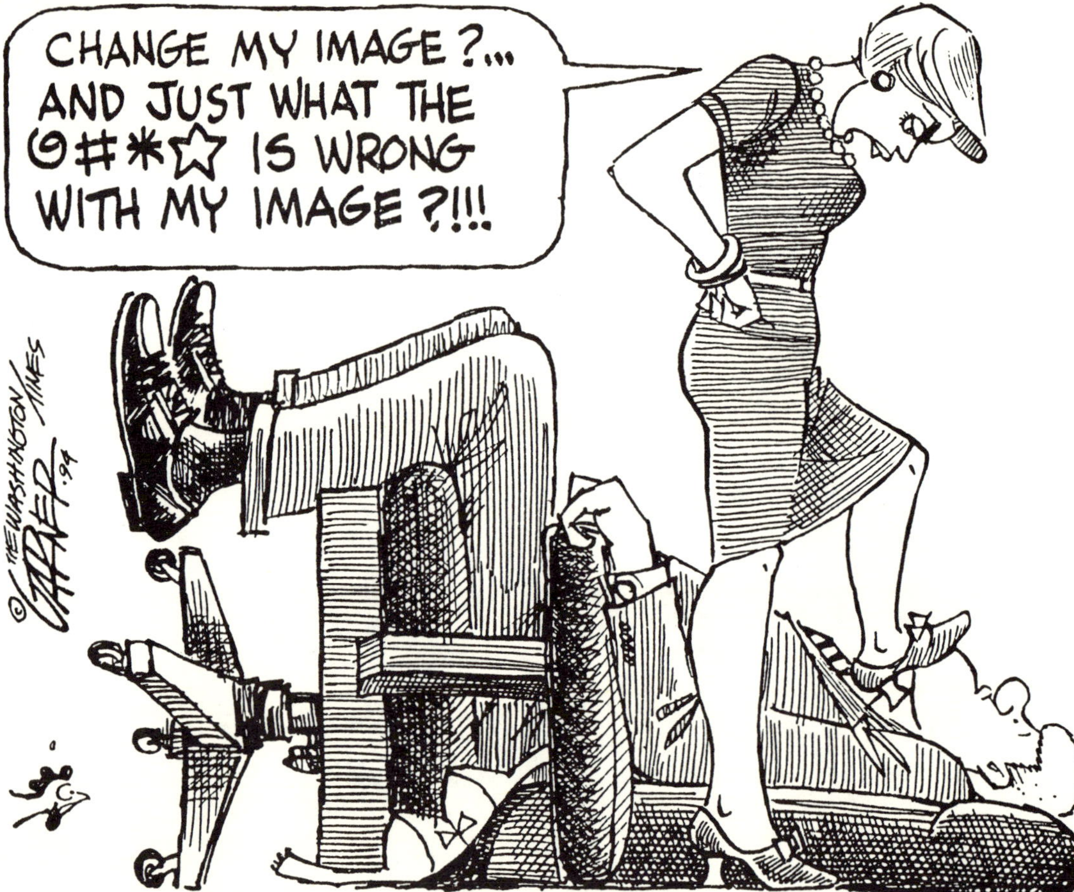
CHANGE MY IMAGE?... AND JUST WHAT THE @#*☆ IS WRONG WITH MY IMAGE?!!!
© THE WASHINGTON TIMES
GARNER '94

Whitewater

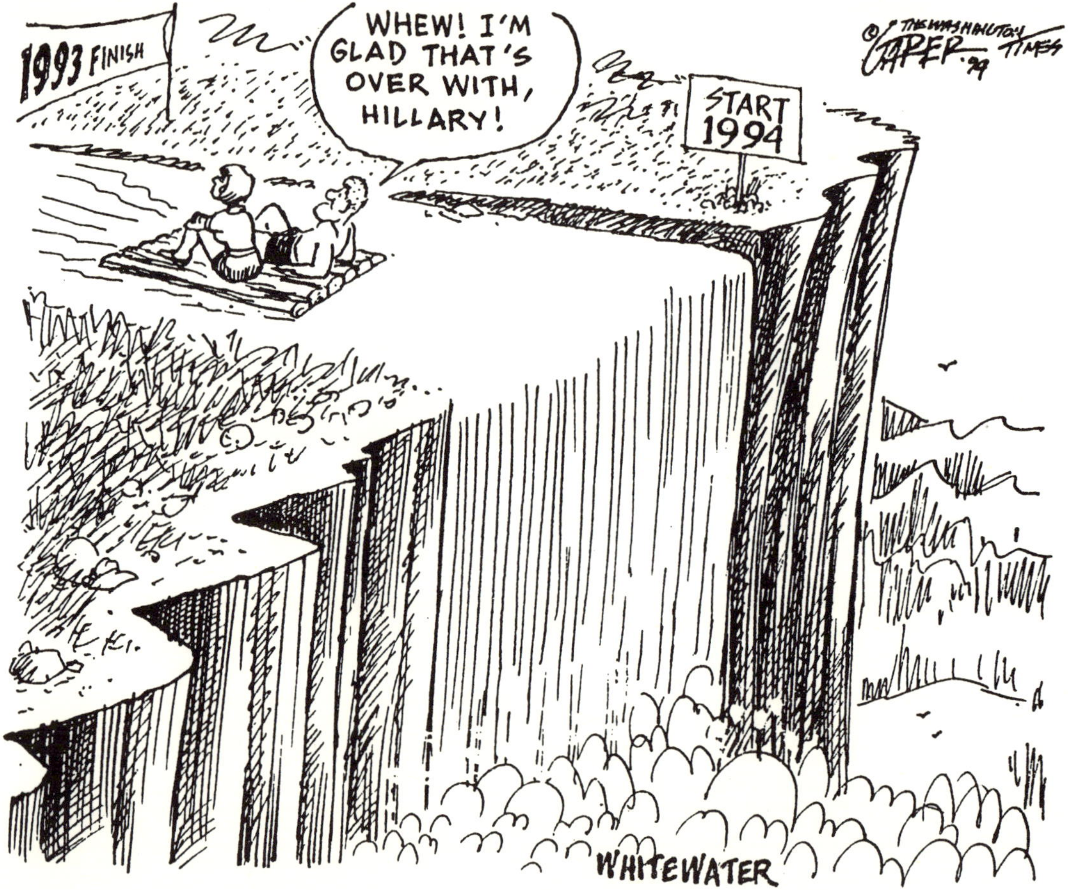
1993 FINISH
WHEW! I'M GLAD THAT'S OVER WITH, HILLARY!
START 1994
WHITEWATER

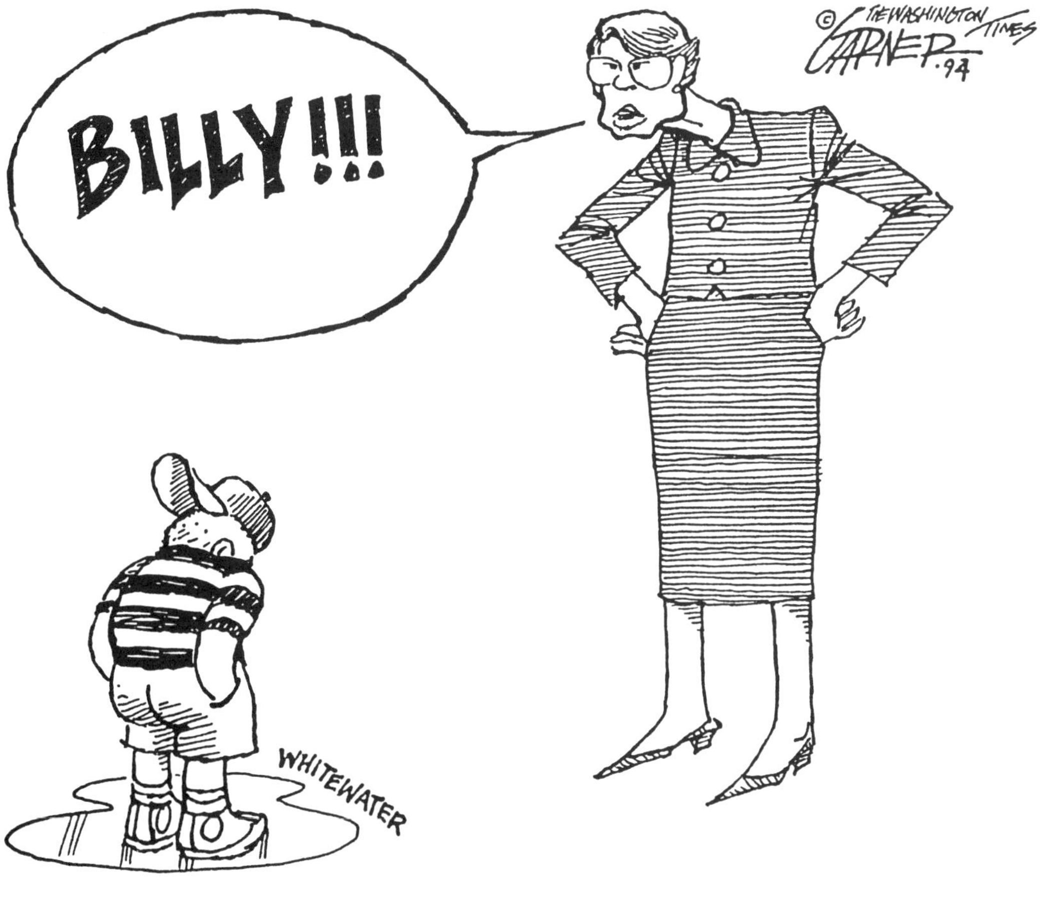
BILLY!!!
WHITEWATER
© THE WASHINGTON TIMES
GARNER '94

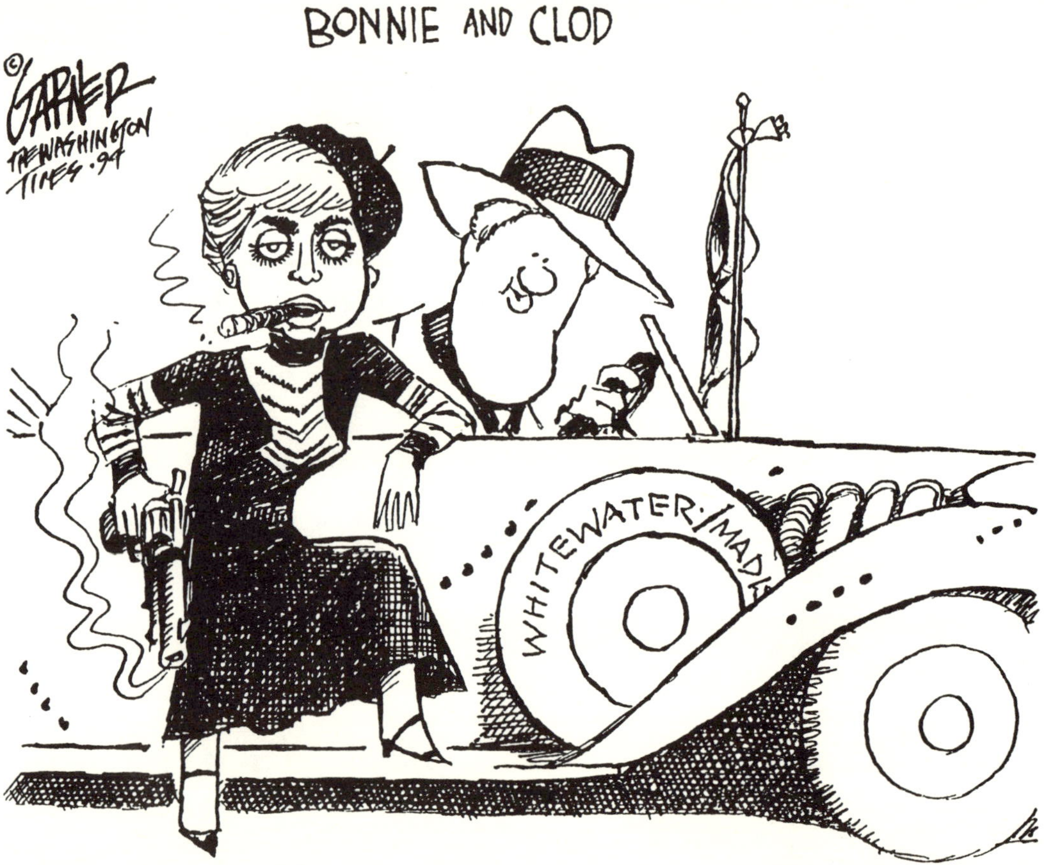
BONNIE AND CLOD
© GARNER THE WASHINGTON TIMES ·94
WHITEWATER/MAD

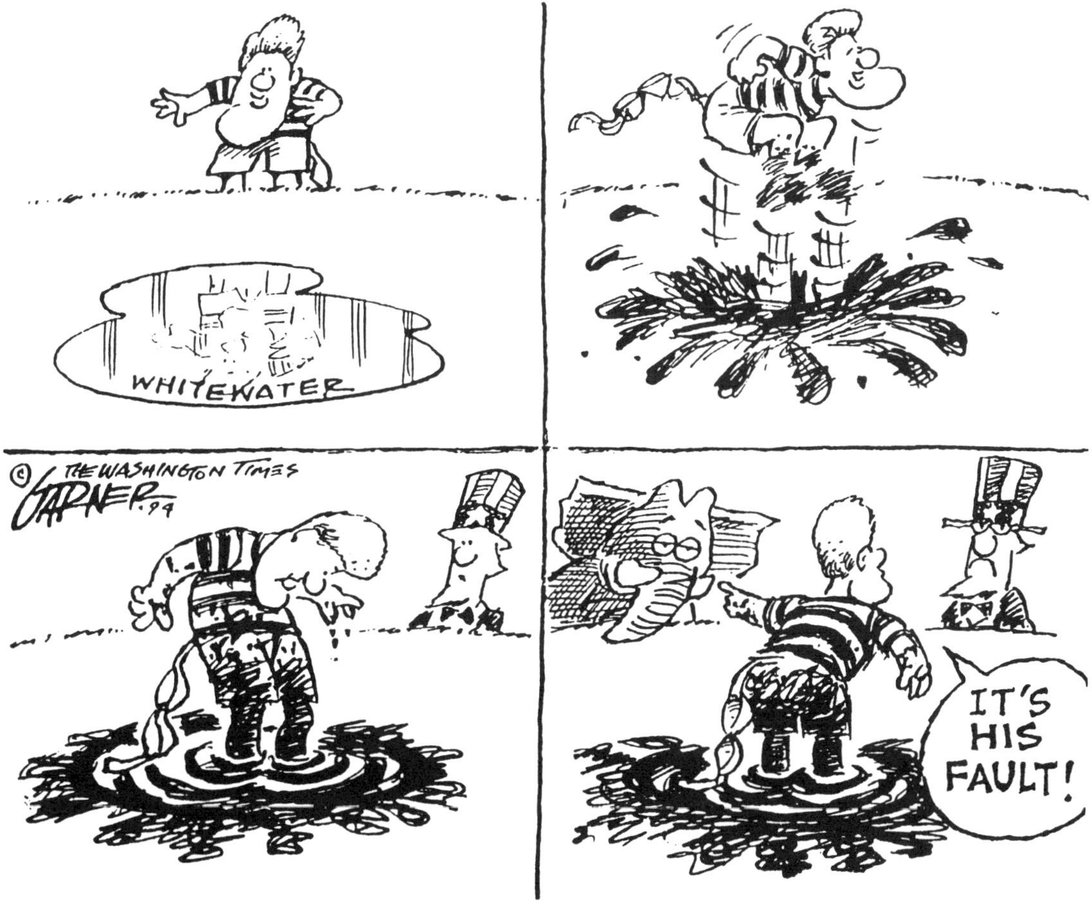
WHITEWATER
© THE WASHINGTON TIMES
GARNER '94
IT'S HIS FAULT!

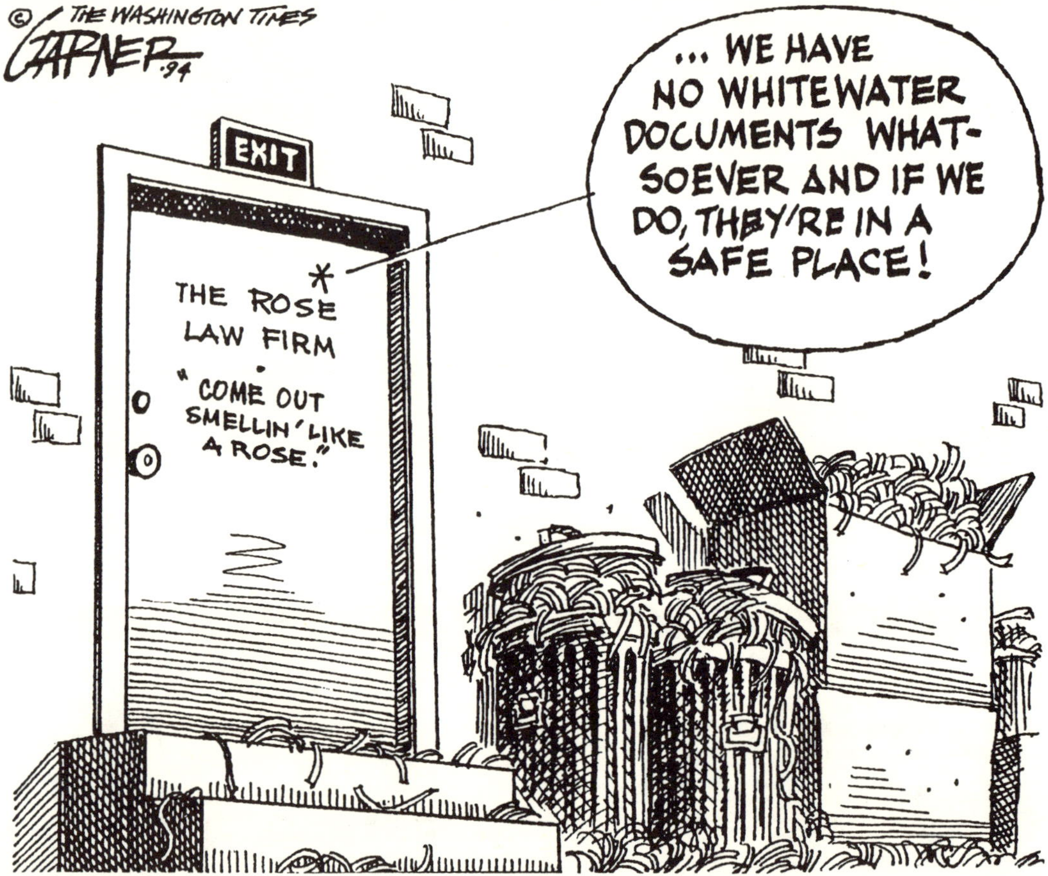
© THE WASHINGTON TIMES
GARNER '94
EXIT
THE ROSE LAW FIRM • "COME OUT SMELLIN' LIKE A ROSE."
... WE HAVE NO WHITEWATER DOCUMENTS WHATSOEVER AND IF WE DO, THEY'RE IN A SAFE PLACE!

Foreign Affairs

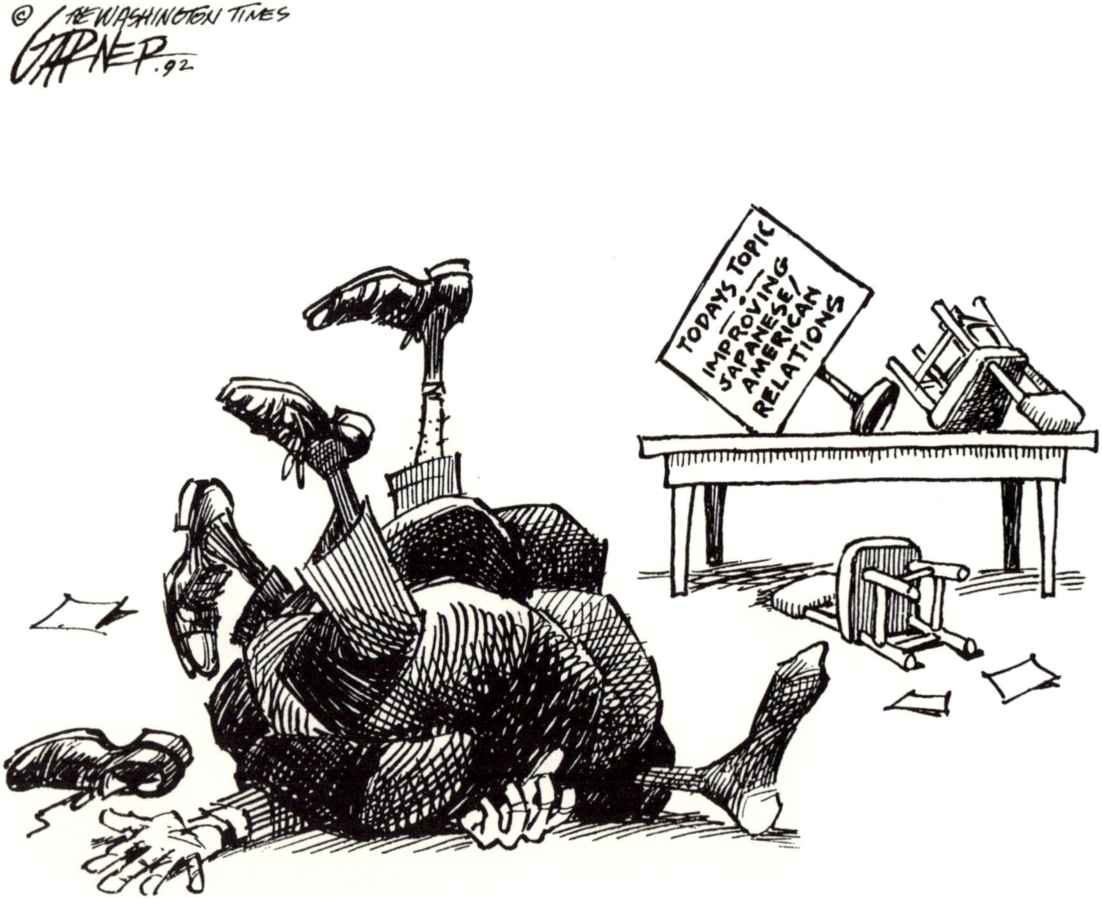
© THE WASHINGTON TIMES
GARNER '92
TODAYS TOPIC
IMPROVING JAPANESE/AMERICAN RELATIONS

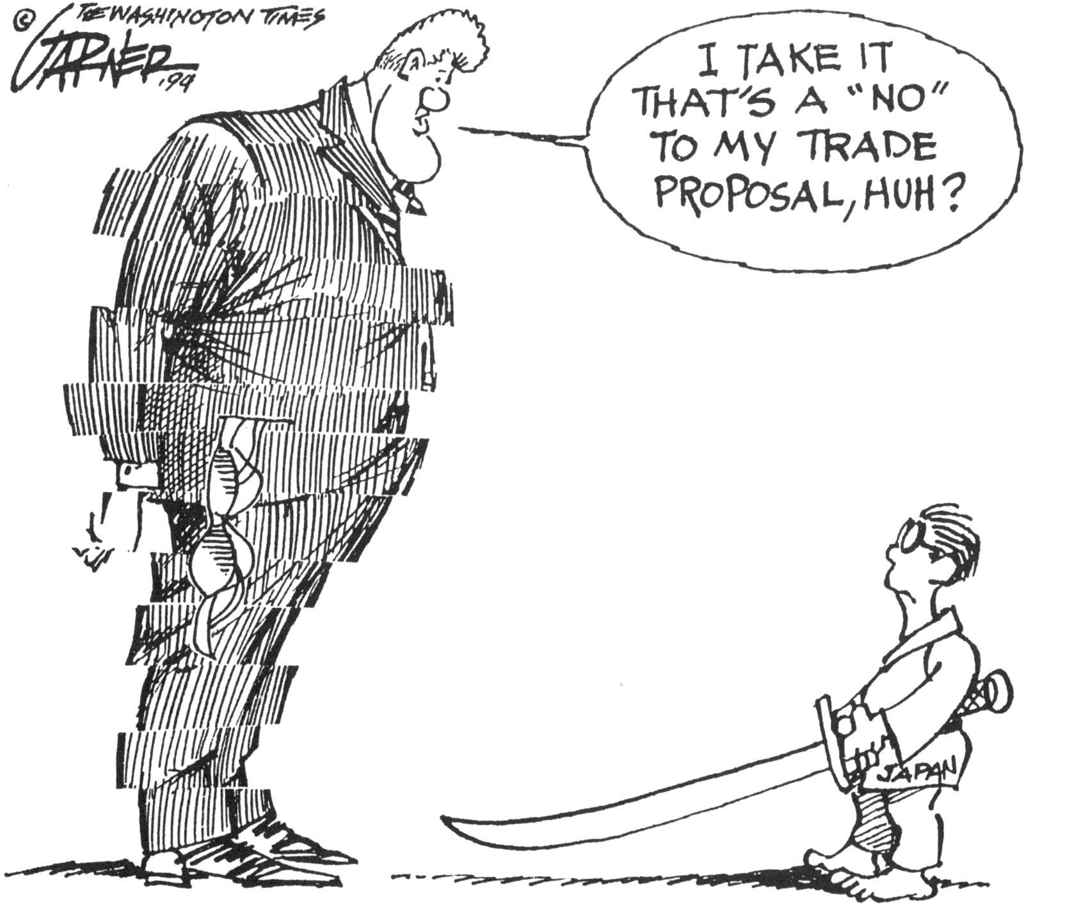
© THE WASHINGTON TIMES
GARNER '94
I TAKE IT THAT'S A "NO" TO MY TRADE PROPOSAL, HUH?
JAPAN

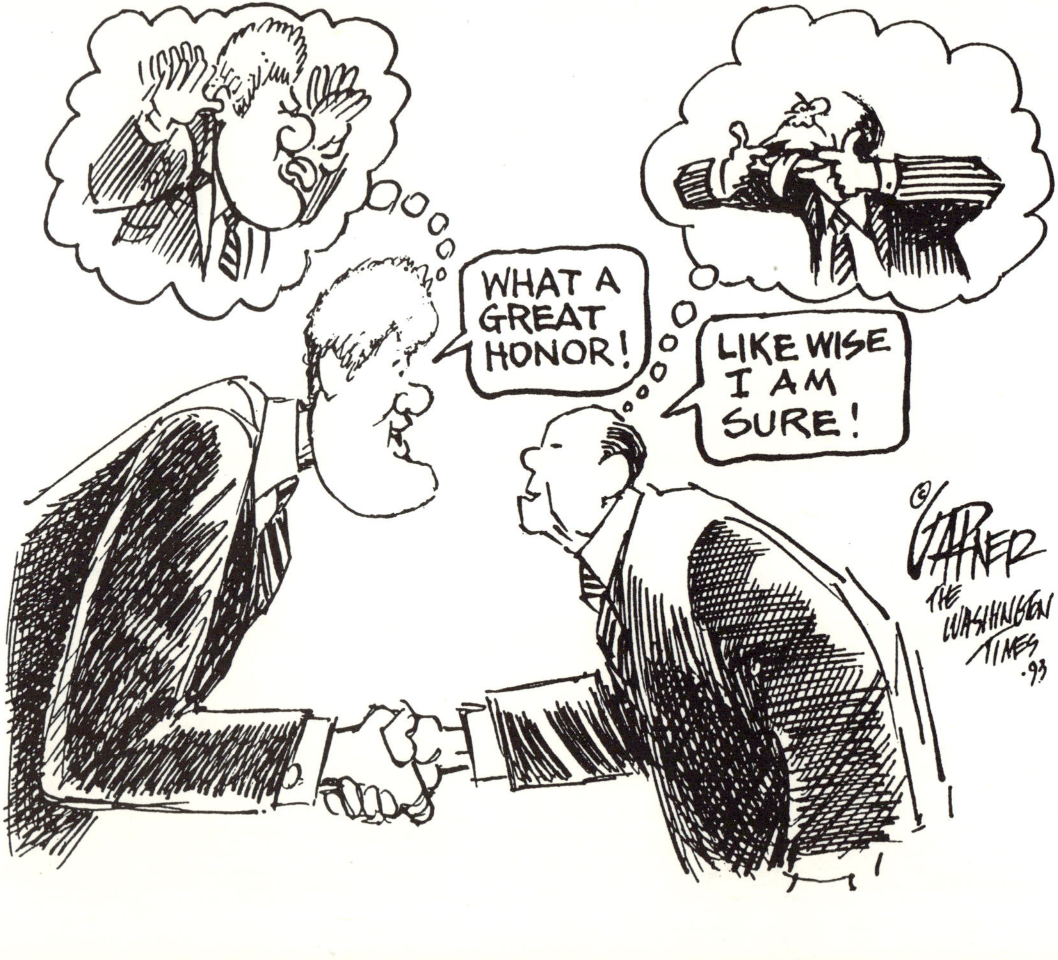
WHAT A GREAT HONOR!
LIKE WISE I AM SURE!
©
GARNER
THE WASHINGTON TIMES
·93

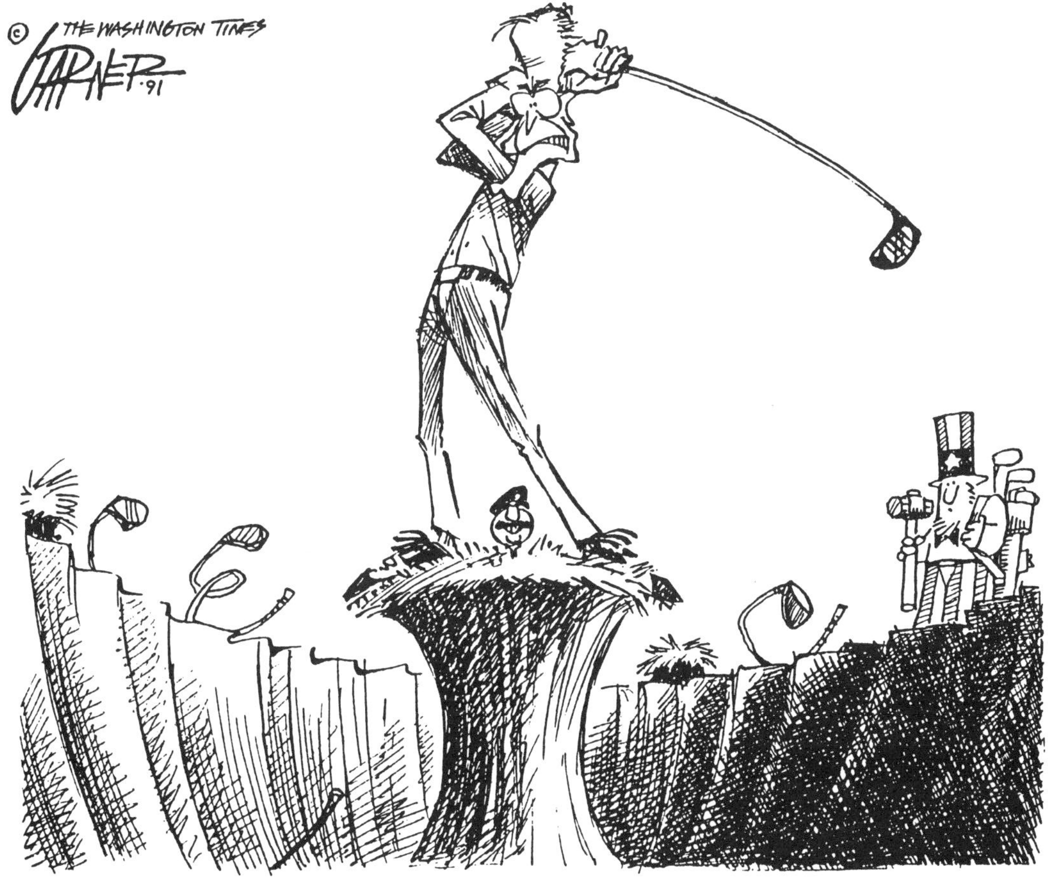
© THE WASHINGTON TIMES
GARNER '91

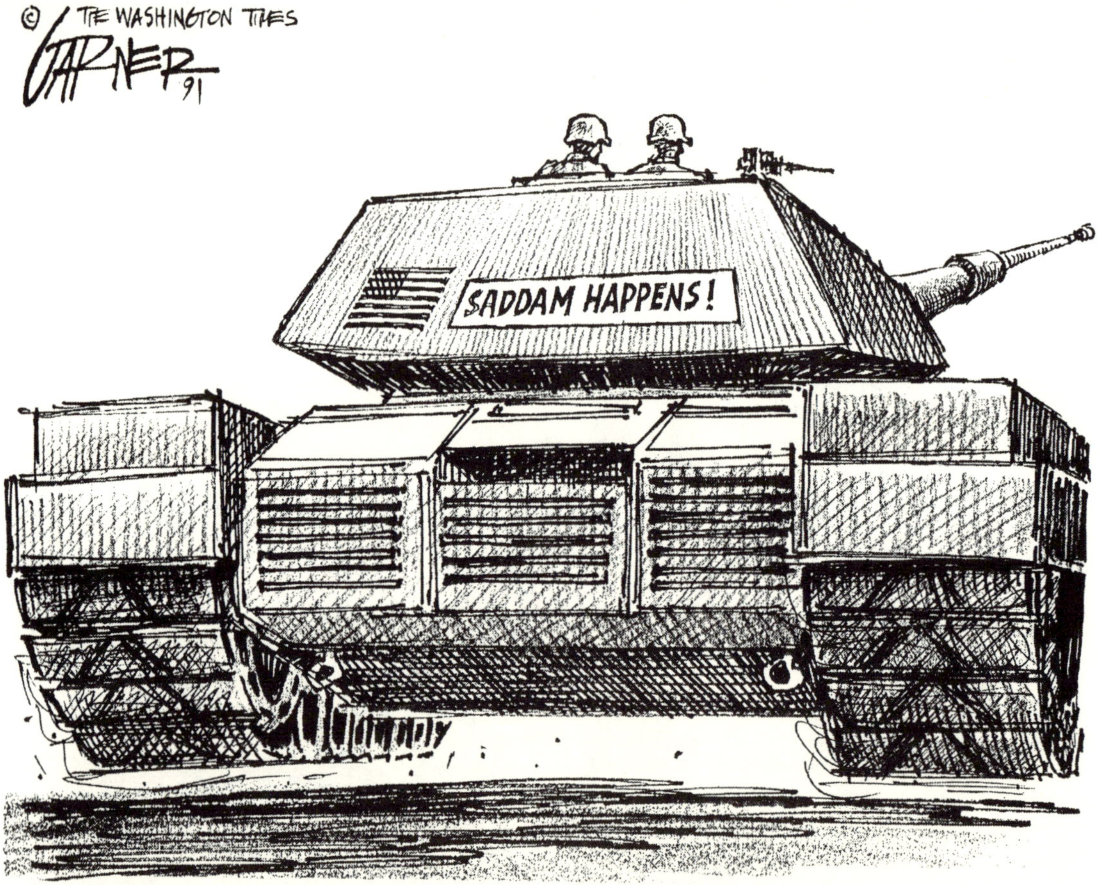
© THE WASHINGTON TIMES
GARNER 91
SADDAM HAPPENS!

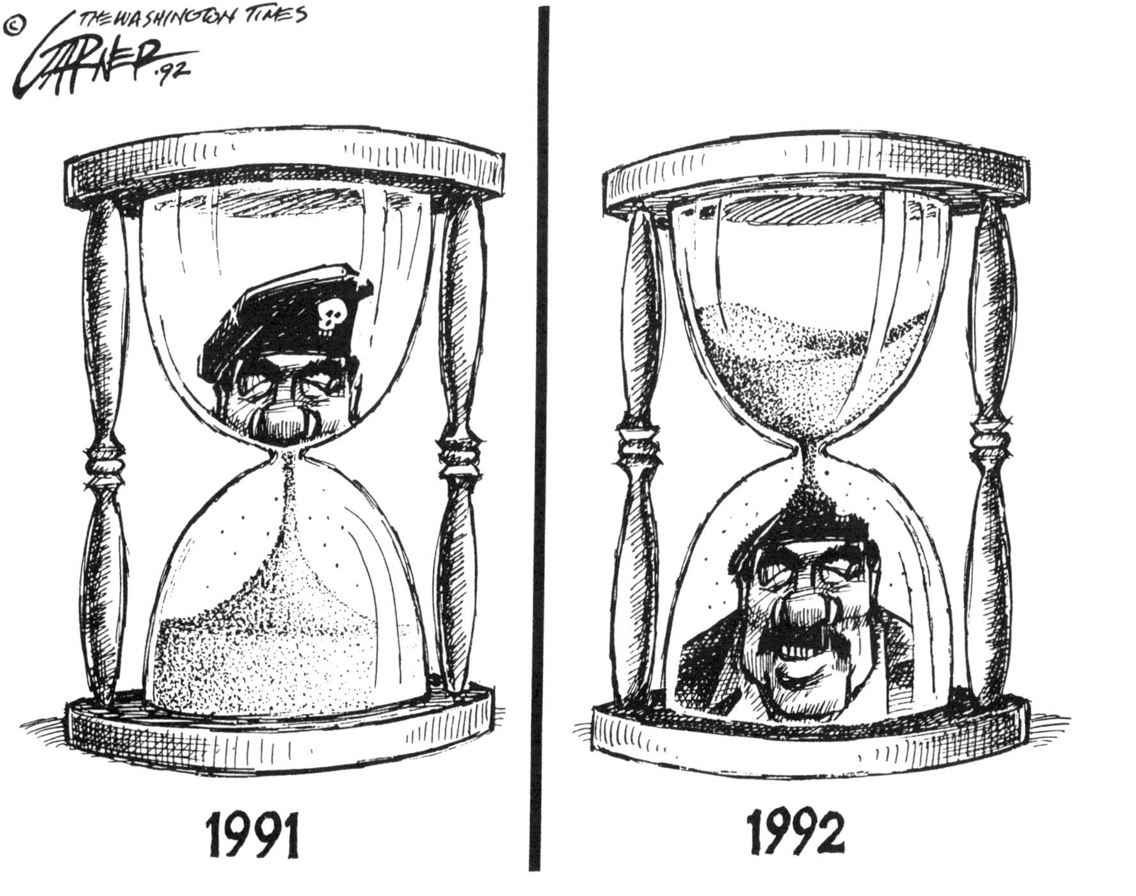
© THE WASHINGTON TIMES
GARNER '92
1991
1992

HAITI
© THE WASHINGTON TIMES
GARNER '94

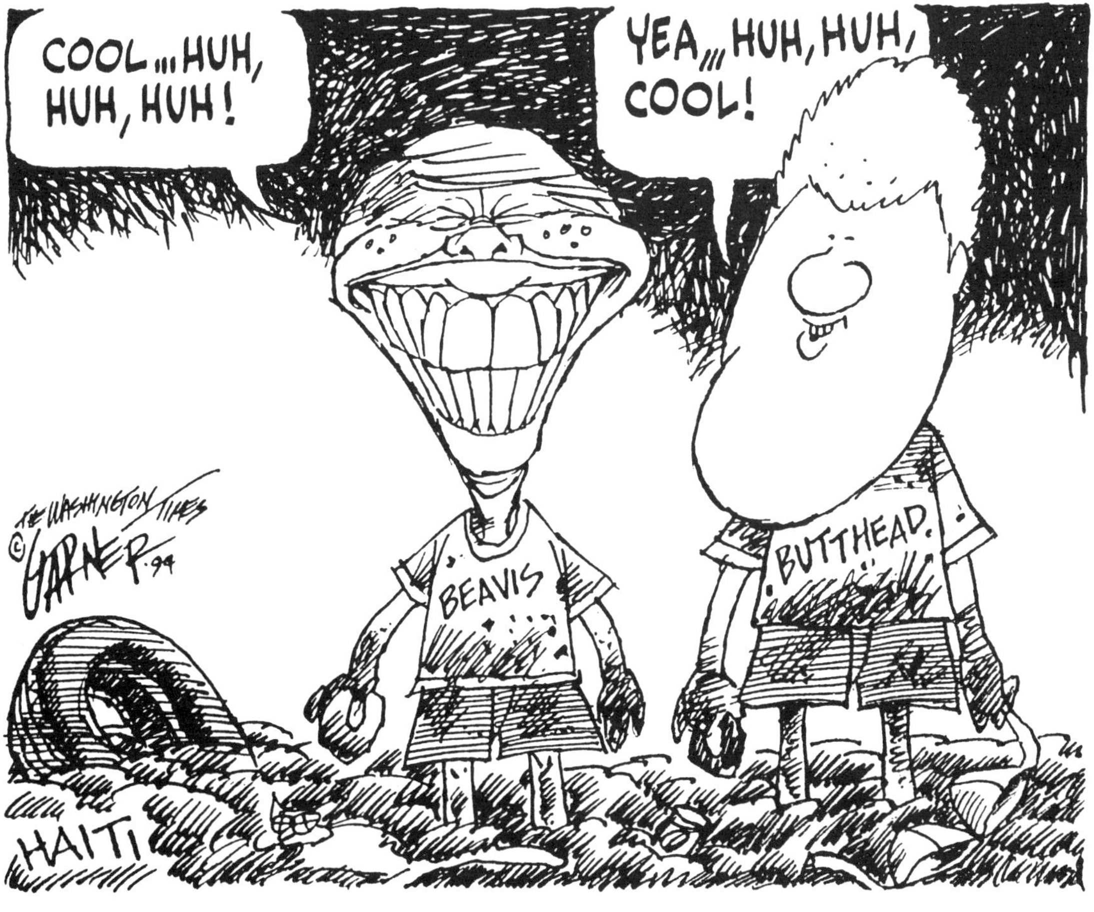
COOL... HUH, HUH, HUH!
YEA... HUH, HUH, COOL!
BEAVIS
BUTTHEAD
HAITI

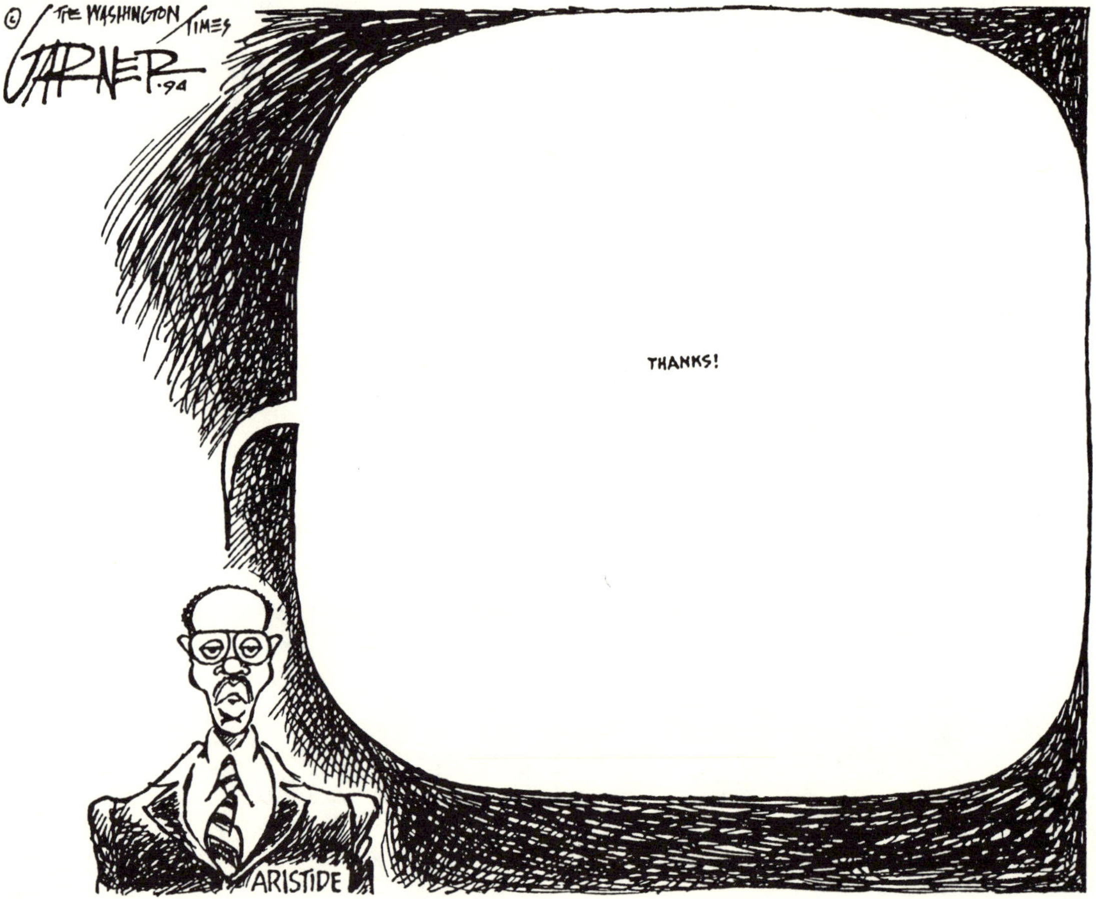
© THE WASHINGTON TIMES
GARNER ·94
THANKS!
ARISTIDE

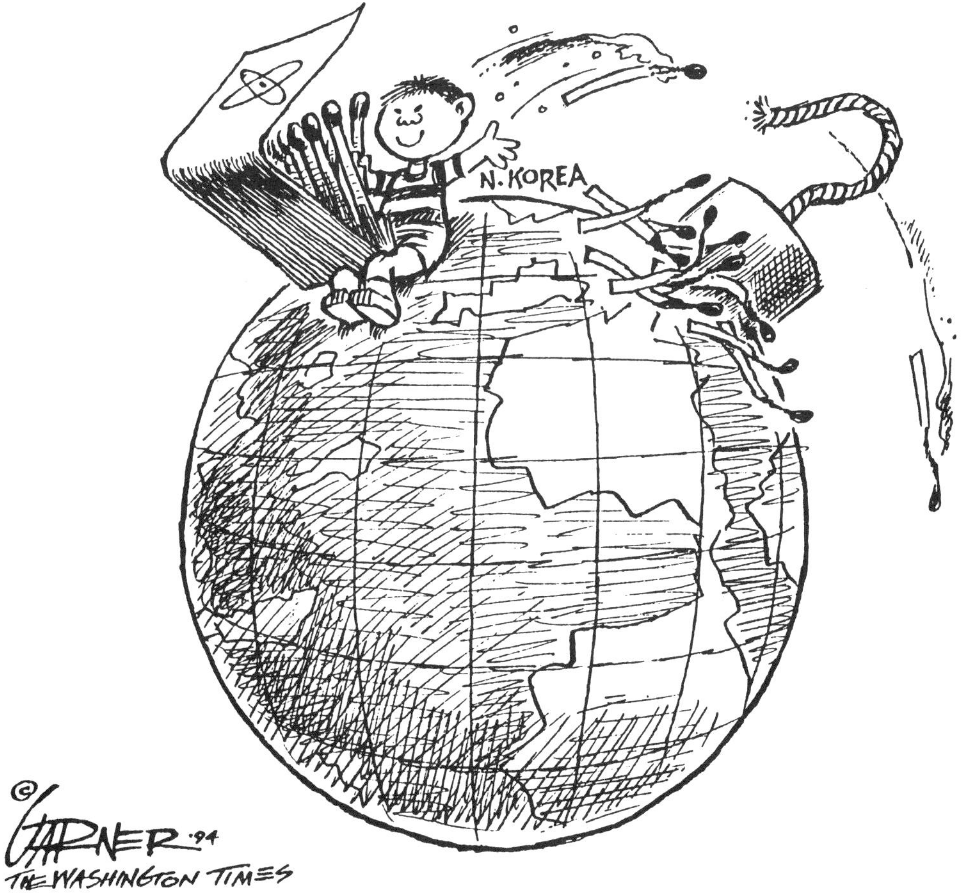
N. KOREA
© GARNER '94
THE WASHINGTON TIMES

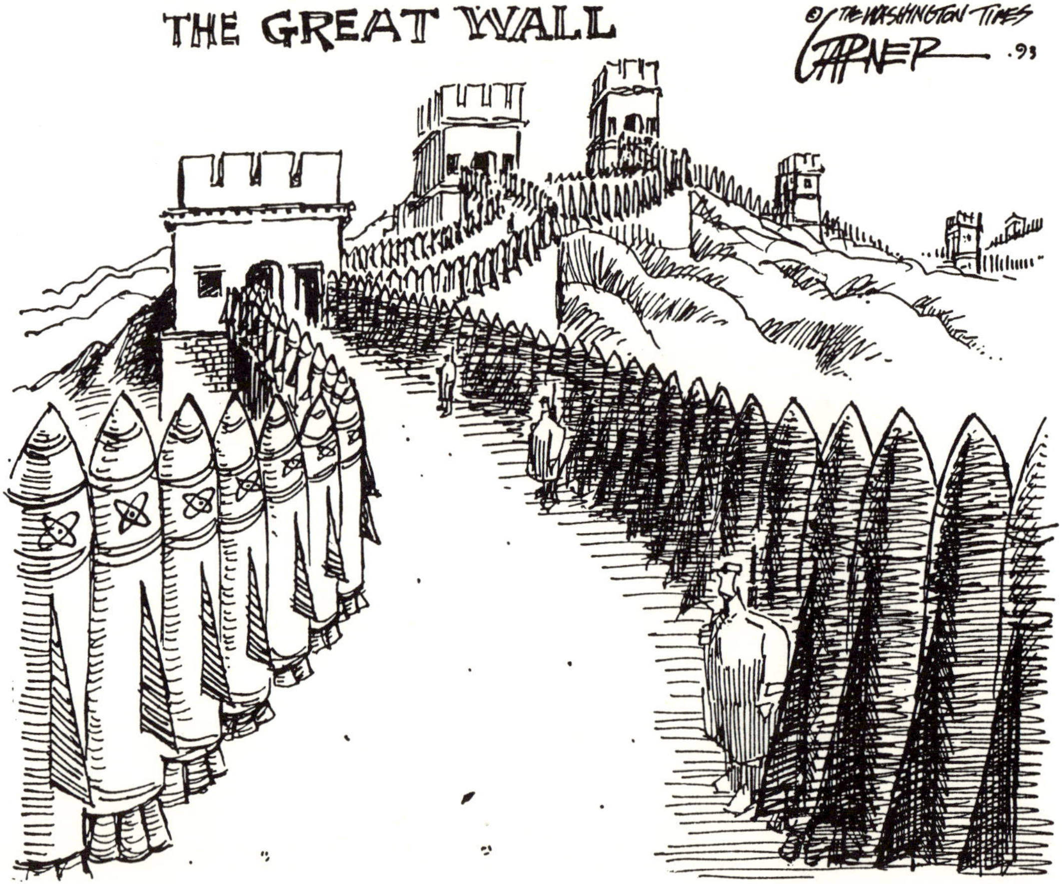
THE GREAT WALL
© THE WASHINGTON TIMES
GARNER '93

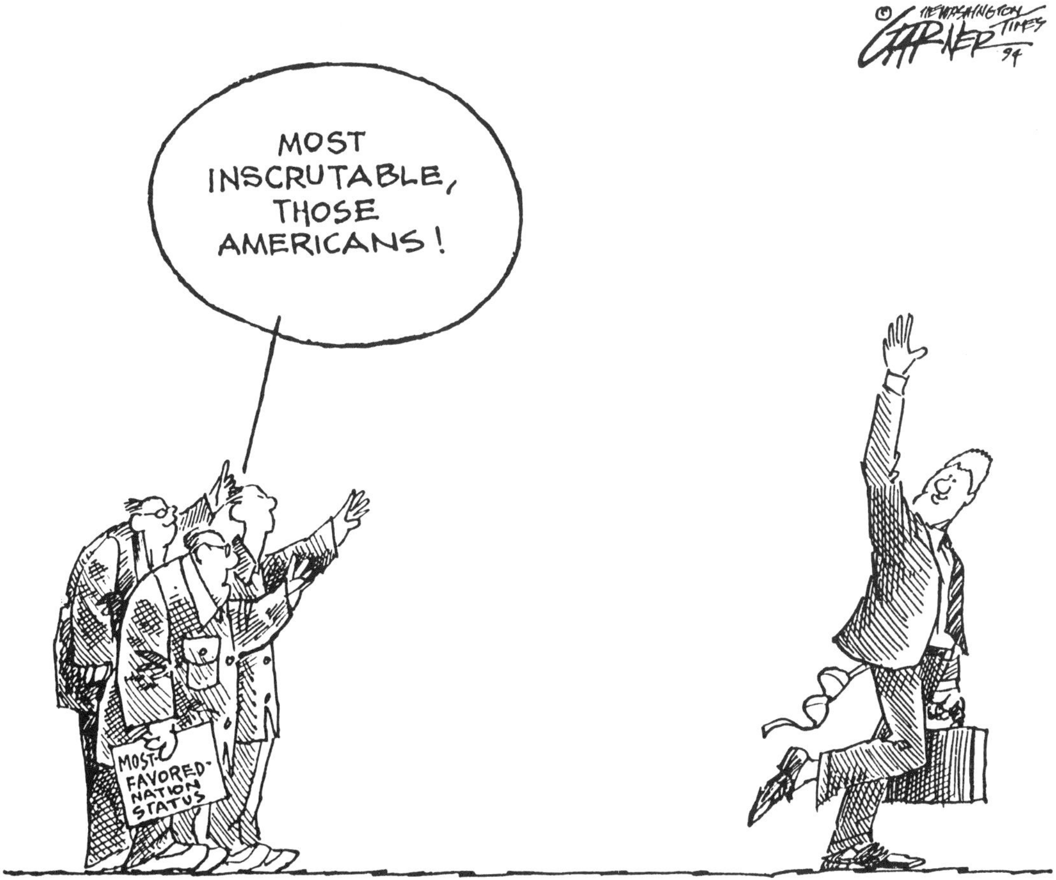
MOST INSCRUTABLE, THOSE AMERICANS!
MOST-FAVORED-NATION STATUS
© GARNER THE WASHINGTON TIMES 94

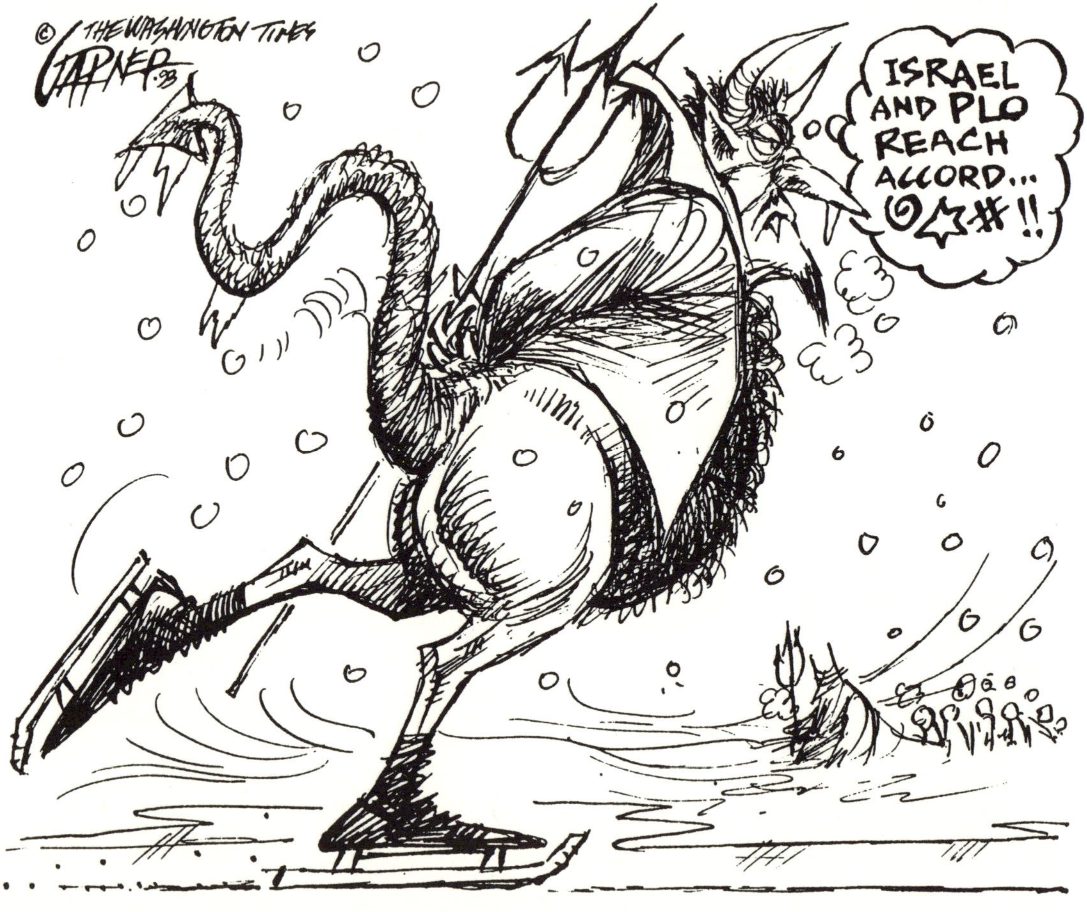
© THE WASHINGTON TIMES
GARNER '93
ISRAEL AND PLO REACH ACCORD...
#!!

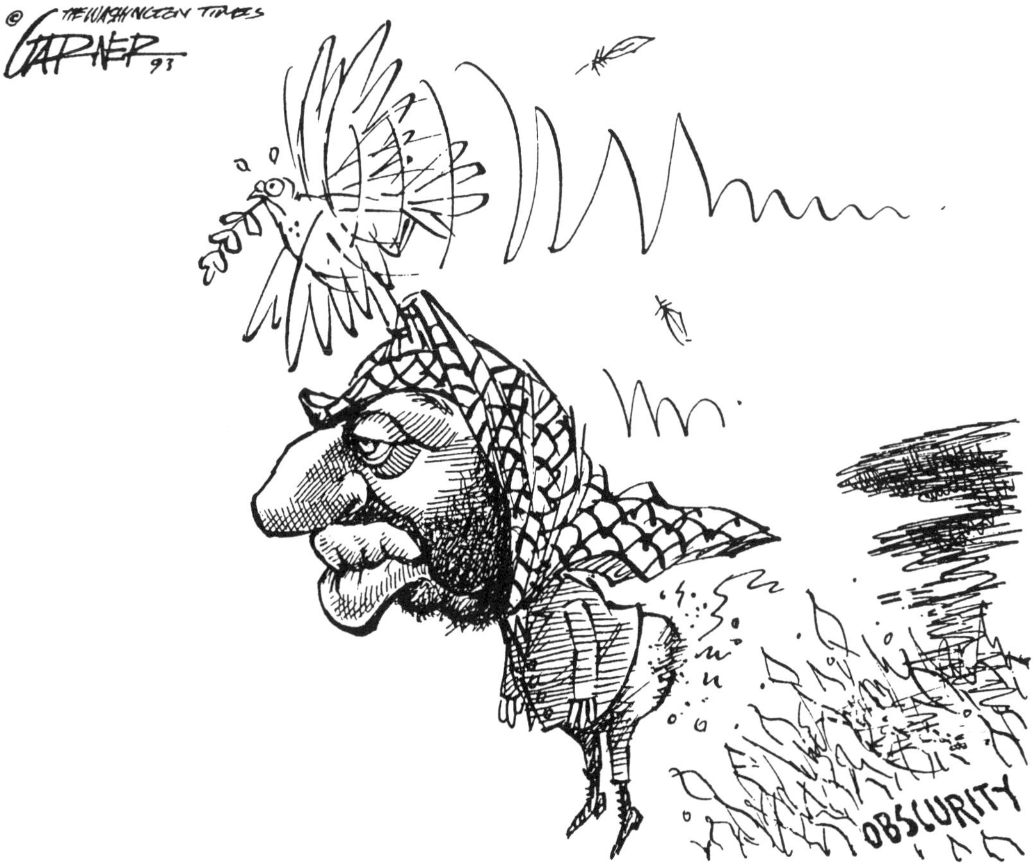
© THE WASHINGTON TIMES
GARNER 93
OBSCURITY

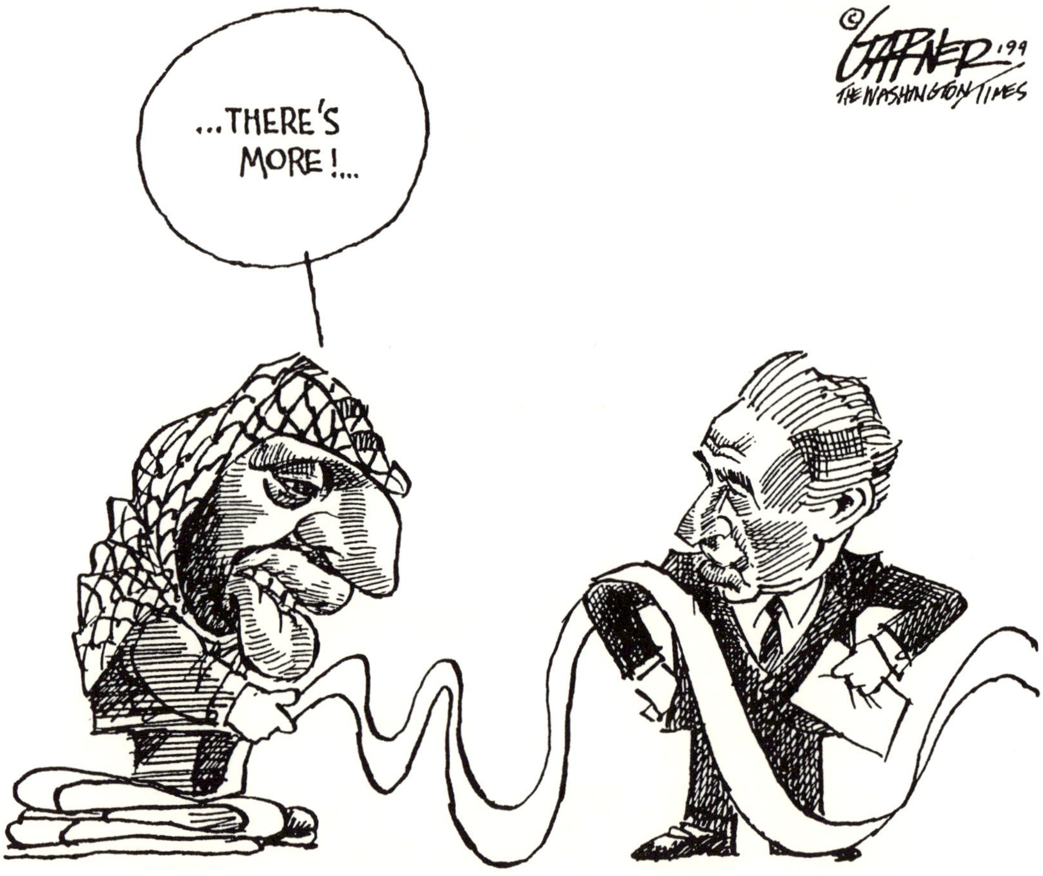
...THERE'S MORE!...
© GARNER '99
THE WASHINGTON TIMES

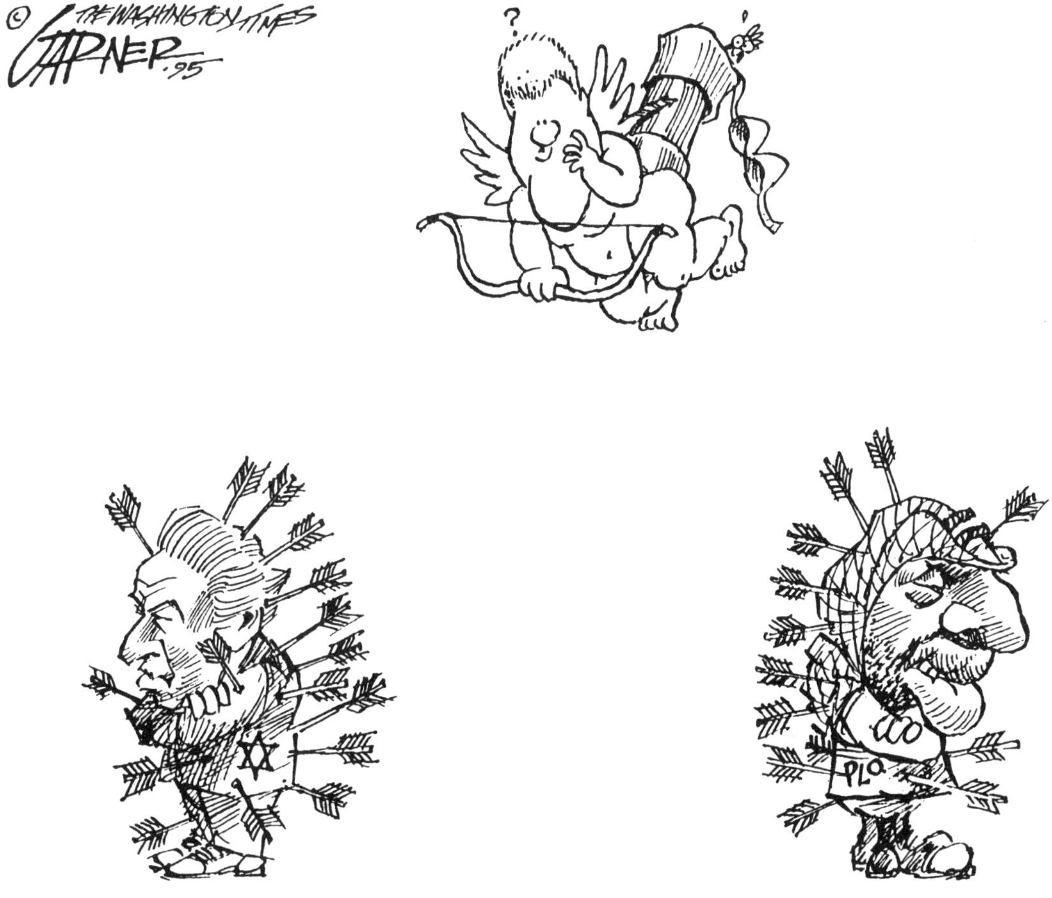
© THE WASHINGTON TIMES
GARNER '95
PLO

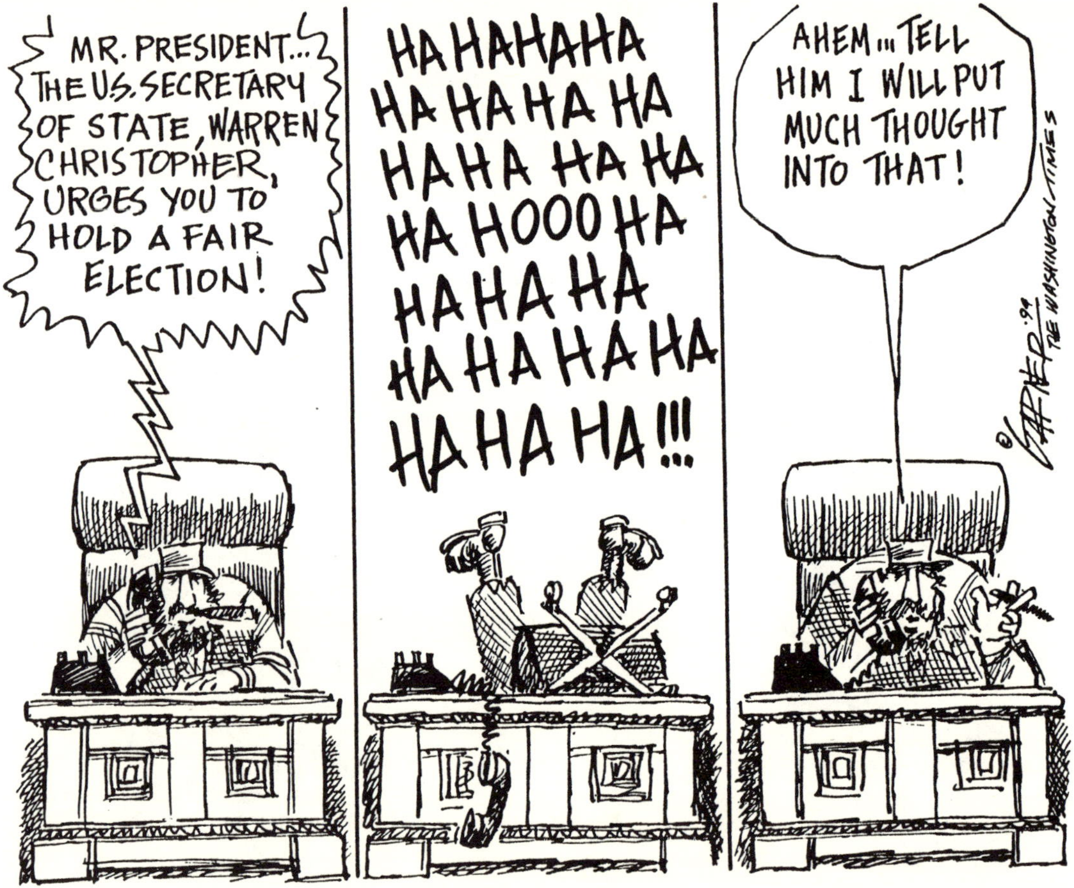
MR. PRESIDENT... THE U.S. SECRETARY OF STATE, WARREN CHRISTOPHER, URGES YOU TO HOLD A FAIR ELECTION!
HA HAHAHA HA HA HA HA HA HA HAHA HA HA HA HA HA HOOO HA HAHAHA HA HA HA HA HA HA HA HA HA!!!
AHEM... TELL HIM I WILL PUT MUCH THOUGHT INTO THAT!
© GARNER '94 THE WASHINGTON TIMES

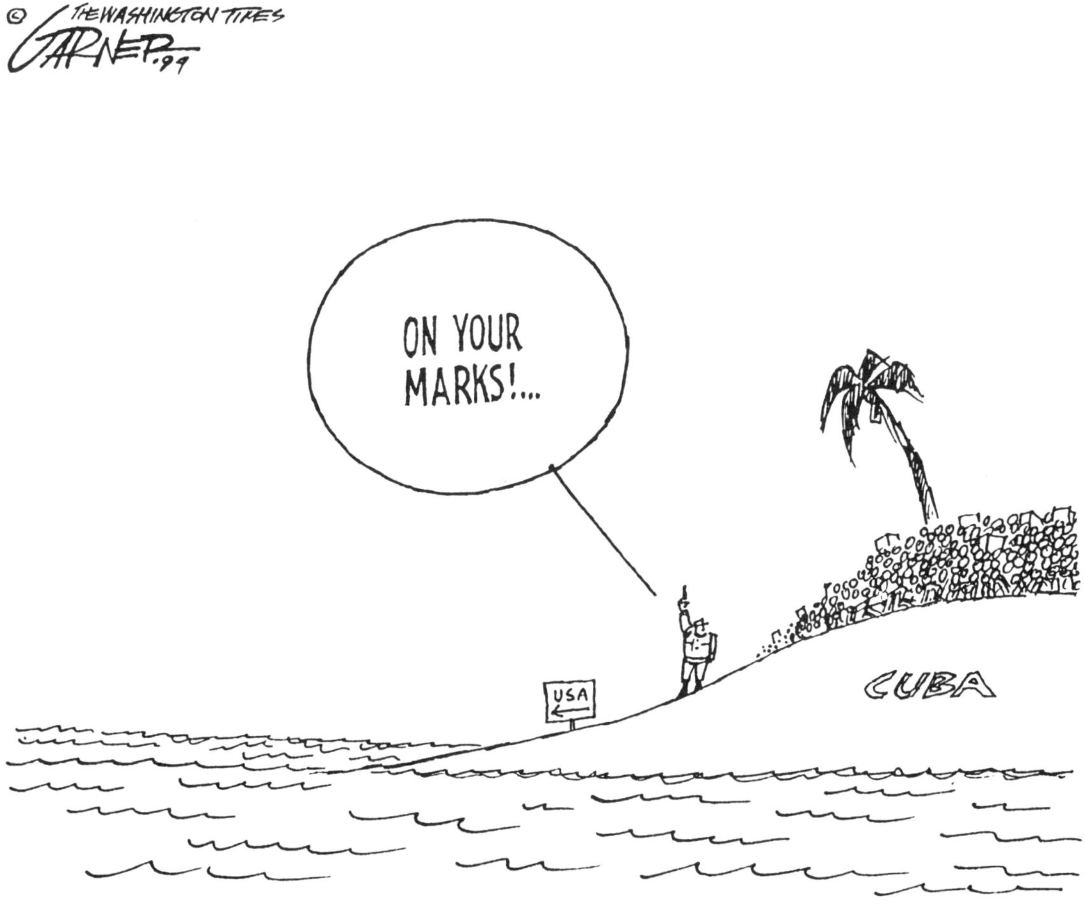
© THE WASHINGTON TIMES
GARNER '99
ON YOUR MARKS!...
USA
CUBA

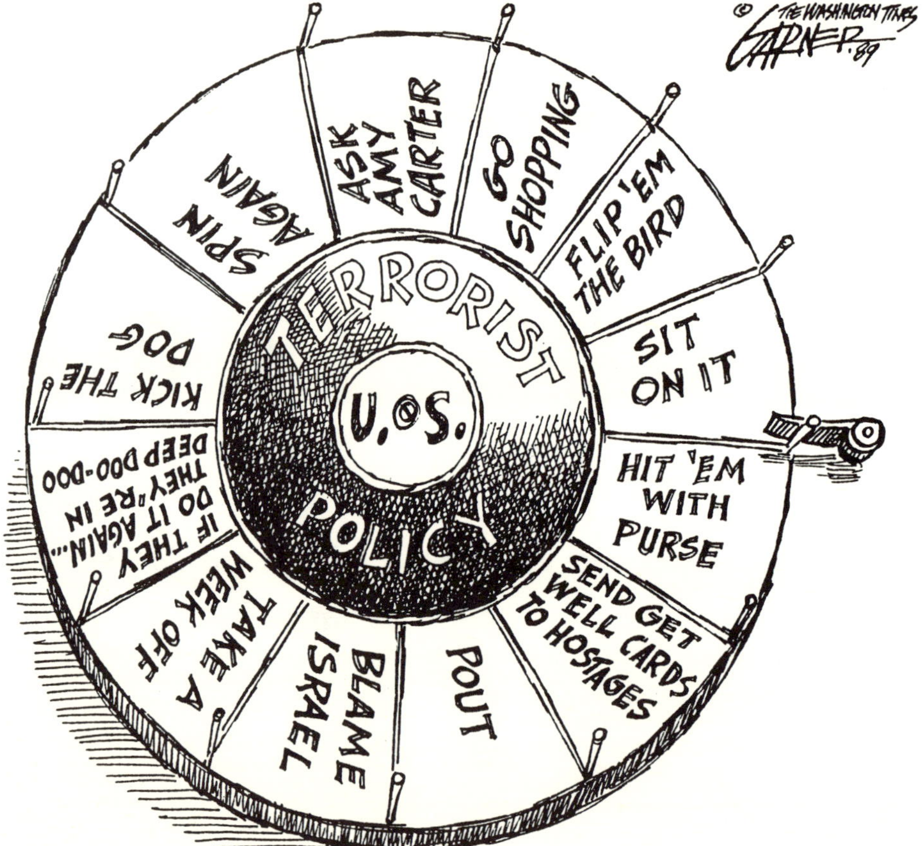
TERRORIST
U.S.
POLICY
SPIN AGAIN
ASK AMY CARTER
GO SHOPPING
FLIP 'EM THE BIRD
SIT ON IT
HIT 'EM WITH PURSE
SEND GET WELL CARDS TO HOSTAGES
POUT
BLAME ISRAEL
TAKE A WEEK OFF
IF THEY DO IT AGAIN... THEY'RE IN DEEP DOO-DOO
KICK THE DOG
© THE WASHINGTON TIMES
GARNER '89

The Media

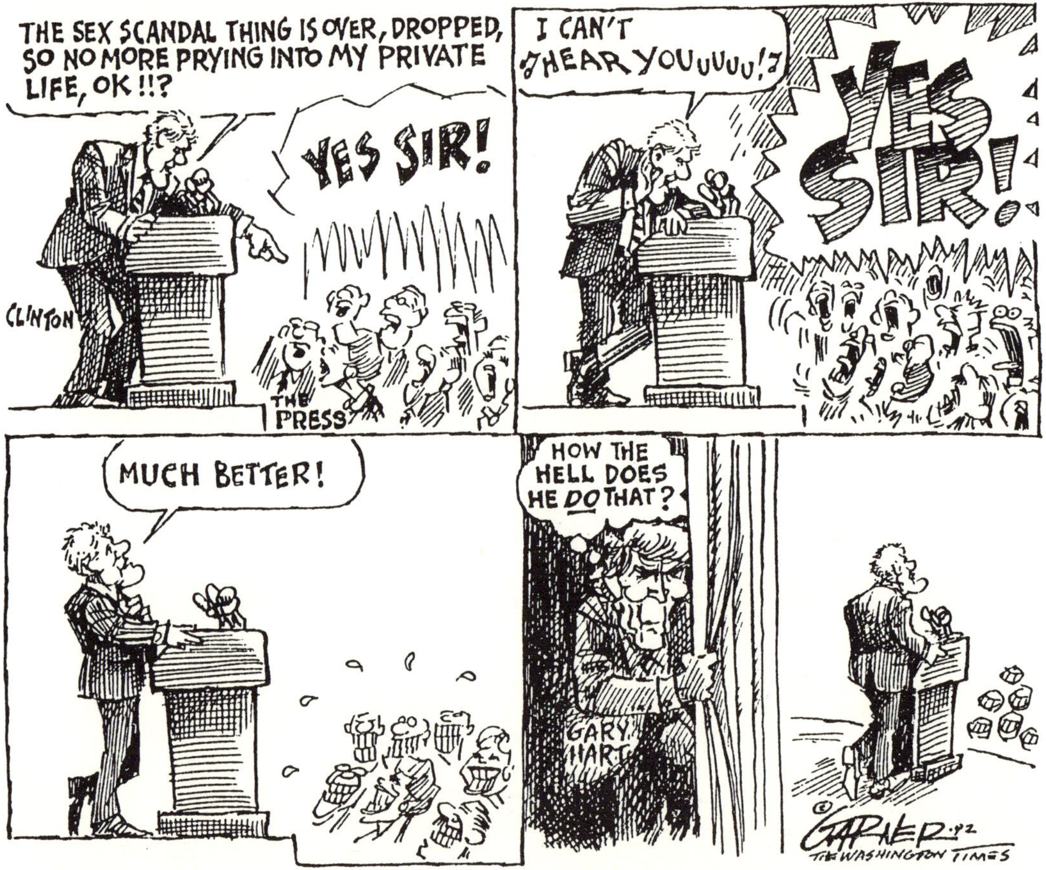
THE SEX SCANDAL THING IS OVER, DROPPED, SO NO MORE PRYING INTO MY PRIVATE LIFE, OK !!?
YES SIR!
CLINTON
THE PRESS
I CAN'T HEAR YOUUUUU!
YES SIR!
MUCH BETTER!
HOW THE HELL DOES HE DO THAT?
GARY HART
© GARNER '92
THE WASHINGTON TIMES

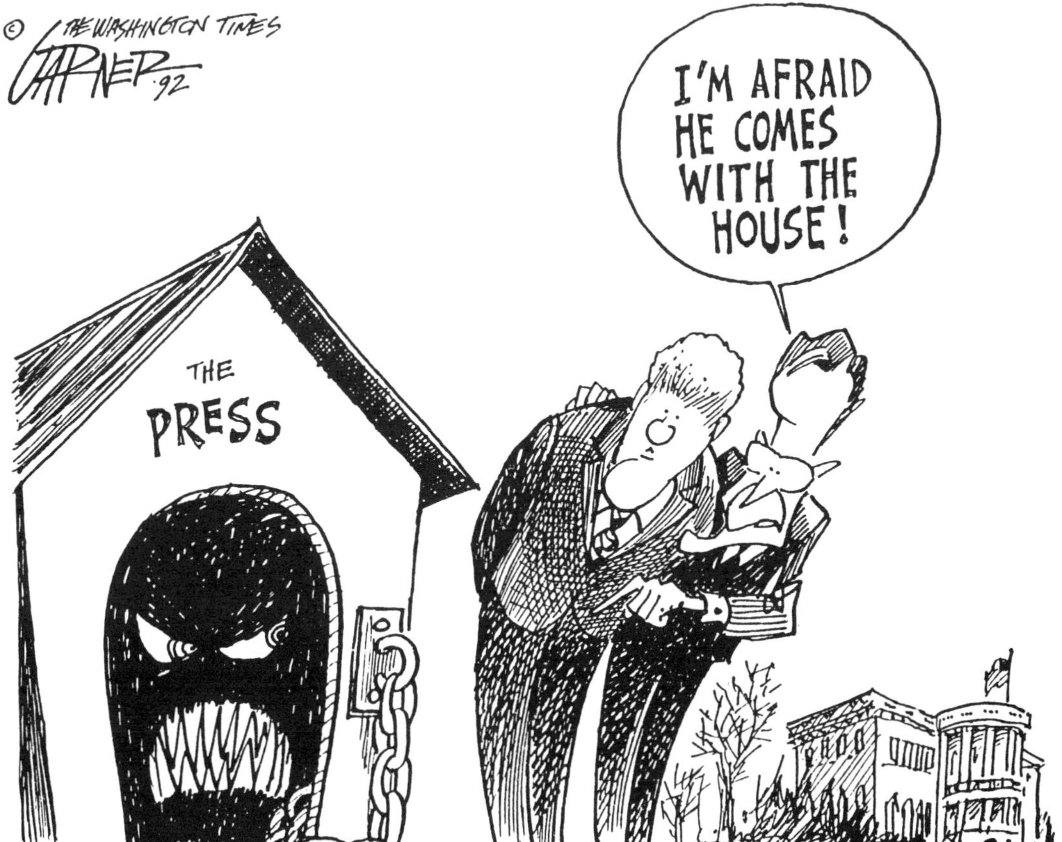
© THE WASHINGTON TIMES
I'M AFRAID HE COMES WITH THE HOUSE!
THE PRESS

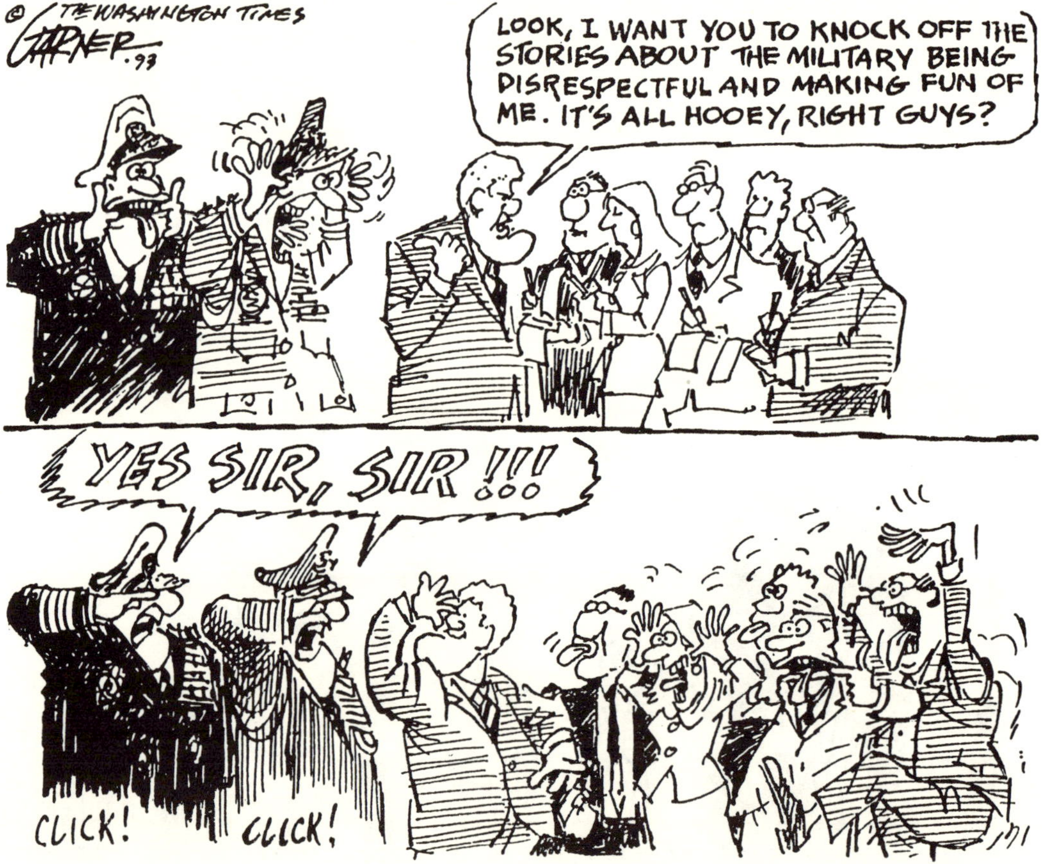
© THE WASHINGTON TIMES
GARNER '93
LOOK, I WANT YOU TO KNOCK OFF THE STORIES ABOUT THE MILITARY BEING DISRESPECTFUL AND MAKING FUN OF ME. IT'S ALL HOOEY, RIGHT GUYS?
YES SIR, SIR!!!
CLICK!
CLICK!

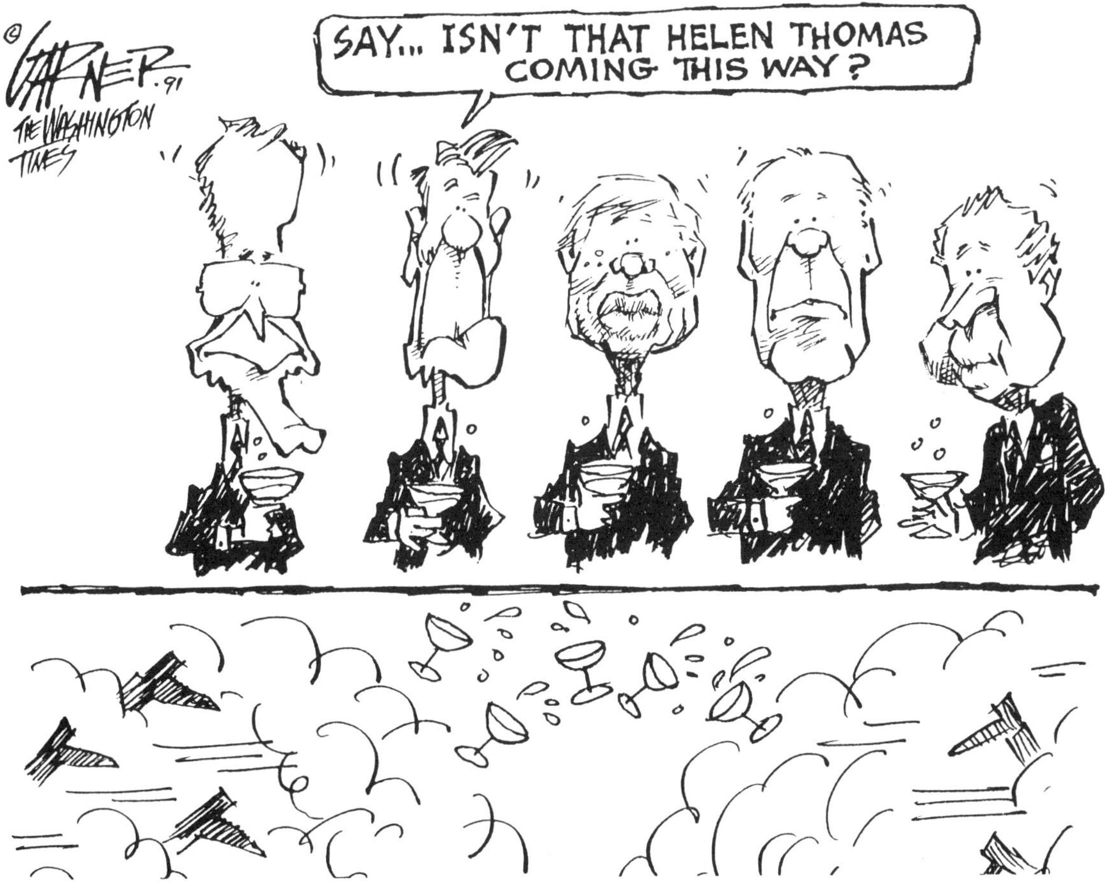
SAY... ISN'T THAT HELEN THOMAS COMING THIS WAY?
© GARNER '91 THE WASHINGTON TIMES

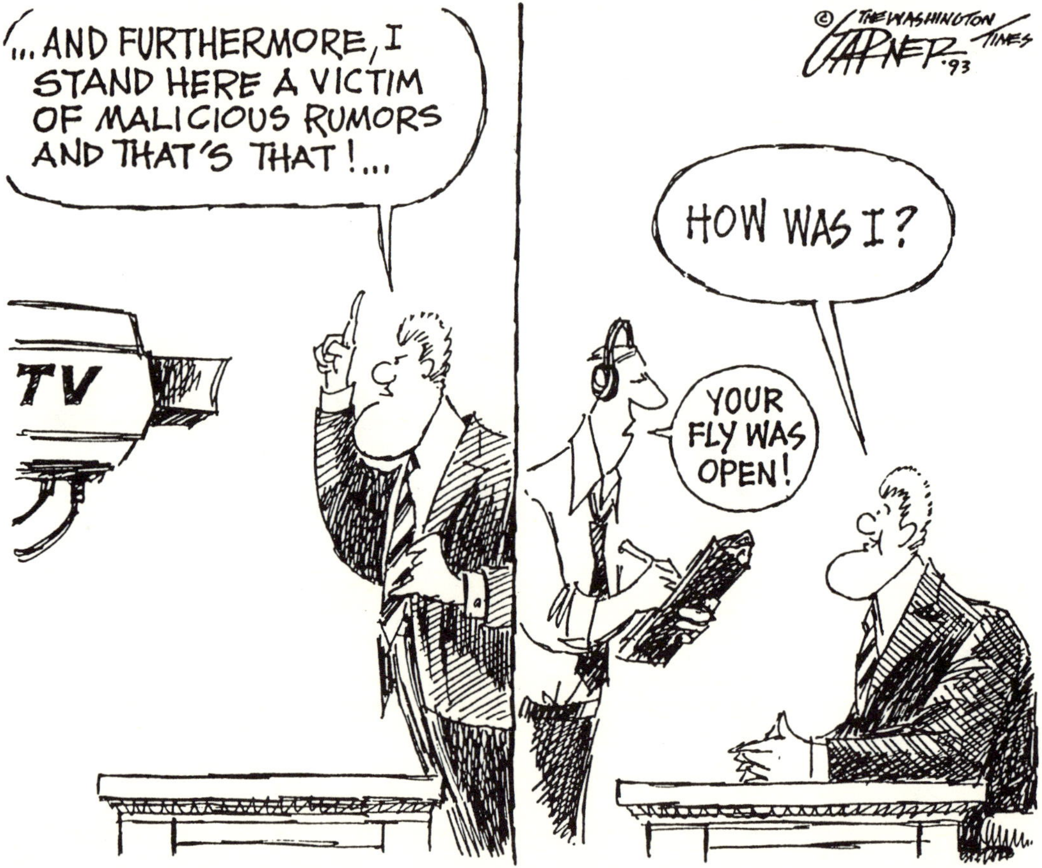
©
THE WASHINGTON TIMES
'93
...AND FURTHERMORE, I STAND HERE A VICTIM OF MALICIOUS RUMORS AND THAT'S THAT!...
TV
HOW WAS I?
YOUR FLY WAS OPEN!

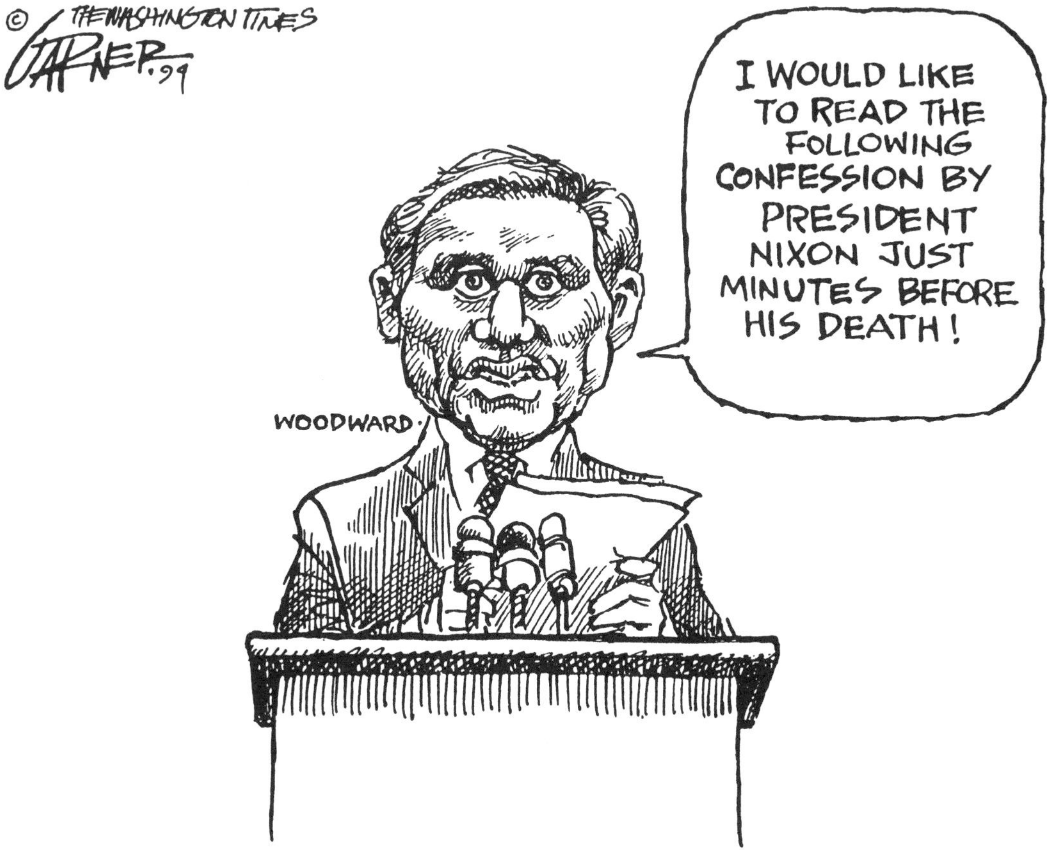
© THE WASHINGTON TIMES
GARNER '99
I WOULD LIKE TO READ THE FOLLOWING CONFESSION BY PRESIDENT NIXON JUST MINUTES BEFORE HIS DEATH!
WOODWARD

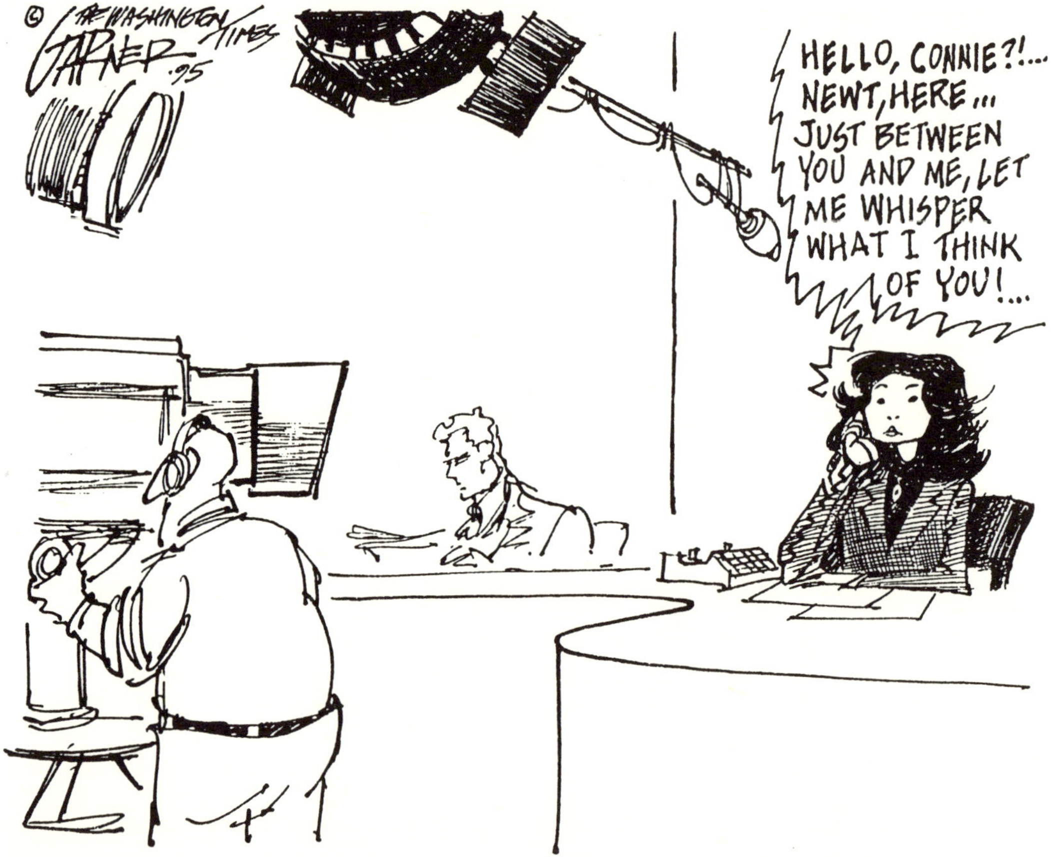
© THE WASHINGTON TIMES GARNER '95
HELLO, CONNIE?!... NEWT, HERE... JUST BETWEEN YOU AND ME, LET ME WHISPER WHAT I THINK OF YOU!...

The Military

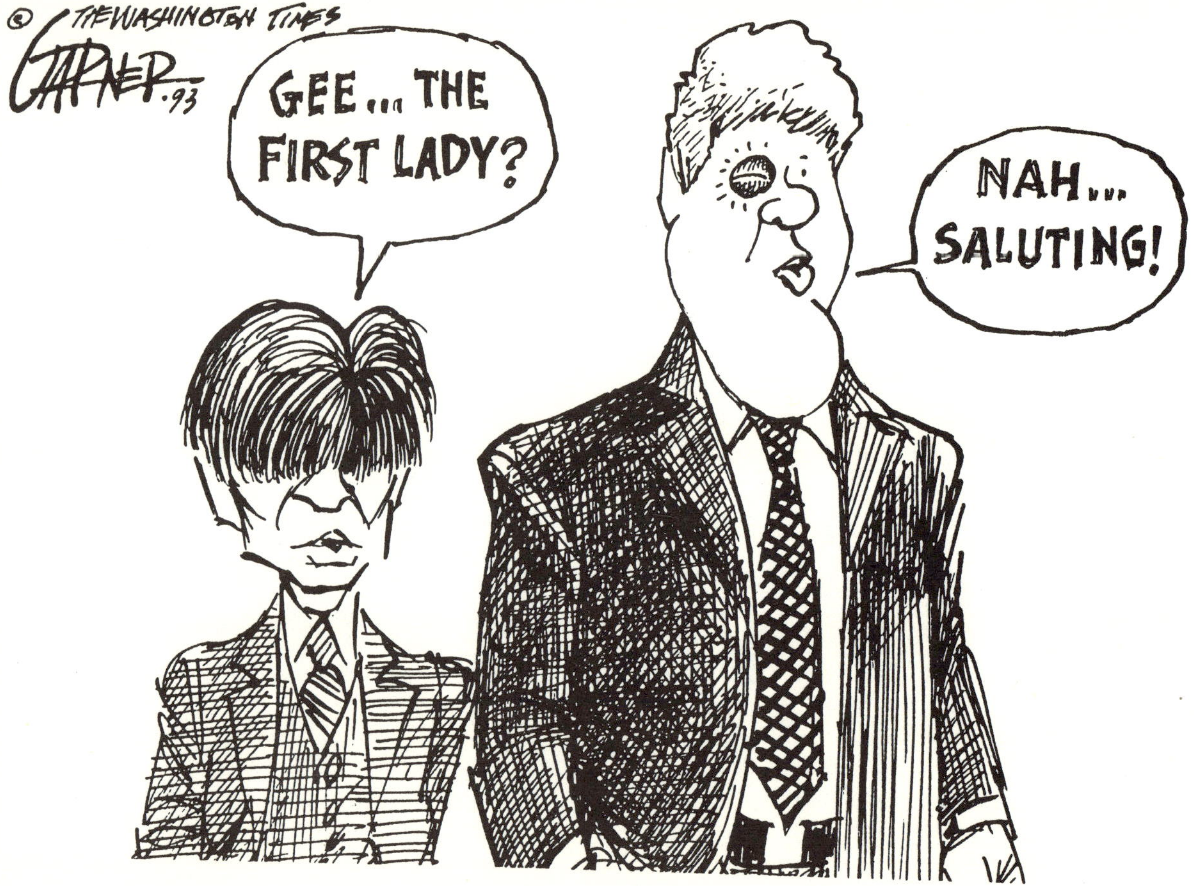
© THE WASHINGTON TIMES
GARNER '93
GEE... THE FIRST LADY?
NAH... SALUTING!

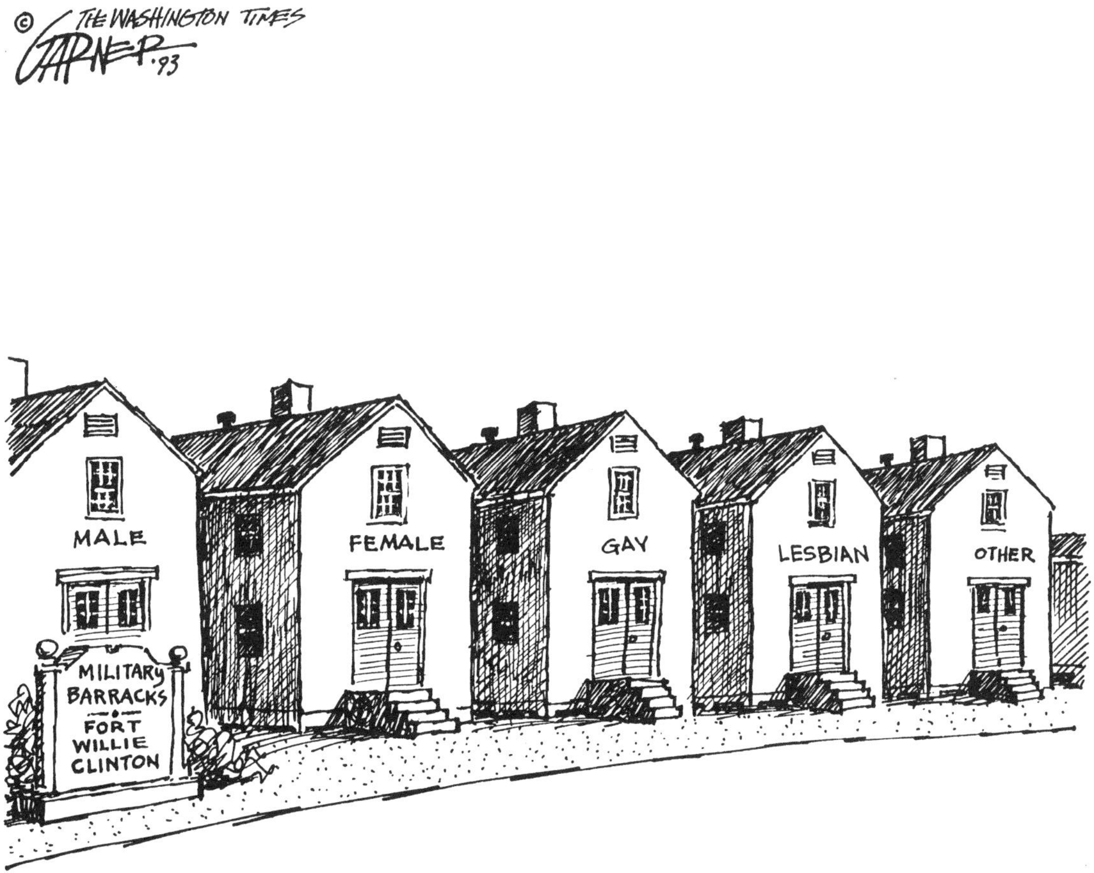
© THE WASHINGTON TIMES
GARNER '93
MALE
FEMALE
GAY
LESBIAN
OTHER
MILITARY BARRACKS
FORT WILLIE CLINTON

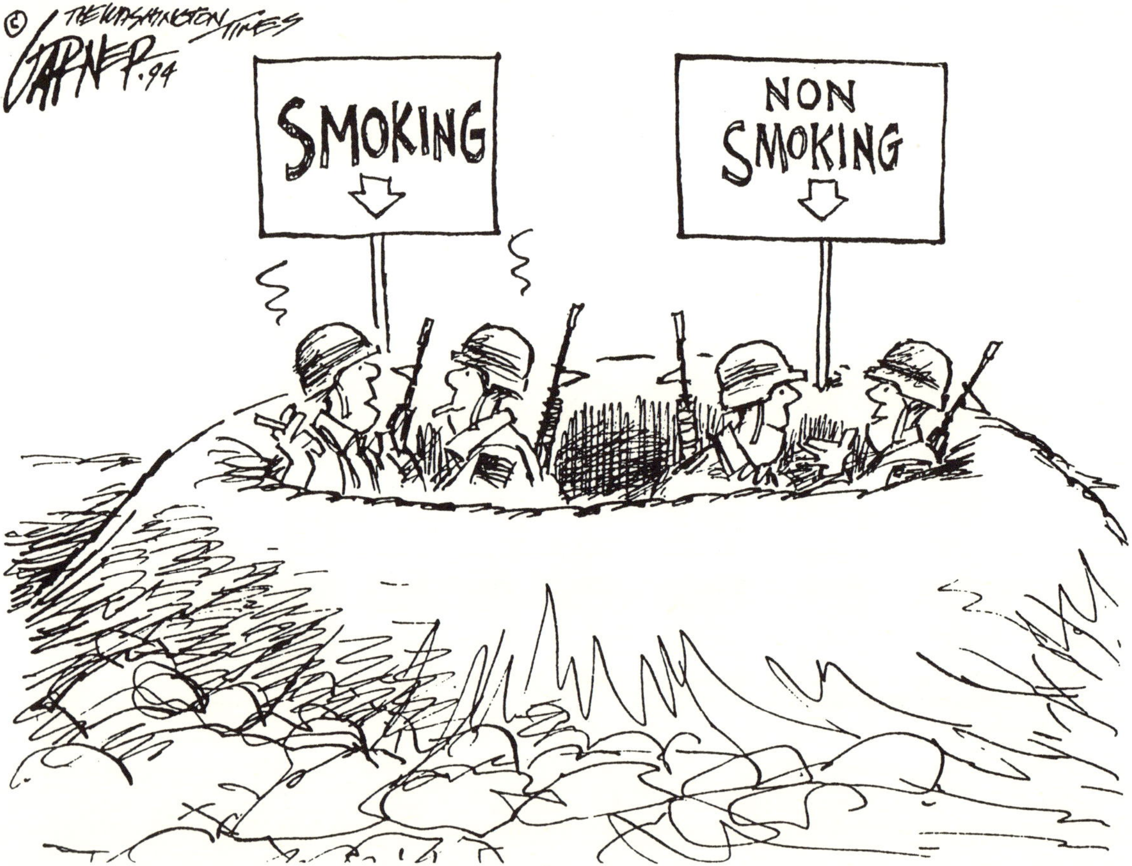
© THE WASHINGTON TIMES
GARNER '94
SMOKING
NON SMOKING

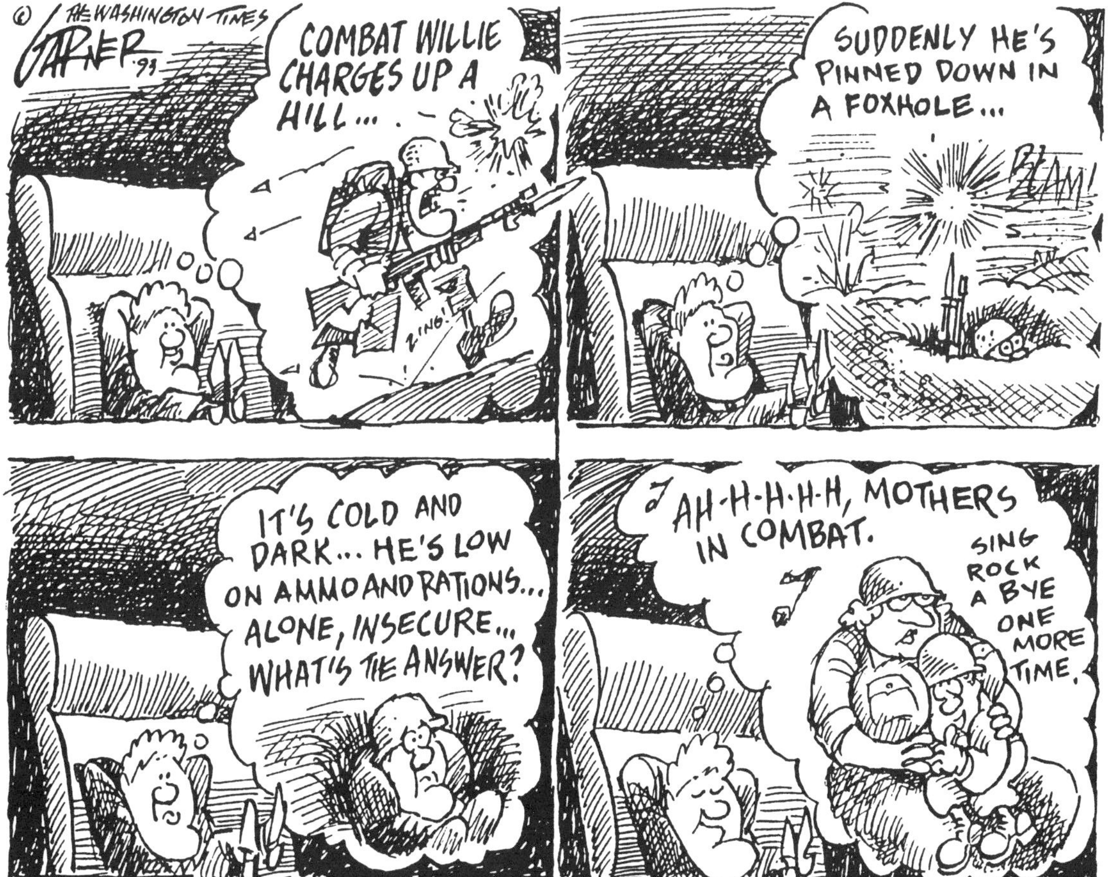
© THE WASHINGTON TIMES
GARNER '93
COMBAT WILLIE CHARGES UP A HILL...
ZING!
SUDDENLY HE'S PINNED DOWN IN A FOXHOLE...
BLAM!
IT'S COLD AND DARK... HE'S LOW ON AMMO AND RATIONS... ALONE, INSECURE... WHAT'S THE ANSWER?
AH-H-H-H-H, MOTHERS IN COMBAT.
SING ROCK A BYE ONE MORE TIME.

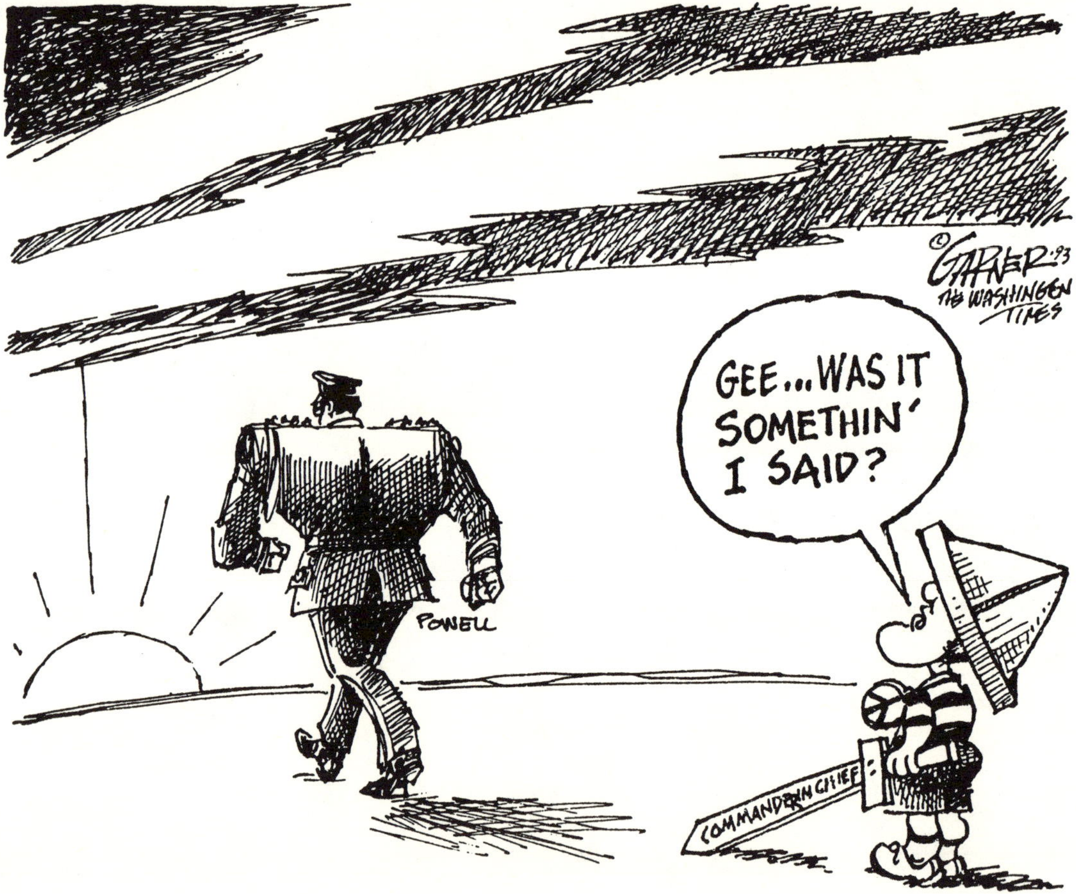
© GARNER '93 THE WASHINGTON TIMES
GEE...WAS IT SOMETHIN' I SAID?
POWELL
COMMANDER IN CHIEF

D.C.

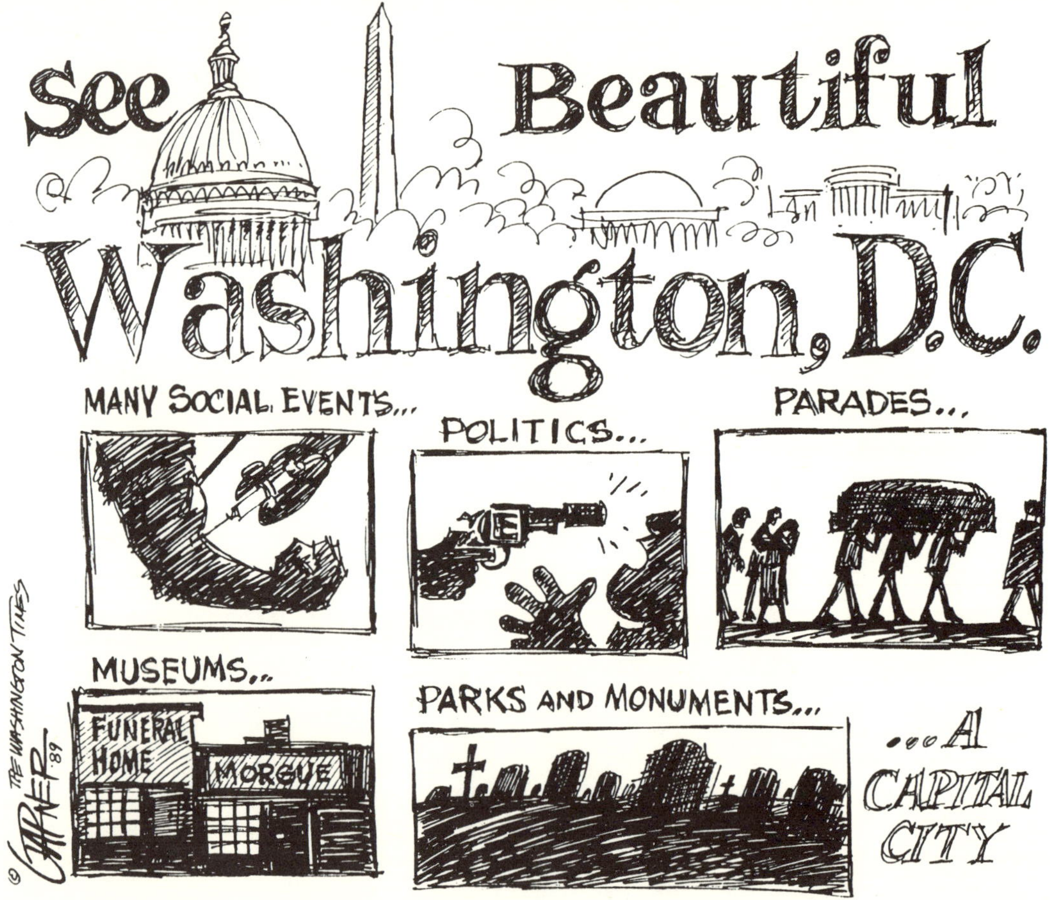
See Beautiful Washington, D.C.
MANY SOCIAL EVENTS...
POLITICS...
PARADES...
MUSEUMS...
FUNERAL HOME
MORGUE
PARKS AND MONUMENTS...
...A CAPITAL CITY
© GARNER '89 THE WASHINGTON TIMES

AN ENDANGERED SPECIES

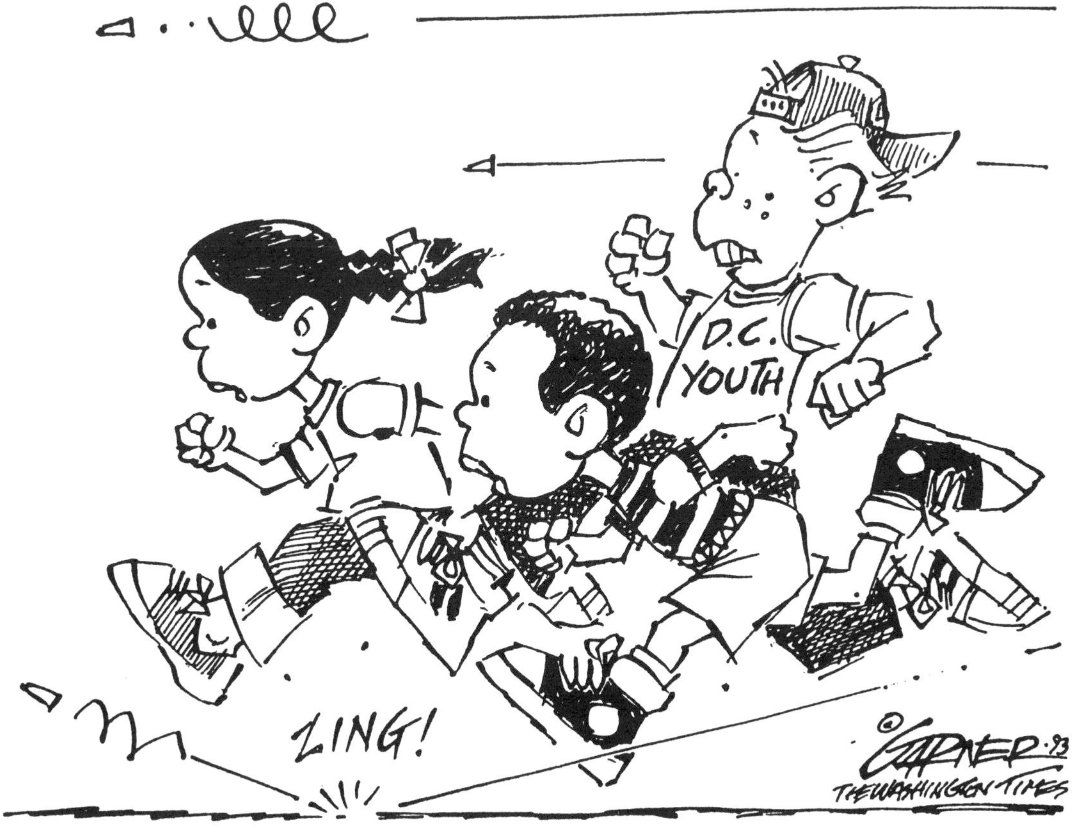

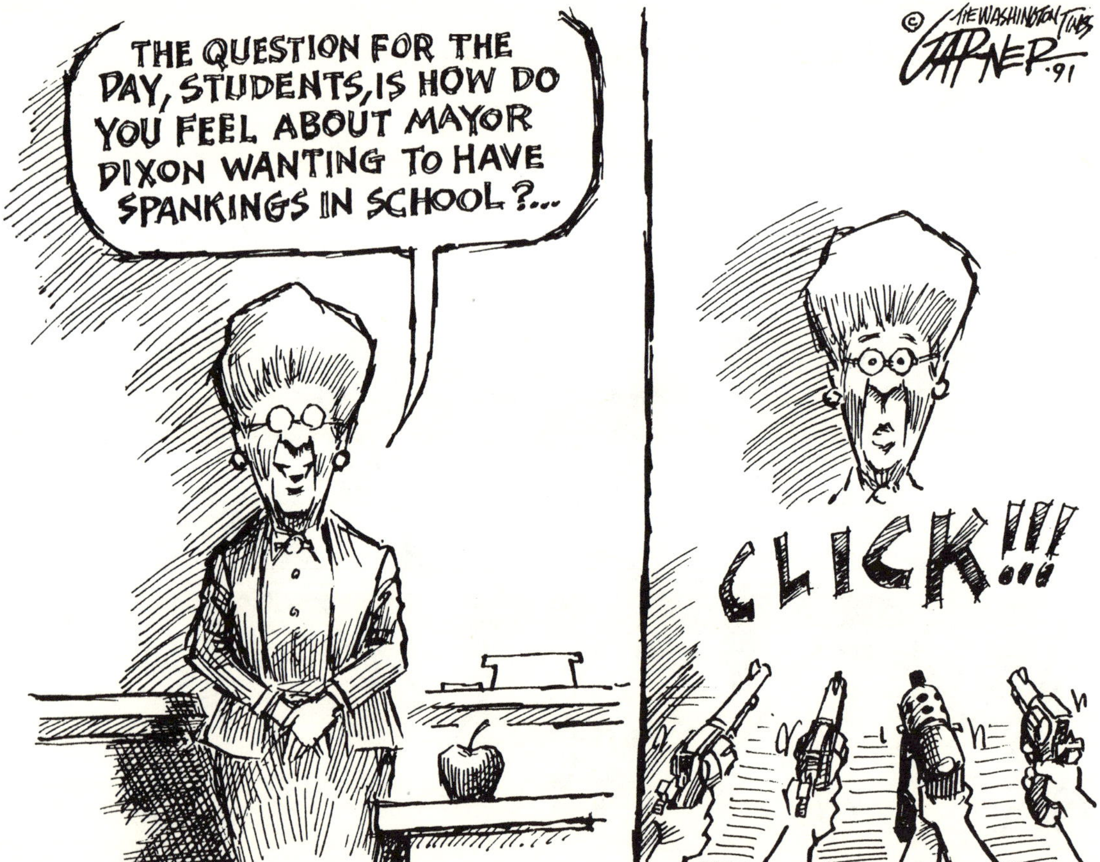
THE QUESTION FOR THE DAY, STUDENTS, IS HOW DO YOU FEEL ABOUT MAYOR DIXON WANTING TO HAVE SPANKINGS IN SCHOOL?...
CLICK!!!
© THE WASHINGTON TIMES GARNER '91

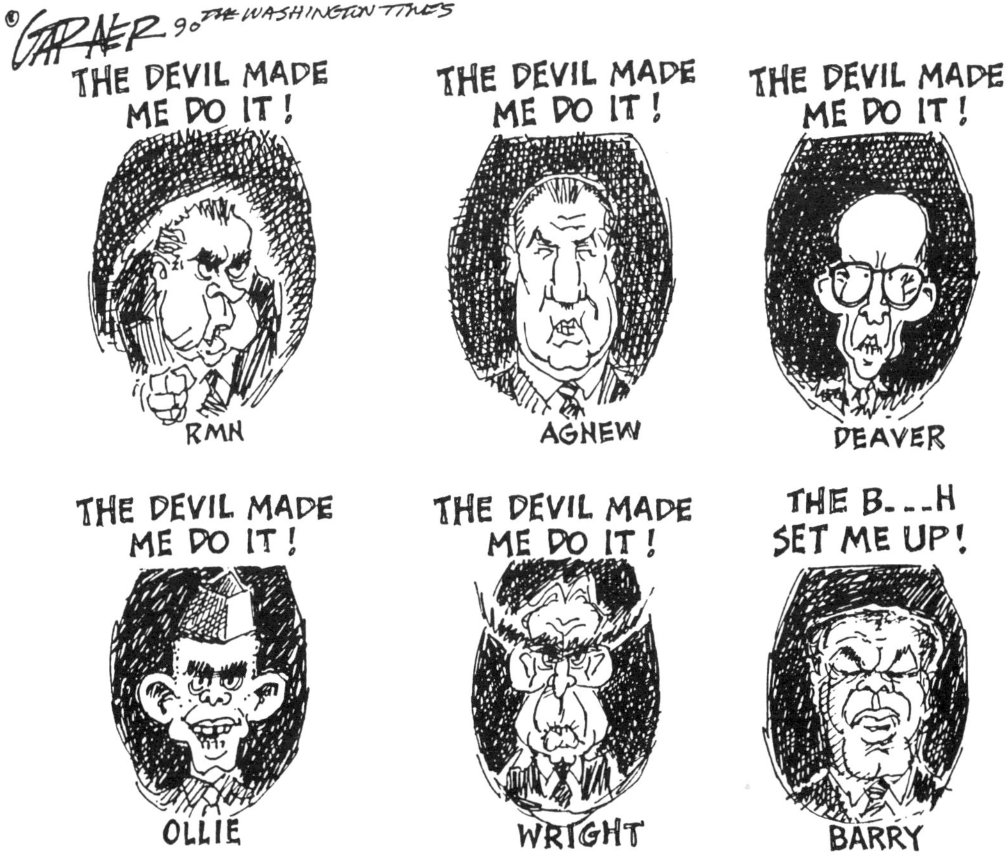
© GARNER 90 THE WASHINGTON TIMES
THE DEVIL MADE ME DO IT!
RMN
THE DEVIL MADE ME DO IT!
AGNEW
THE DEVIL MADE ME DO IT!
DEAVER
THE DEVIL MADE ME DO IT!
OLLIE
THE DEVIL MADE ME DO IT!
WRIGHT
THE B---H SET ME UP!
BARRY

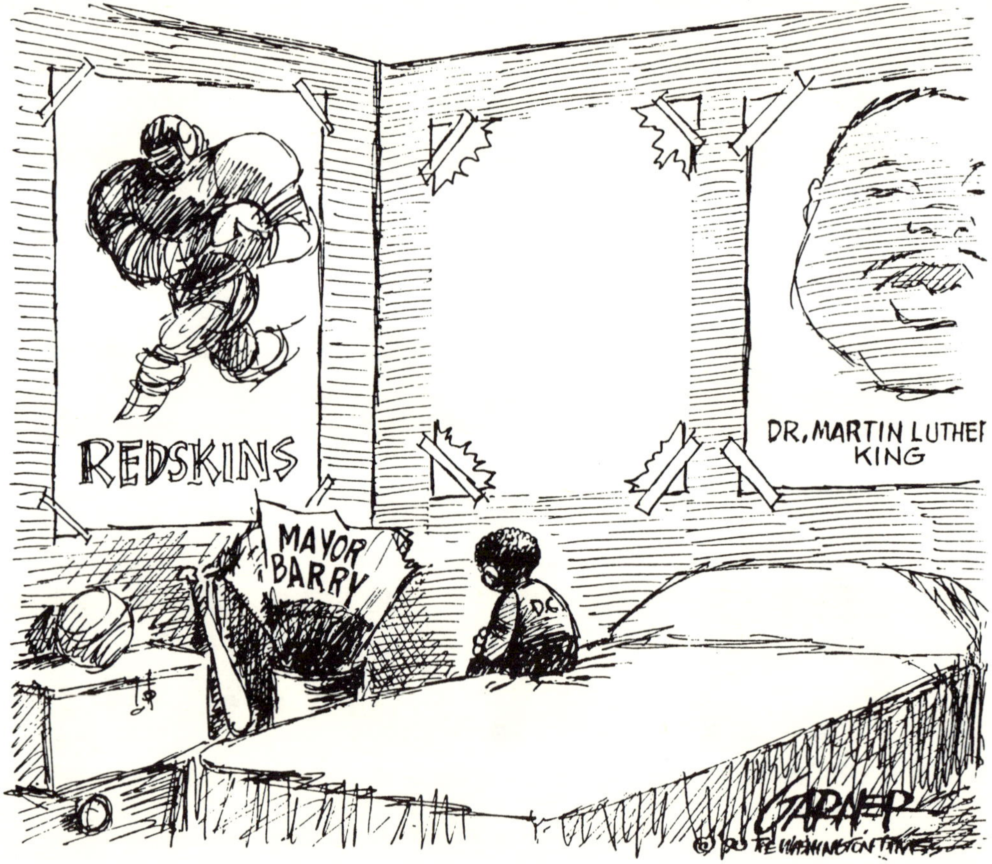
REDSKINS
MAYOR BARRY
D.C.
DR. MARTIN LUTHE
KING
GARNER
THE WASHINGTON TIMES

OJ

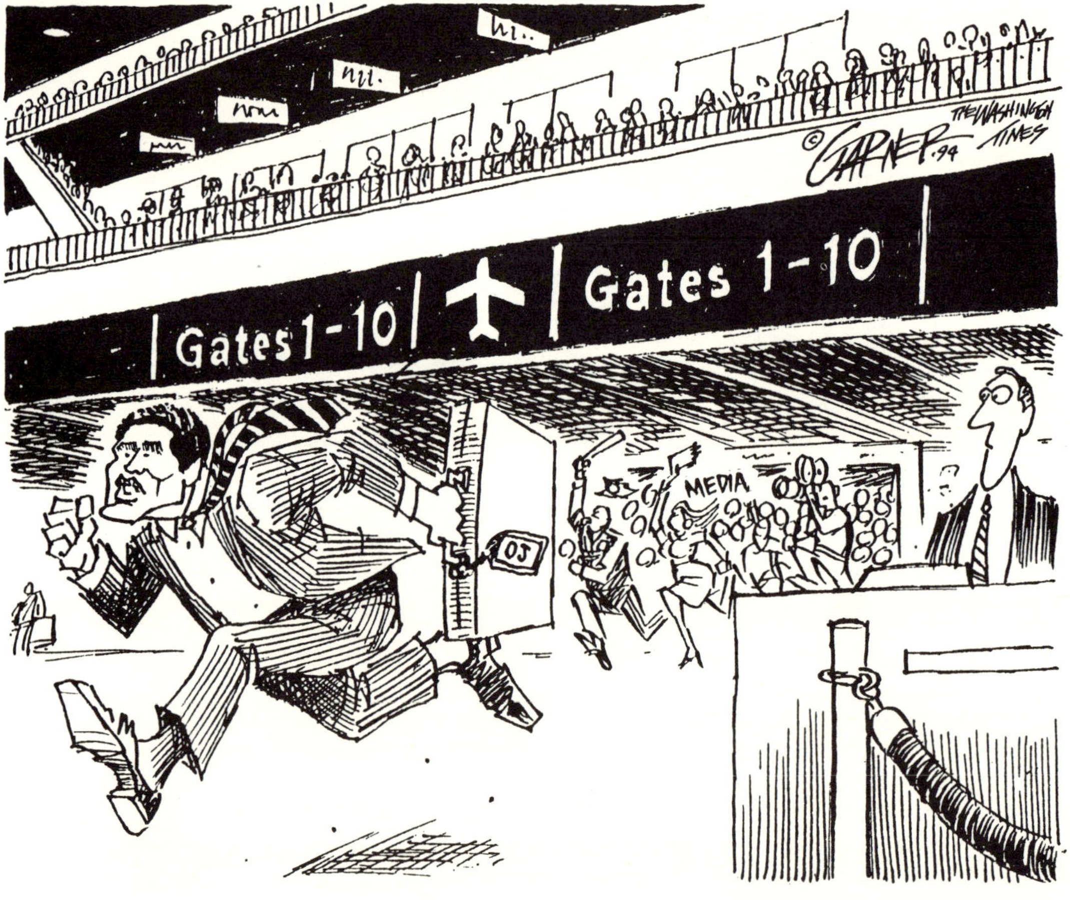
Gates 1-10
Gates 1-10
MEDIA
OJ
© GARNER '94 THE WASHINGTON TIMES

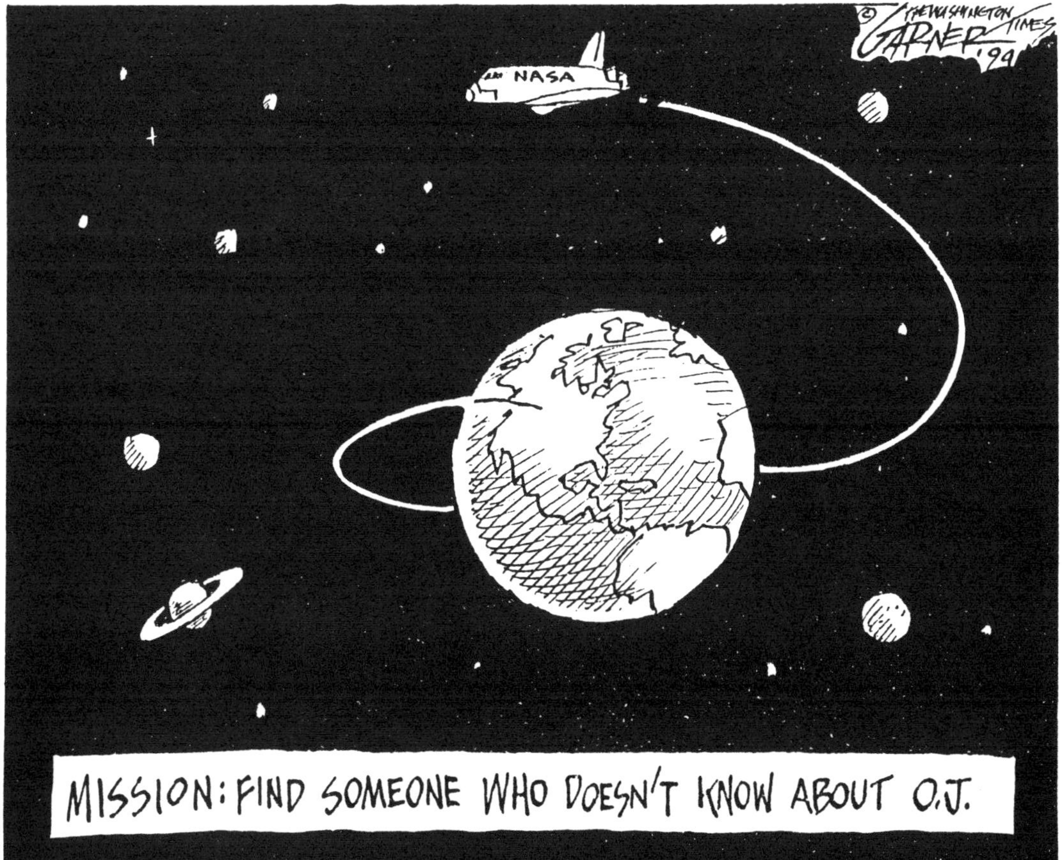

MISSION: FIND SOMEONE WHO DOESN'T KNOW ABOUT O.J.

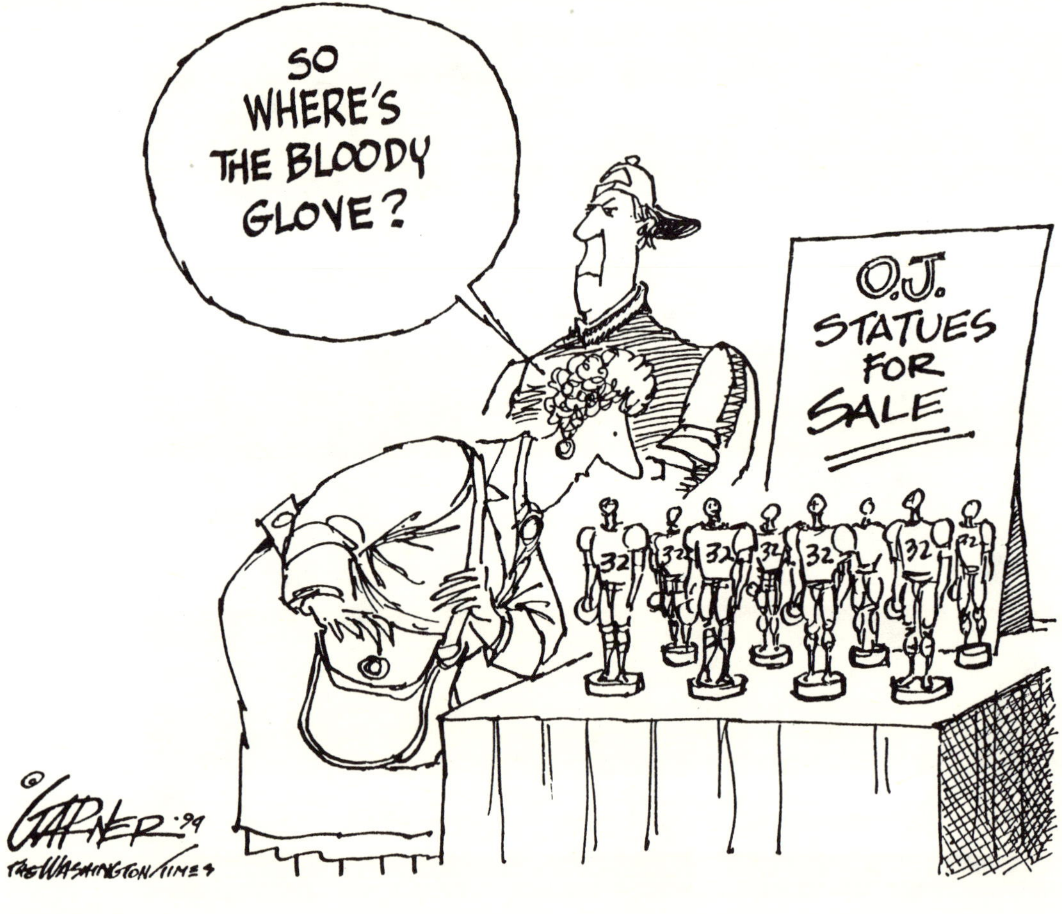
SO WHERE'S THE BLOODY GLOVE?
O.J. STATUES FOR SALE
32
©GARNER '94
THE WASHINGTON TIMES

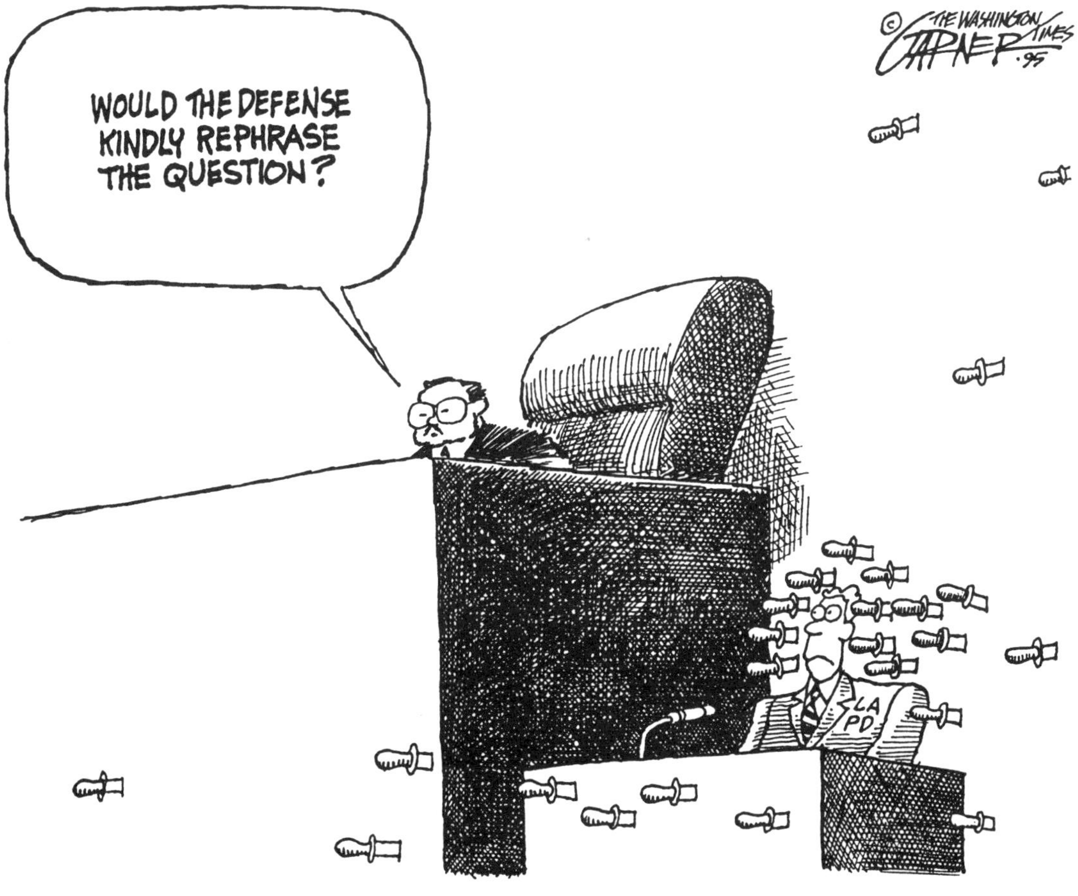
© THE WASHINGTON TIMES
GARNER '95
WOULD THE DEFENSE KINDLY REPHRASE THE QUESTION?
LA PD

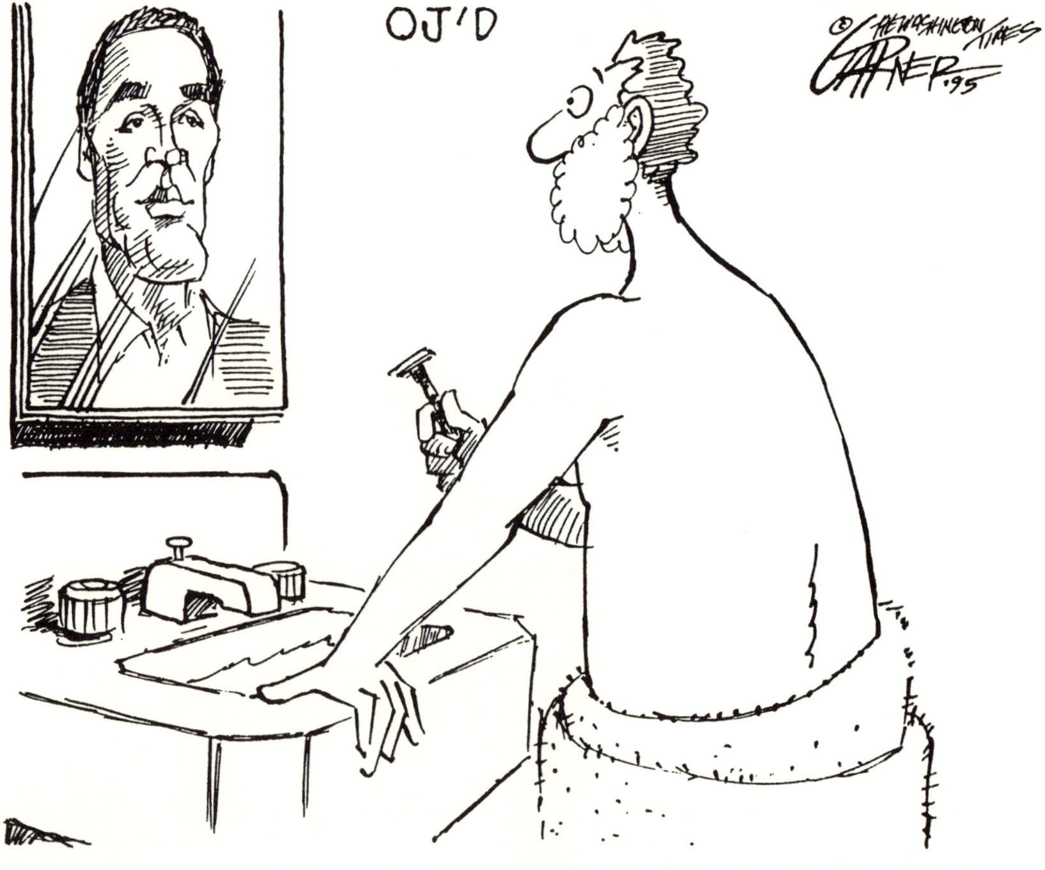
OJ'D
© THE WASHINGTON TIMES
GARNER '95

Sports

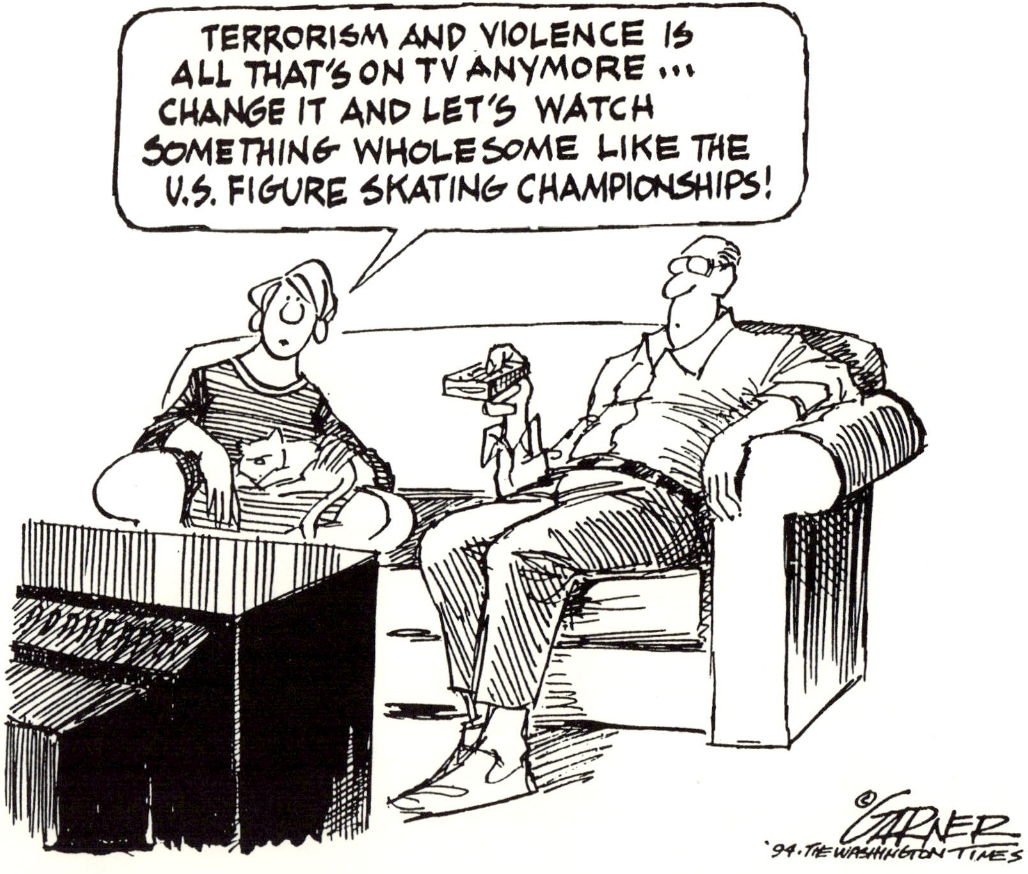
TERRORISM AND VIOLENCE IS ALL THAT'S ON TV ANYMORE ... CHANGE IT AND LET'S WATCH SOMETHING WHOLESOME LIKE THE U.S. FIGURE SKATING CHAMPIONSHIPS!
© GARNER
'94 · THE WASHINGTON TIMES

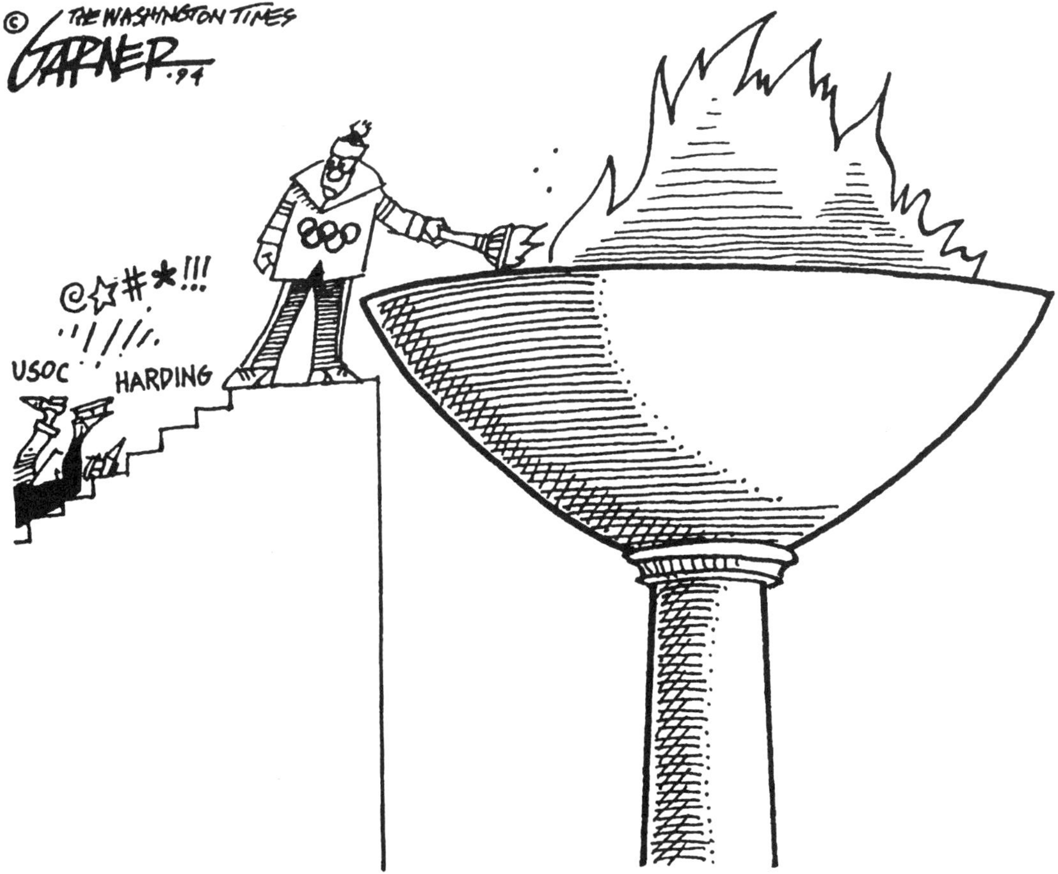
© THE WASHINGTON TIMES
GARNER '94
@☆#*!!!
USOC
HARDING

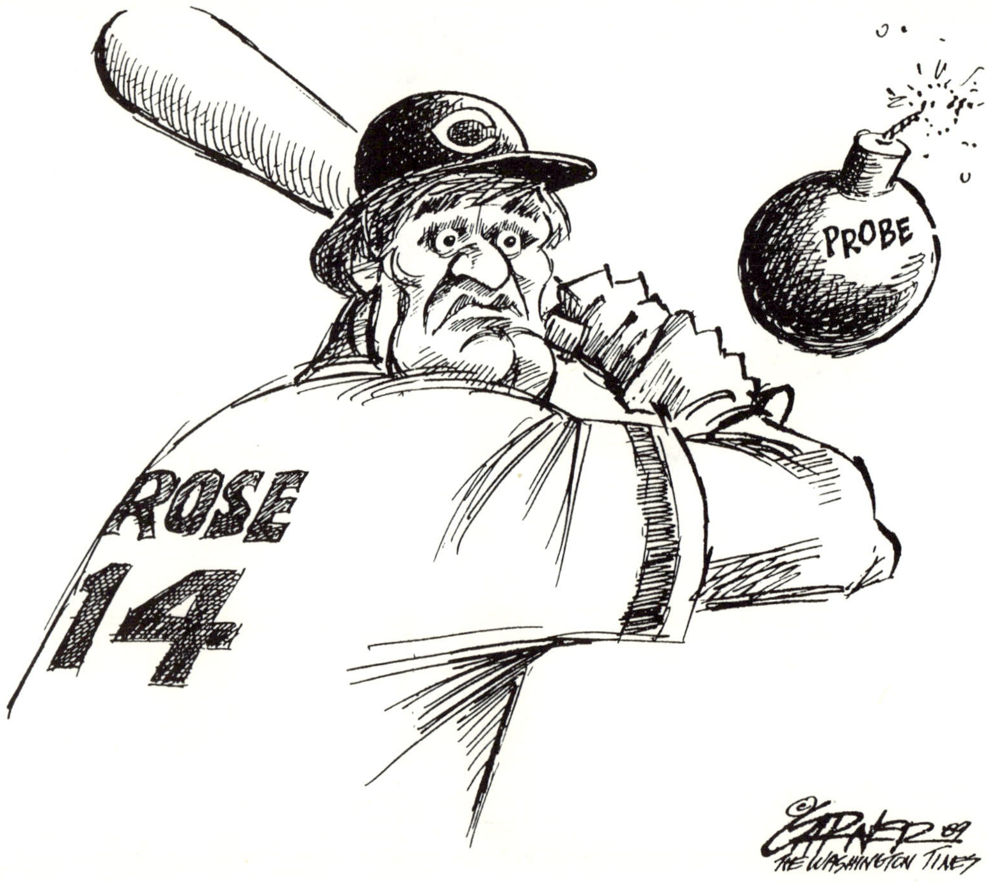
PROBE
ROSE
14
THE WASHINGTON TIMES

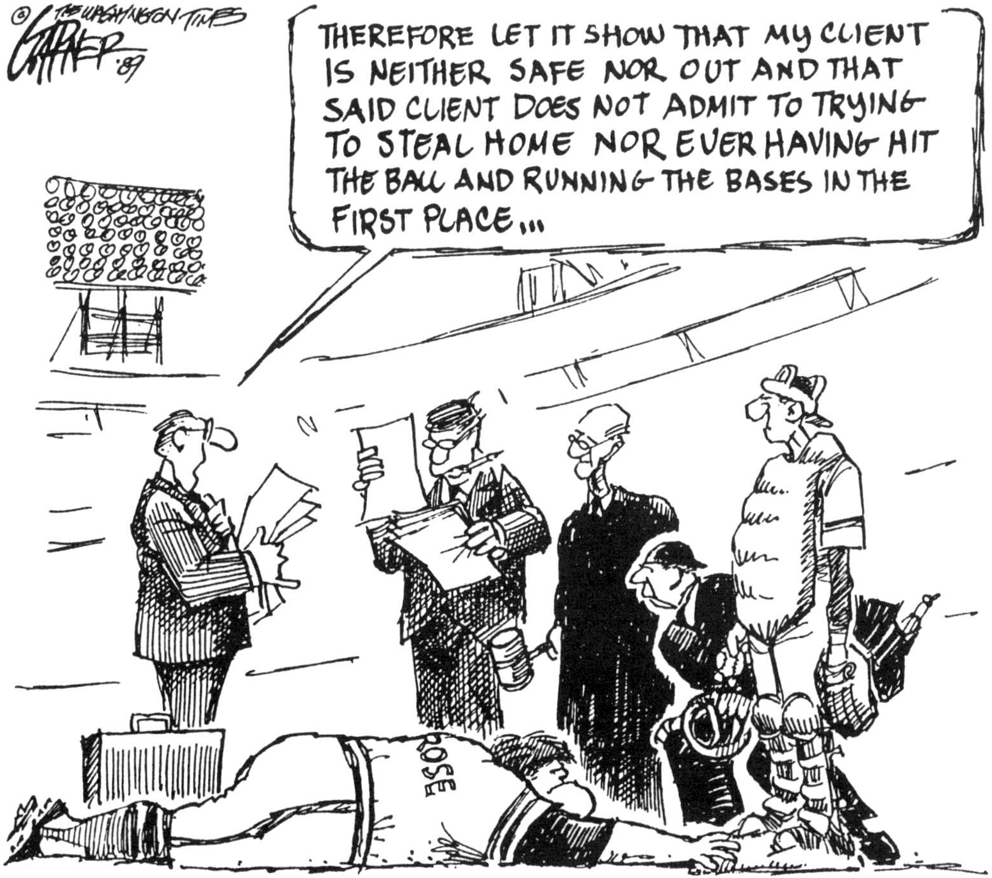
© THE WASHINGTON TIMES GARNER '89
THEREFORE LET IT SHOW THAT MY CLIENT IS NEITHER SAFE NOR OUT AND THAT SAID CLIENT DOES NOT ADMIT TO TRYING TO STEAL HOME NOR EVER HAVING HIT THE BALL AND RUNNING THE BASES IN THE FIRST PLACE...
ROSE

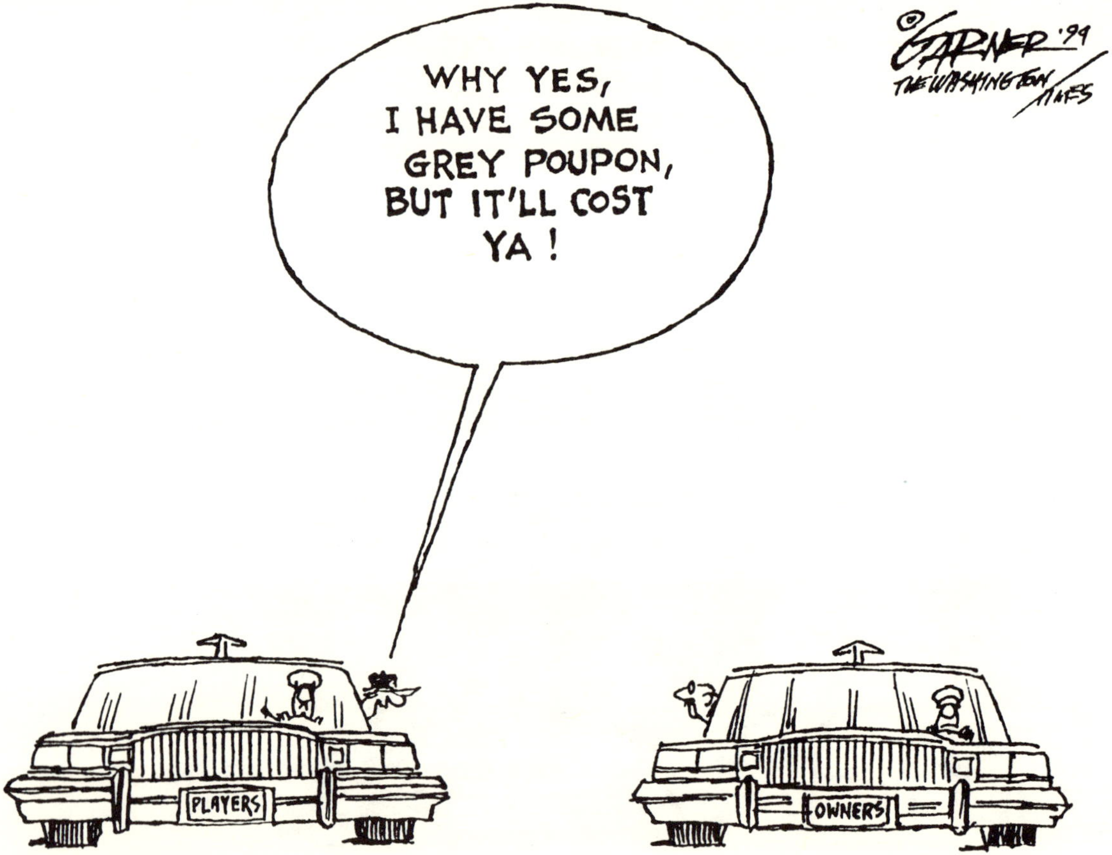
WHY YES, I HAVE SOME GREY POUPON, BUT IT'LL COST YA!
PLAYERS
OWNERS
© GARNER '94 THE WASHINGTON TIMES

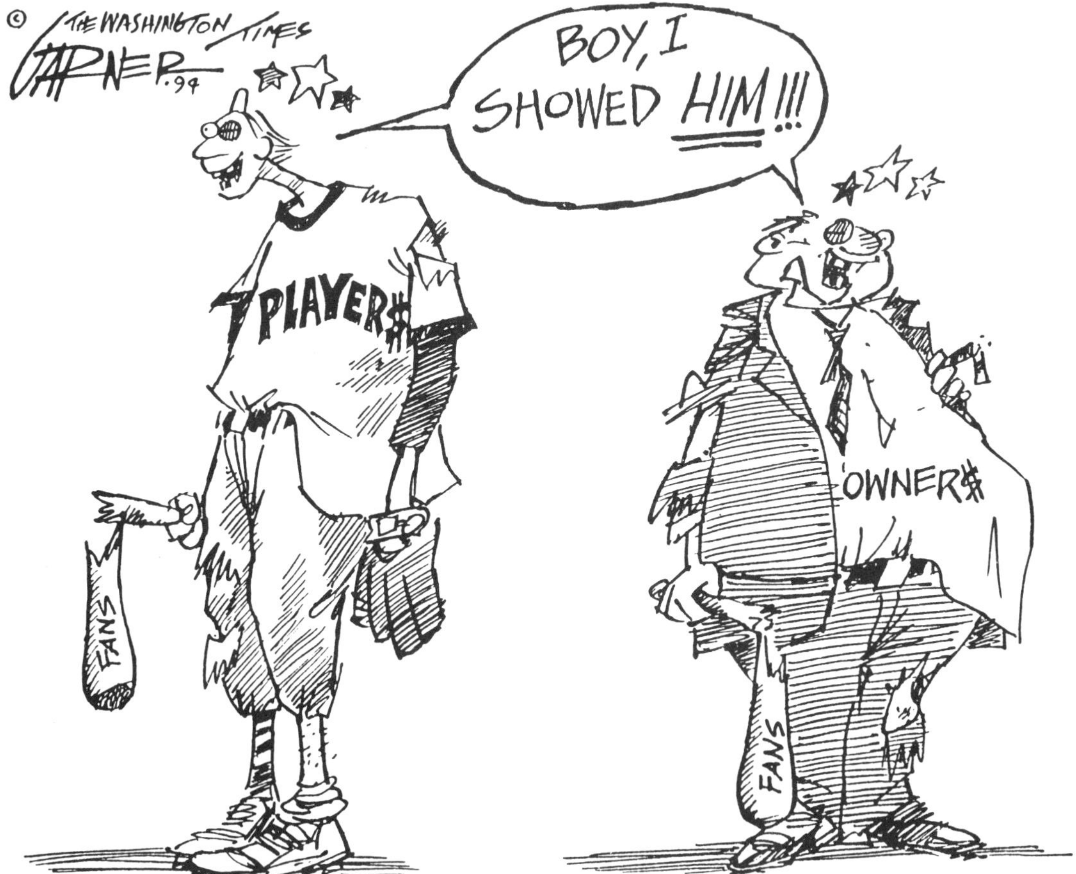
© THE WASHINGTON TIMES
GARNER '94
BOY, I SHOWED HIM!!!
PLAYER$
FANS
OWNER$
FANS

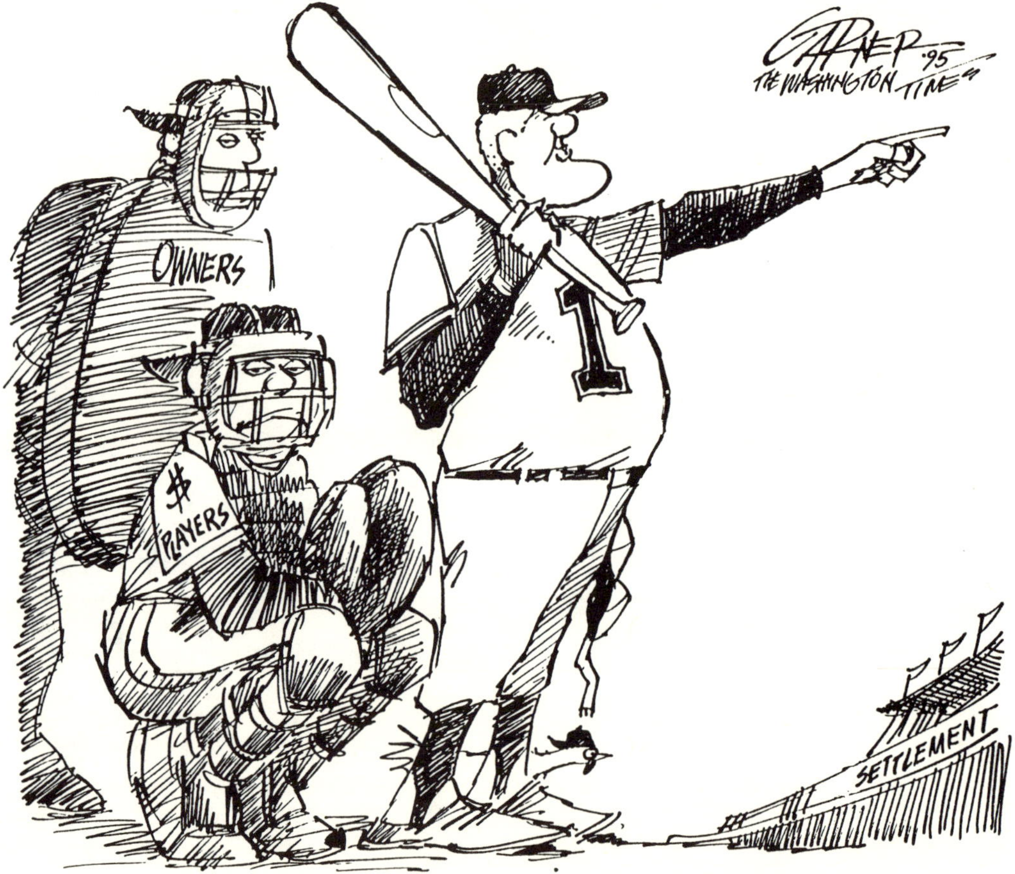

GARNER '95
THE WASHINGTON TIMES
OWNERS
$
PLAYERS
1
SETTLEMENT

'94 Election

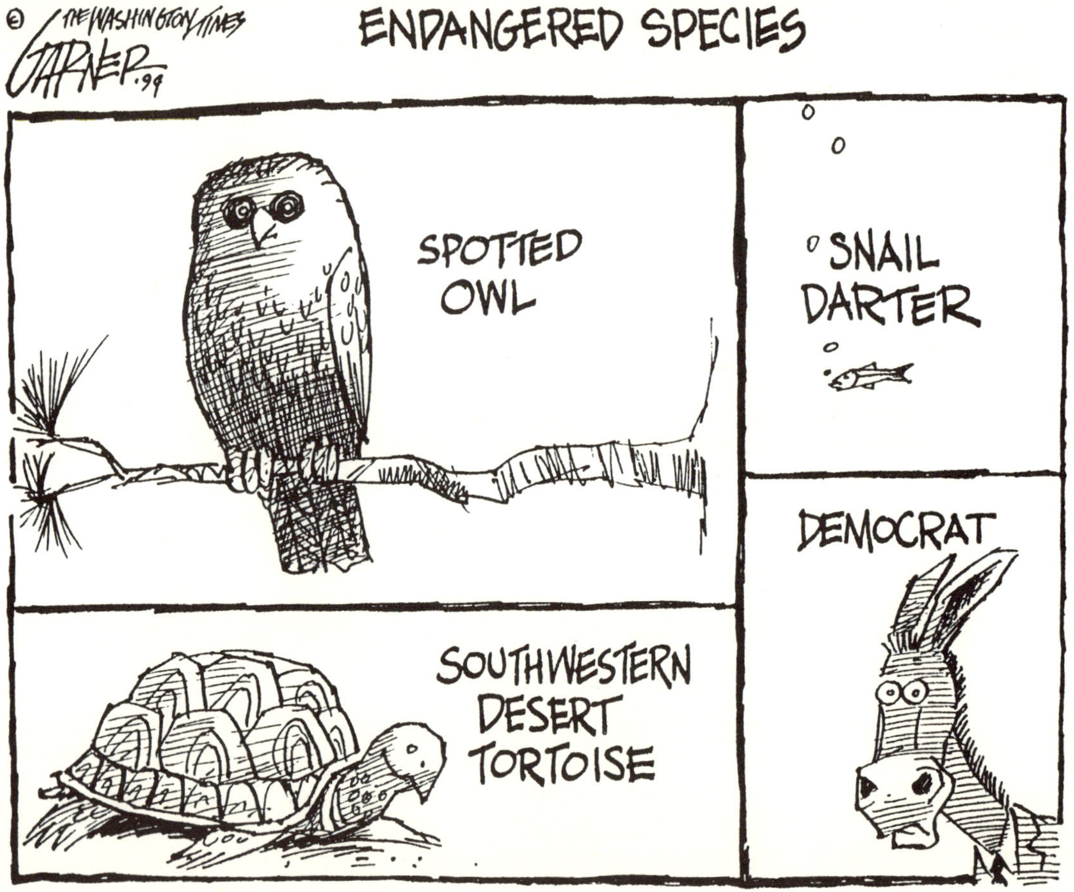
© THE WASHINGTON TIMES
GARNER '94
ENDANGERED SPECIES
SPOTTED OWL
SNAIL DARTER
SOUTHWESTERN DESERT TORTOISE
DEMOCRAT

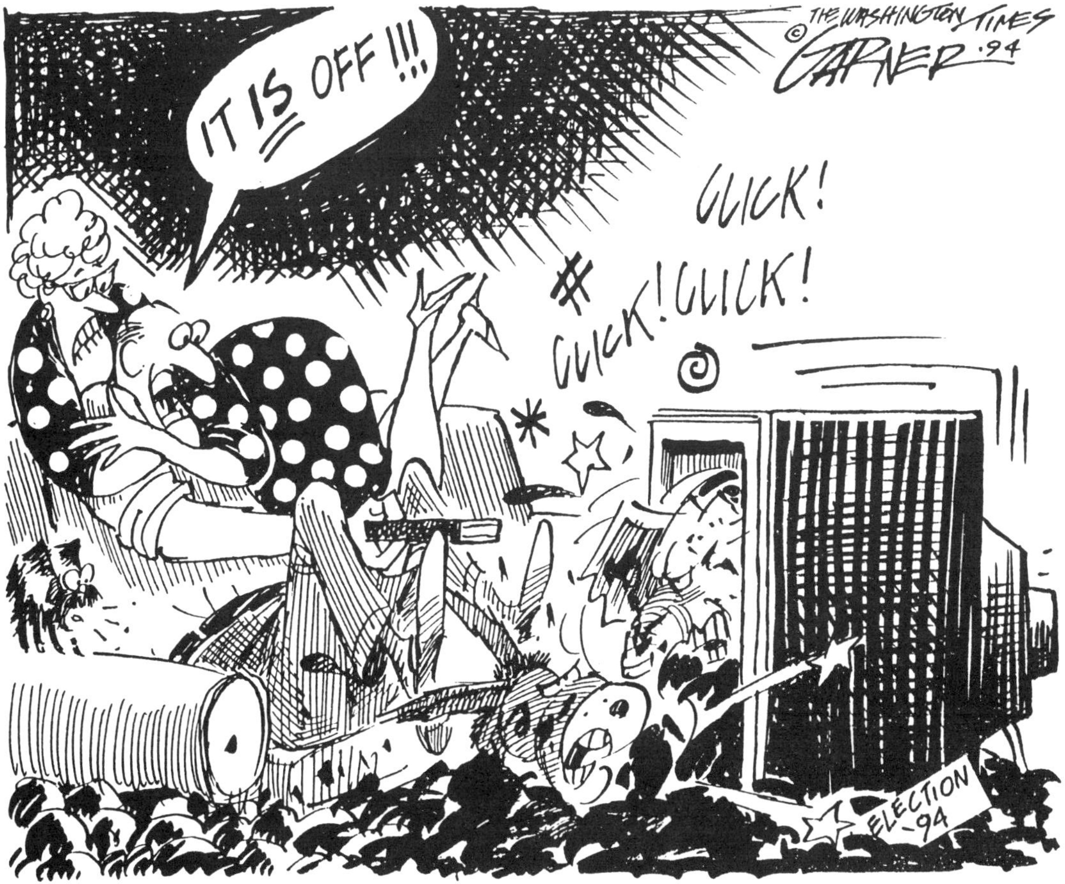

IT IS OFF !!!
CLICK!
CLICK! CLICK!
ELECTION '94
© THE WASHINGTON TIMES
GARNER '94

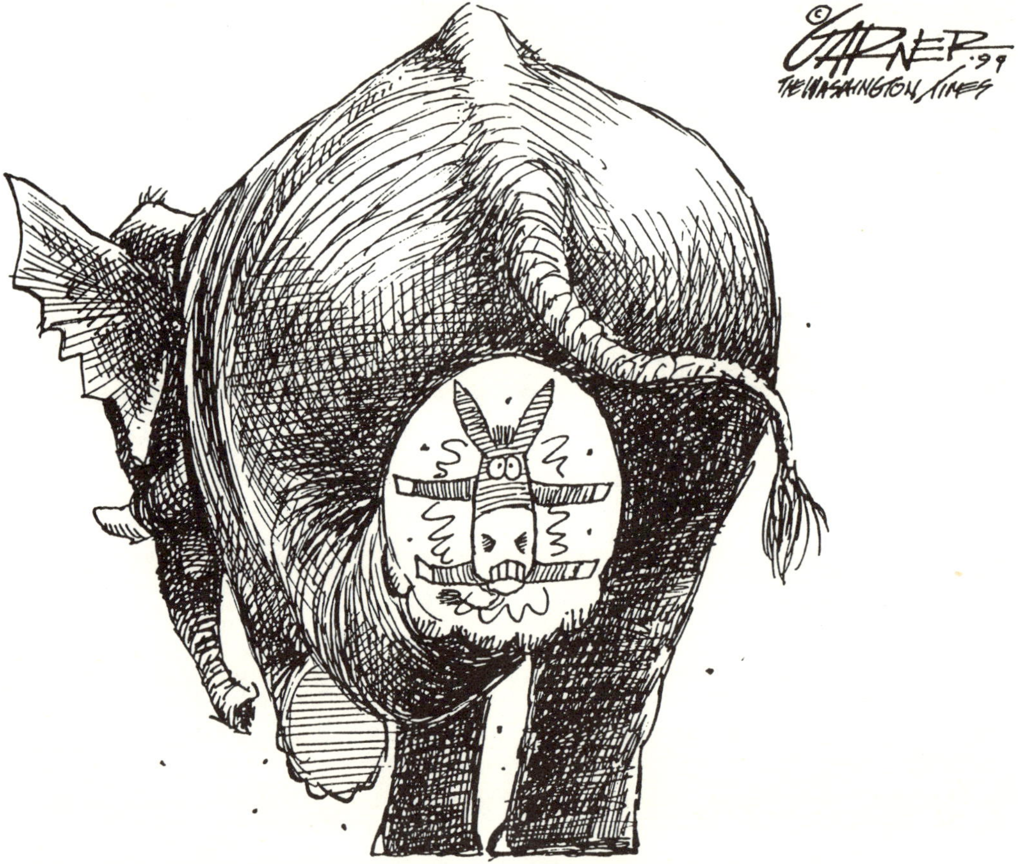
©GARNER '99
THE WASHINGTON TIMES

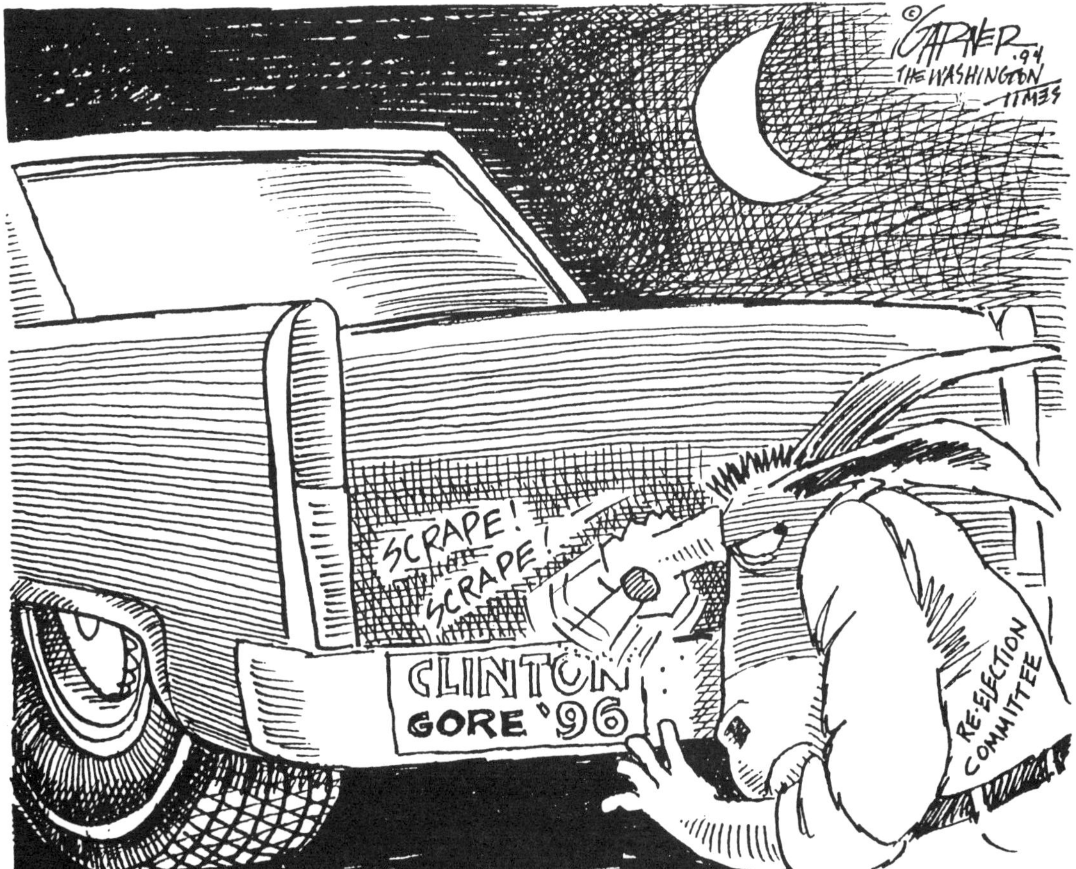

© GARNER '94 THE WASHINGTON TIMES
SCRAPE! SCRAPE!
CLINTON GORE '96
RE-ELECTION COMMITTEE

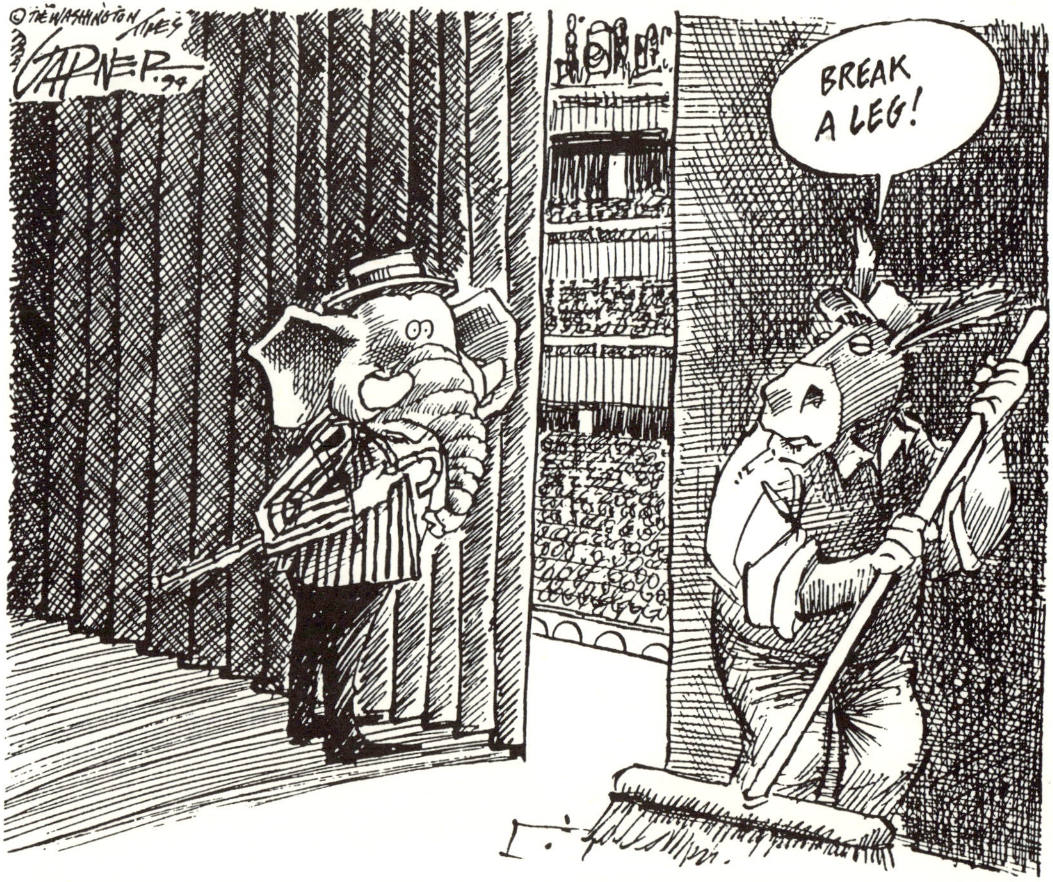
© THE WASHINGTON TIMES
GARNER '94
BREAK A LEG!

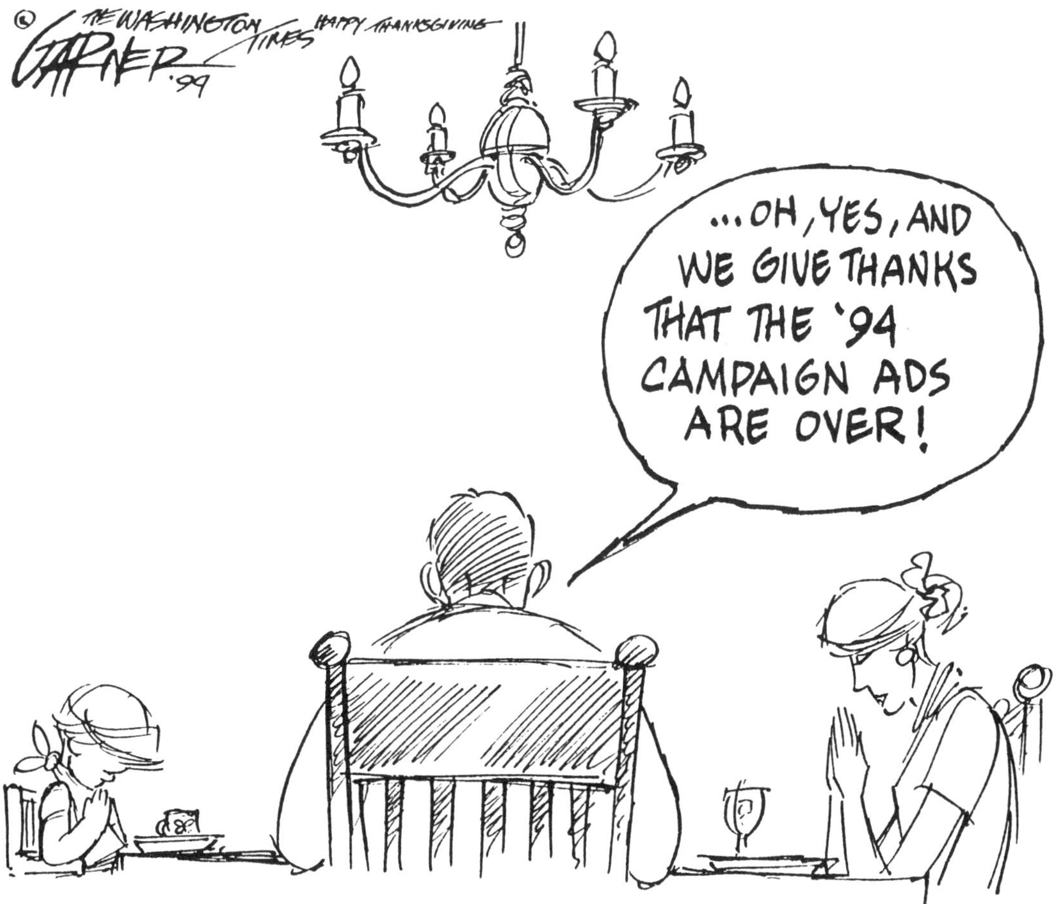
© THE WASHINGTON TIMES HAPPY THANKSGIVING
GARNER '94
...OH, YES, AND WE GIVE THANKS THAT THE '94 CAMPAIGN ADS ARE OVER!

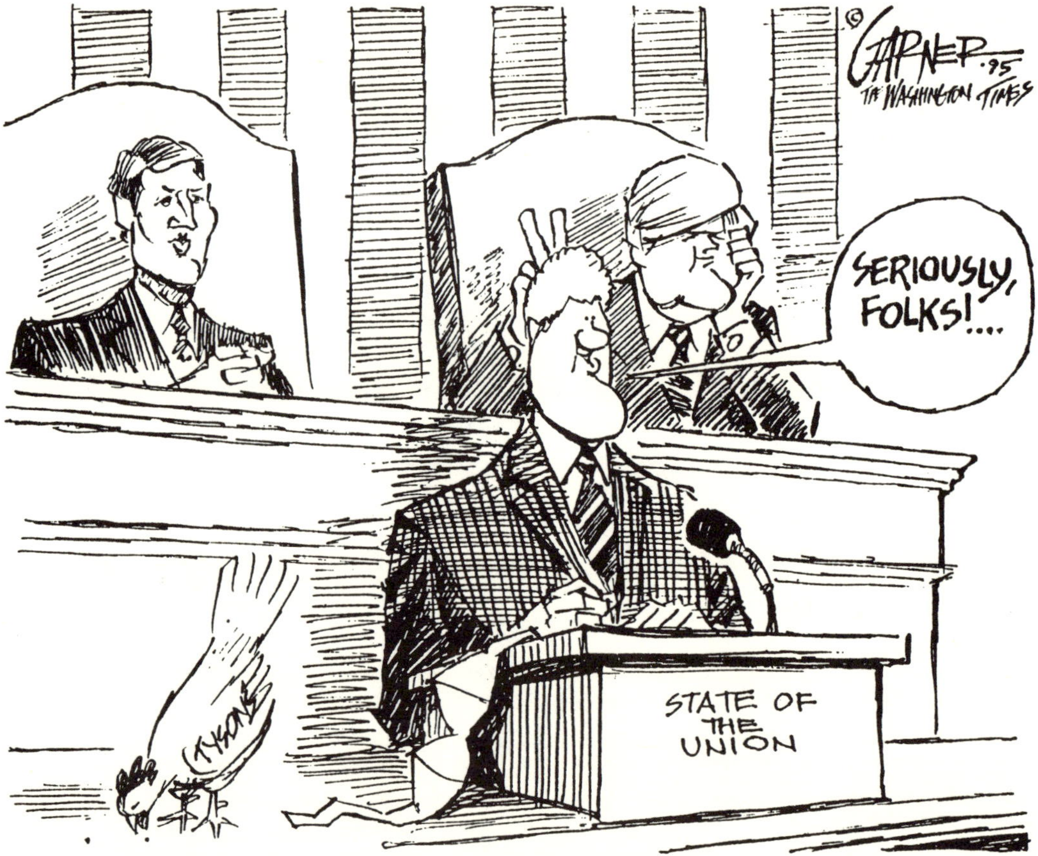
© GARNER '95 THE WASHINGTON TIMES
SERIOUSLY, FOLKS!....
STATE OF THE UNION
TYSONS

. . . and Other Issues

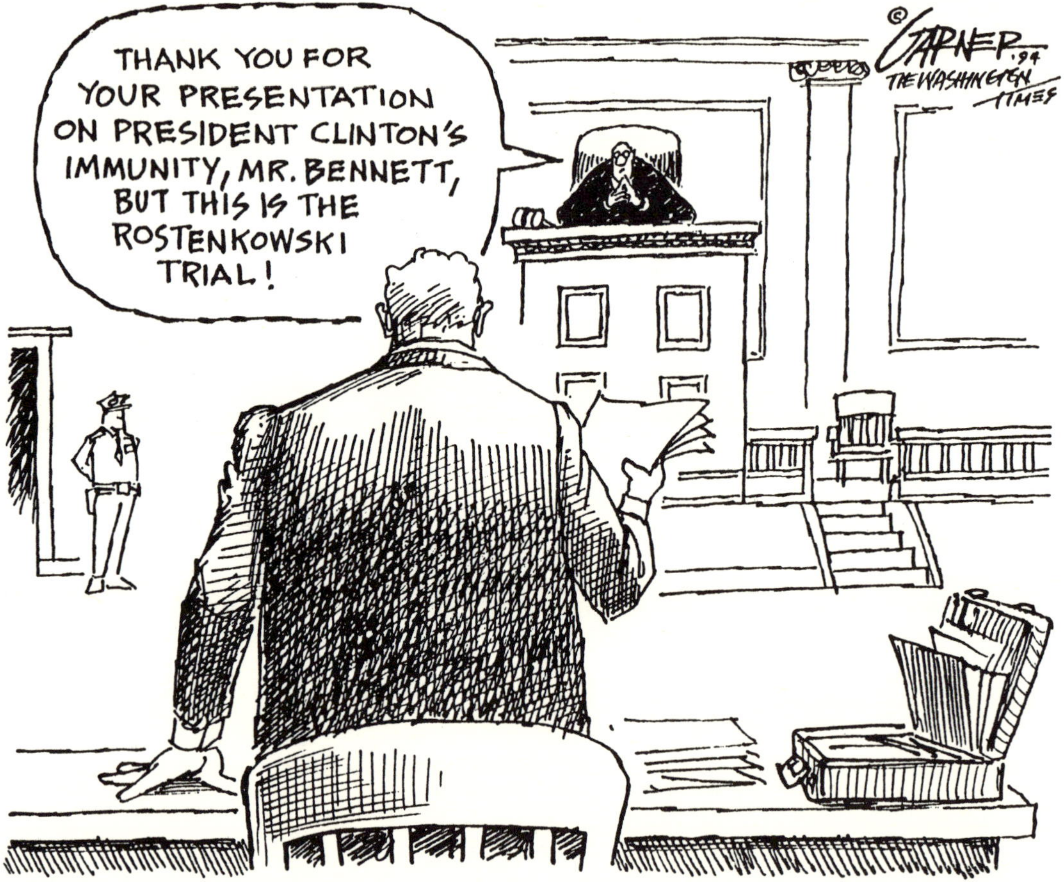
THANK YOU FOR YOUR PRESENTATION ON PRESIDENT CLINTON'S IMMUNITY, MR. BENNETT, BUT THIS IS THE ROSTENKOWSKI TRIAL!
© GARNER '94 THE WASHINGTON TIMES

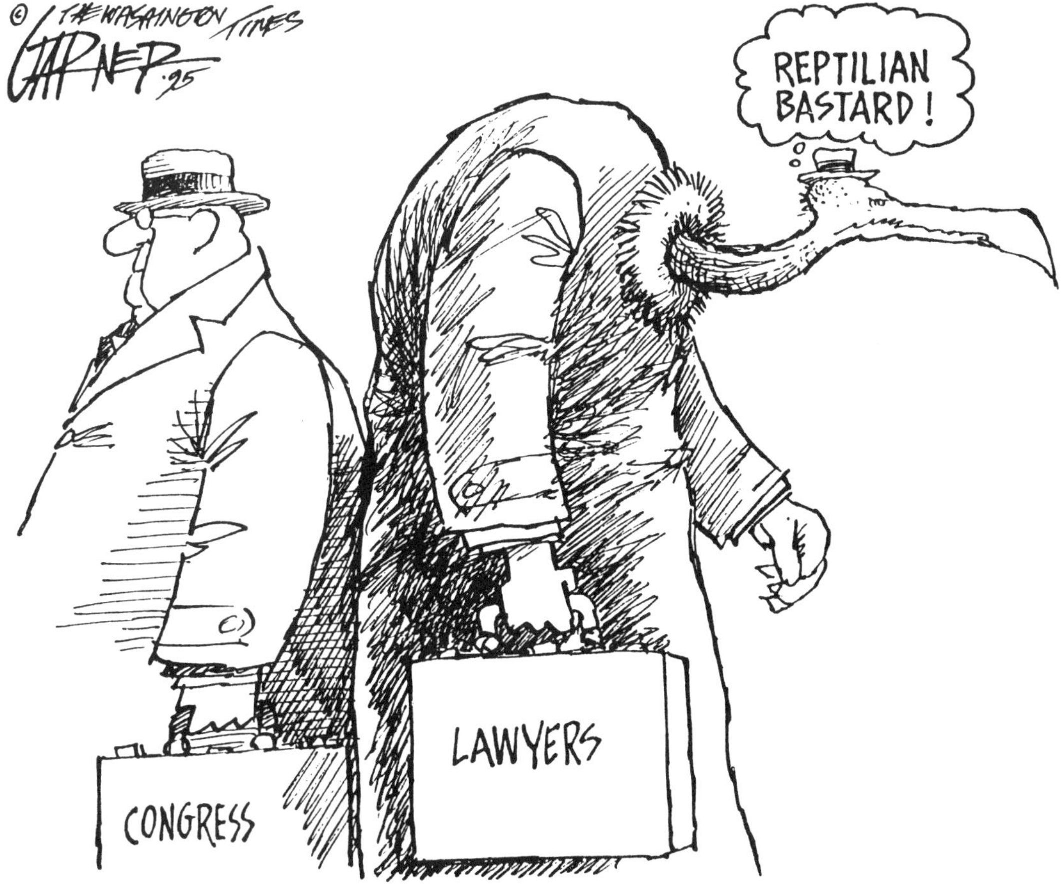
© THE WASHINGTON TIMES
GARNER '95
REPTILIAN BASTARD!
CONGRESS
LAWYERS

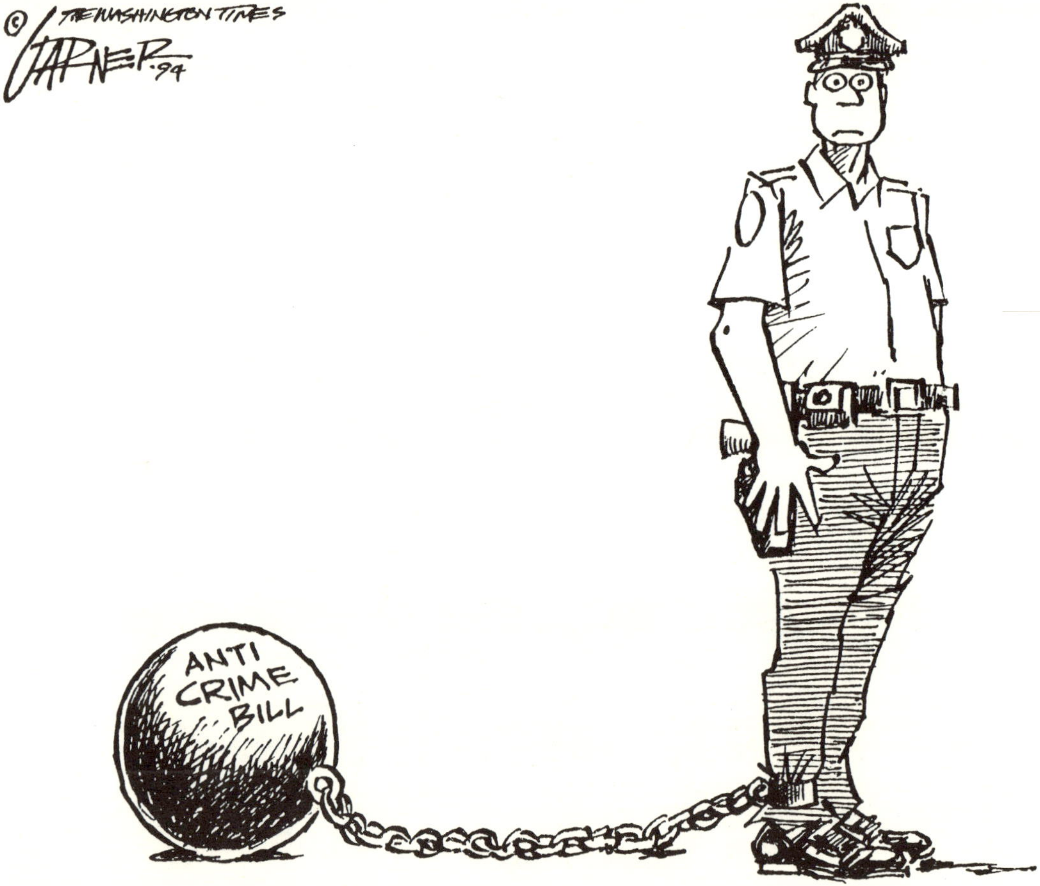
© THE WASHINGTON TIMES
GARNER '94
ANTI
CRIME
BILL

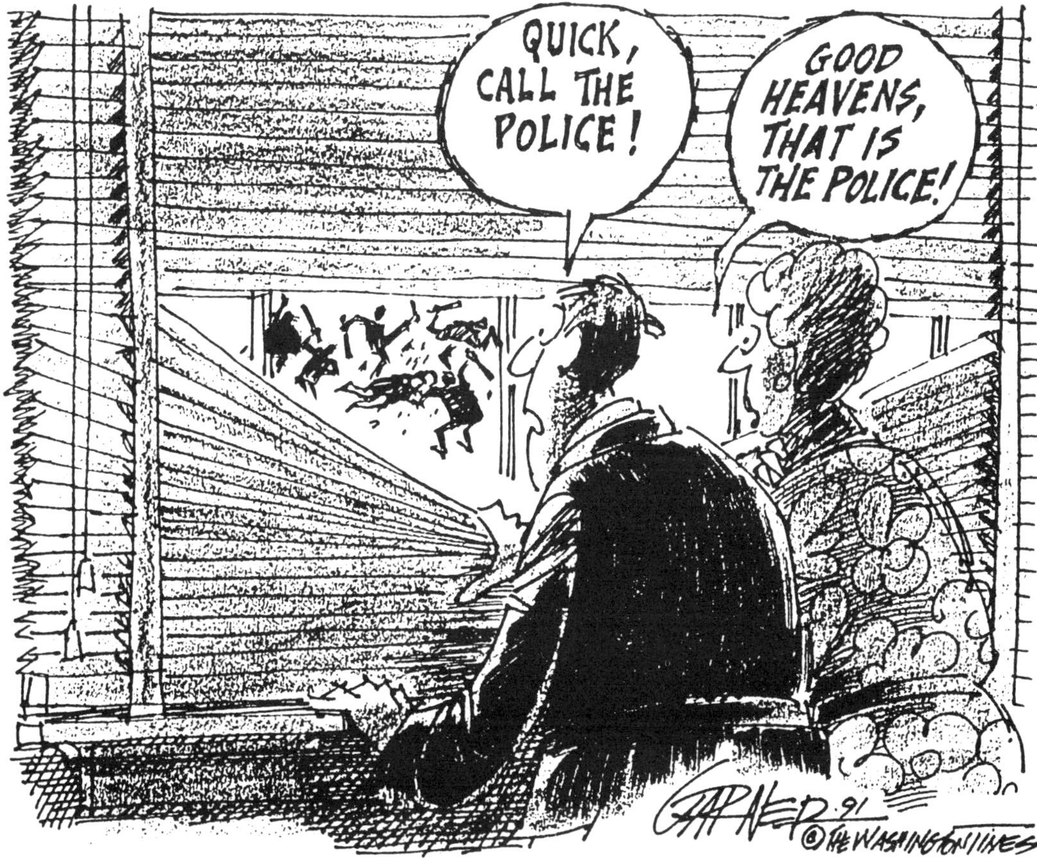
QUICK, CALL THE POLICE!
GOOD HEAVENS, THAT IS THE POLICE!
GARNER ·91
© THE WASHINGTON TIMES

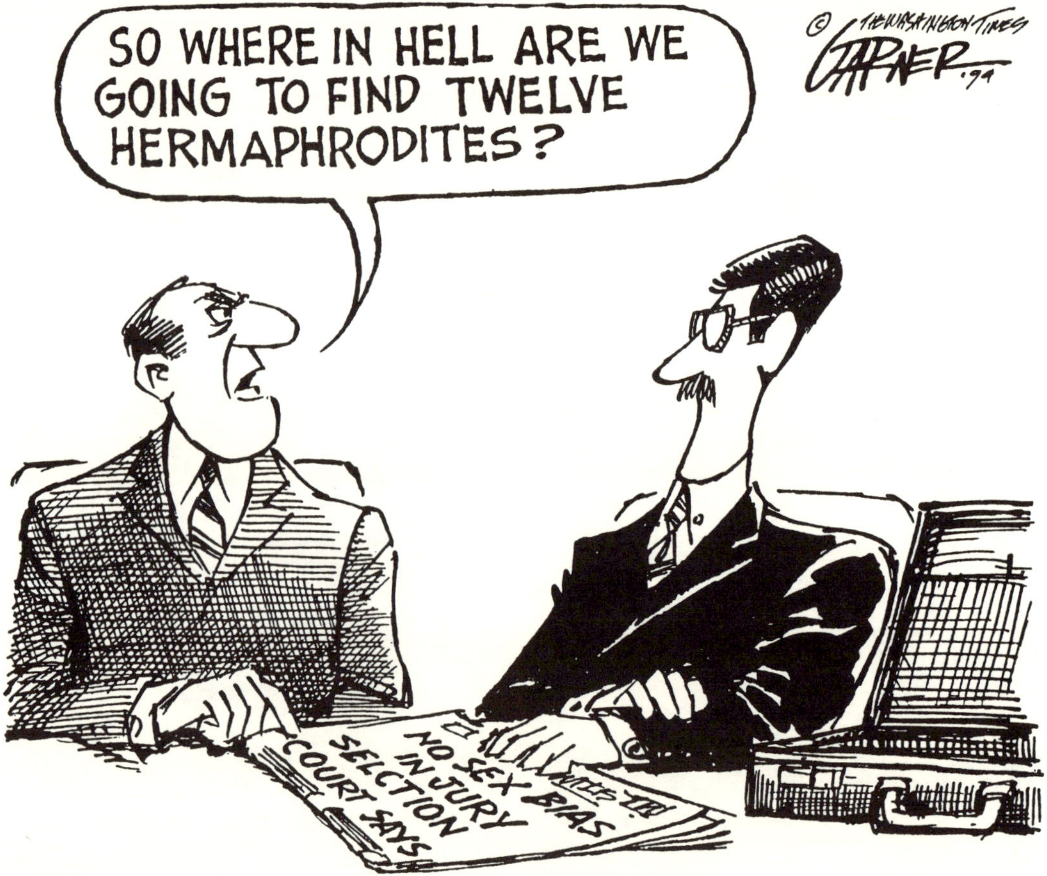

SO WHERE IN HELL ARE WE GOING TO FIND TWELVE HERMAPHRODITES?
© THE WASHINGTON TIMES
GARNER '94
NO SEX BIAS IN JURY SELCTION COURT SAYS

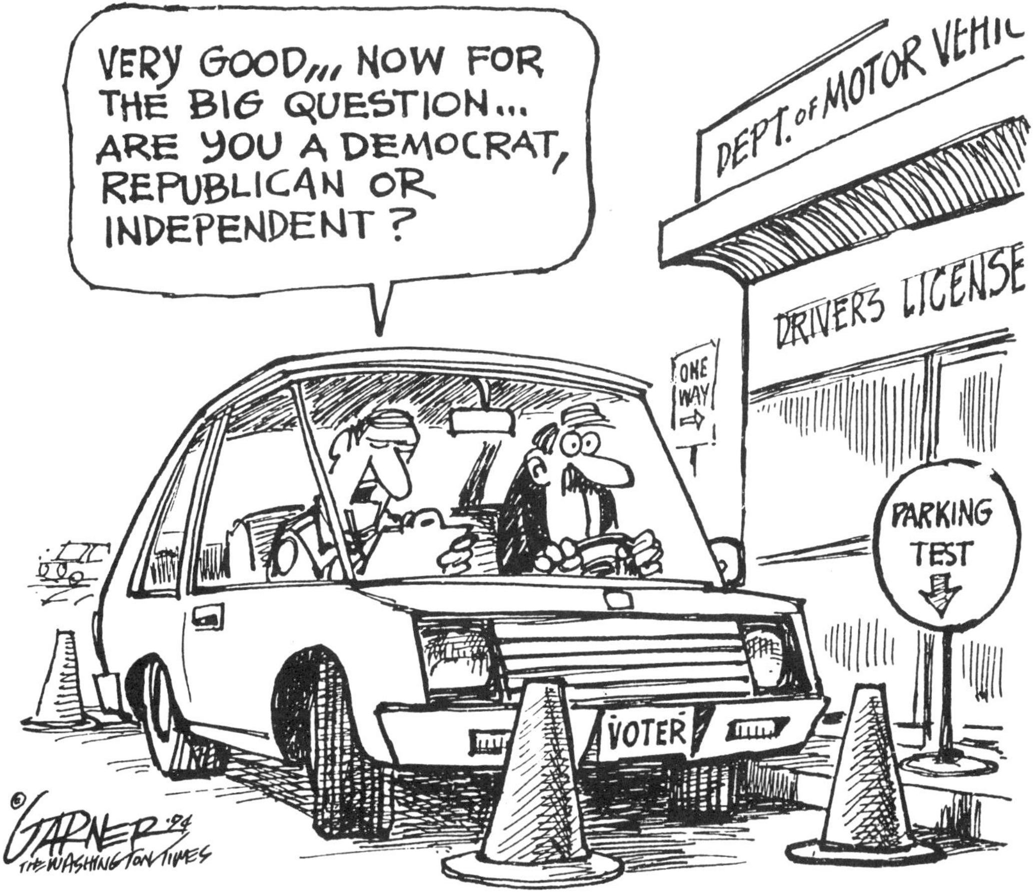
VERY GOOD,,, NOW FOR THE BIG QUESTION... ARE YOU A DEMOCRAT, REPUBLICAN OR INDEPENDENT?
DEPT. of MOTOR VEHIC
DRIVERS LICENSE
ONE WAY
PARKING TEST
VOTER
© GARNER '94 THE WASHINGTON TIMES

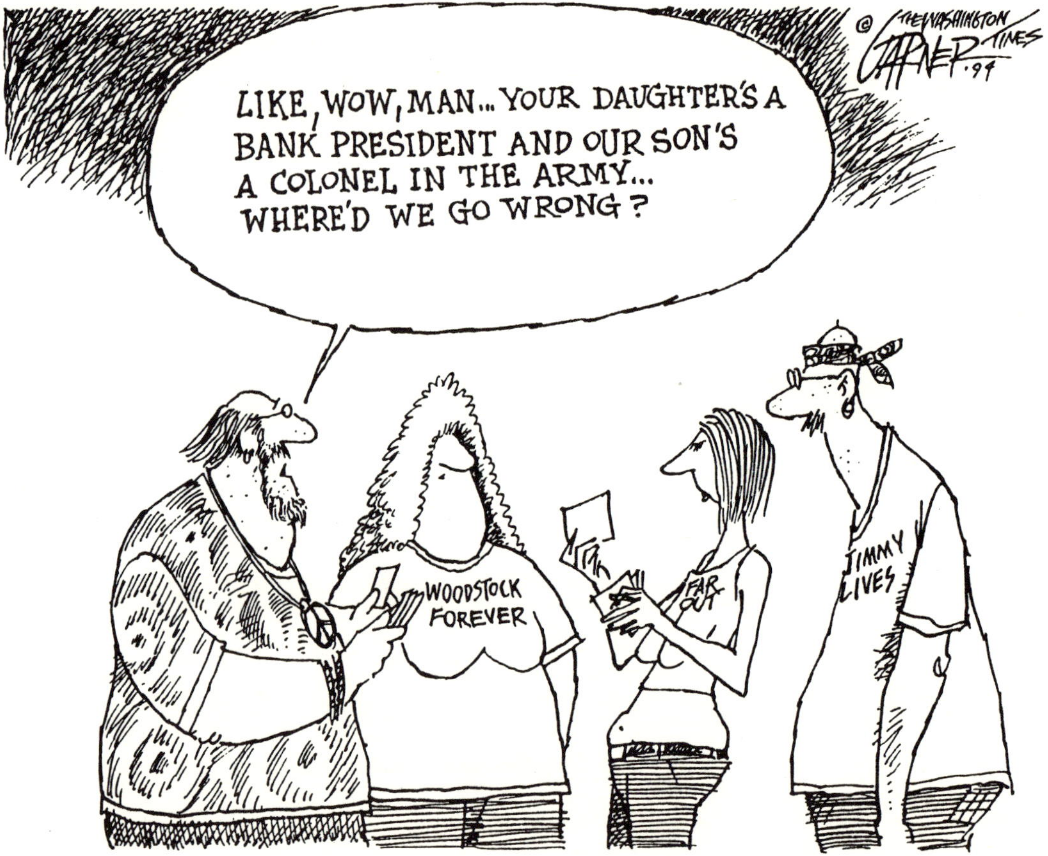
LIKE, WOW, MAN... YOUR DAUGHTER'S A BANK PRESIDENT AND OUR SON'S A COLONEL IN THE ARMY... WHERE'D WE GO WRONG?
© THE WASHINGTON TIMES GARNER '94
WOODSTOCK FOREVER
FAR OUT
JIMMY LIVES

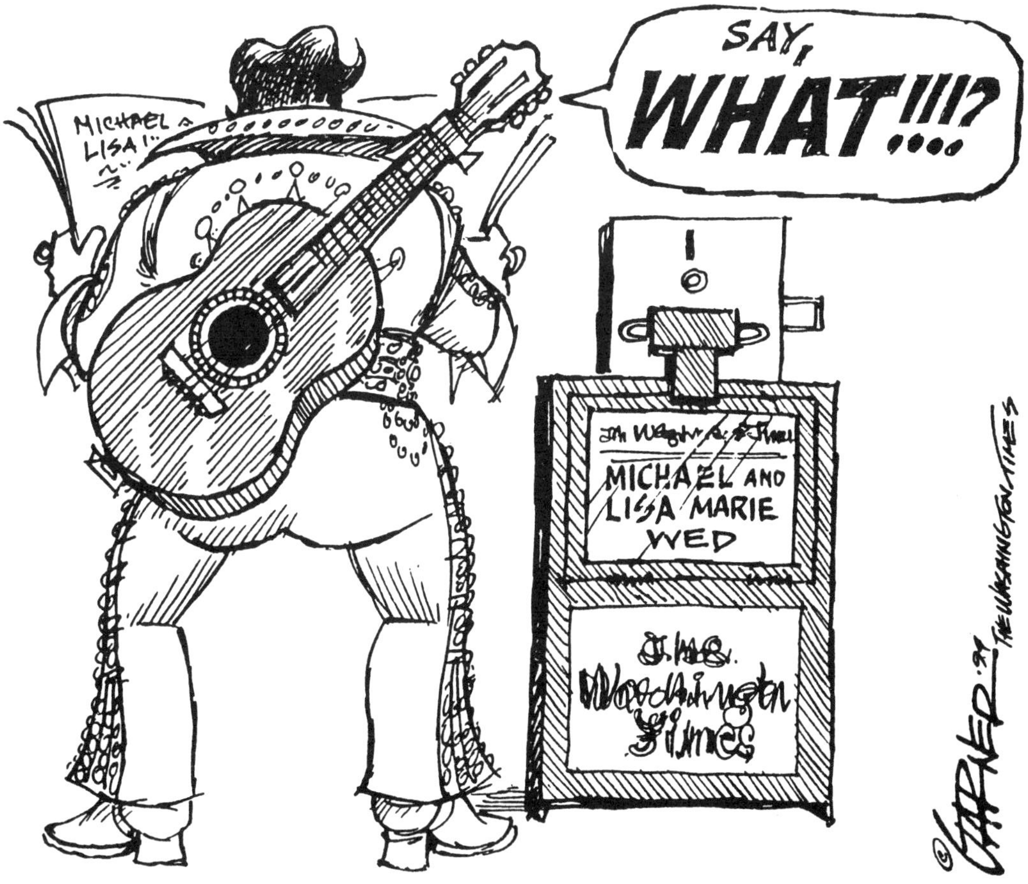

SAY, WHAT!!!?....
MICHAEL
LISA
MICHAEL AND LISA MARIE WED
THE WASHINGTON TIMES

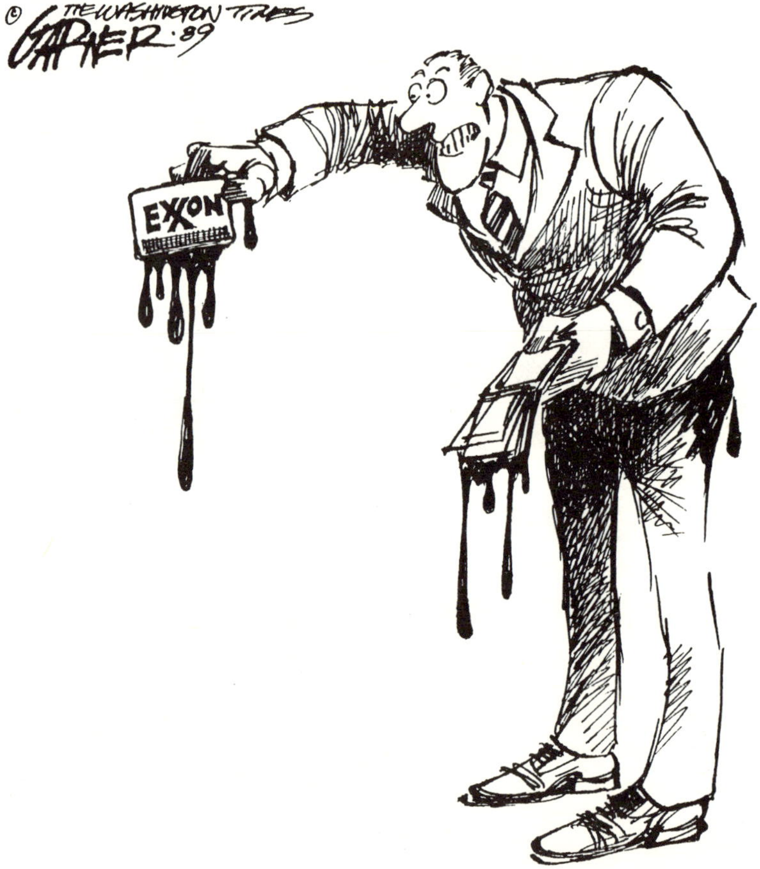
© THE WASHINGTON TIMES
GARNER '89
EXXON

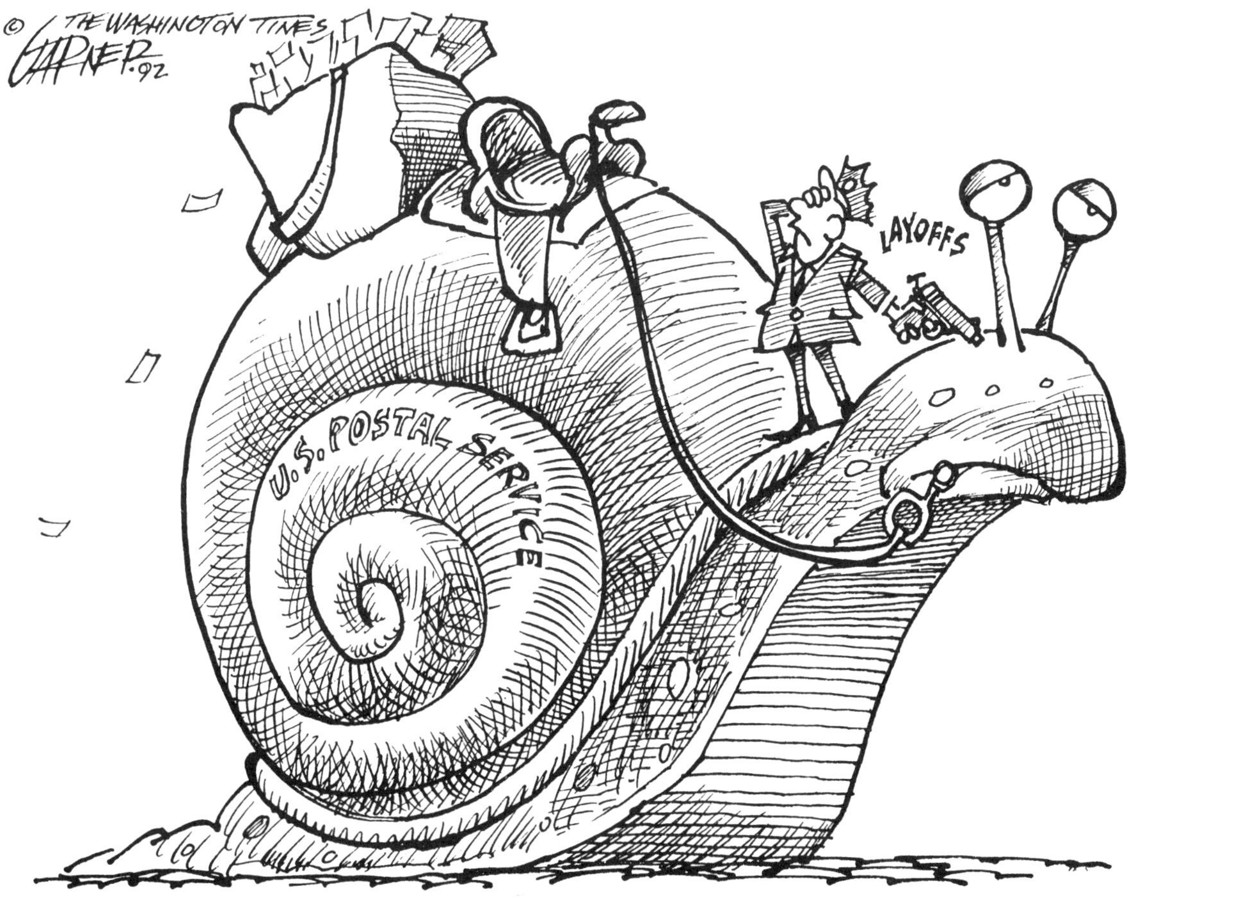
© THE WASHINGTON TIMES
GARNER '92
LAYOFFS
U.S. POSTAL SERVICE

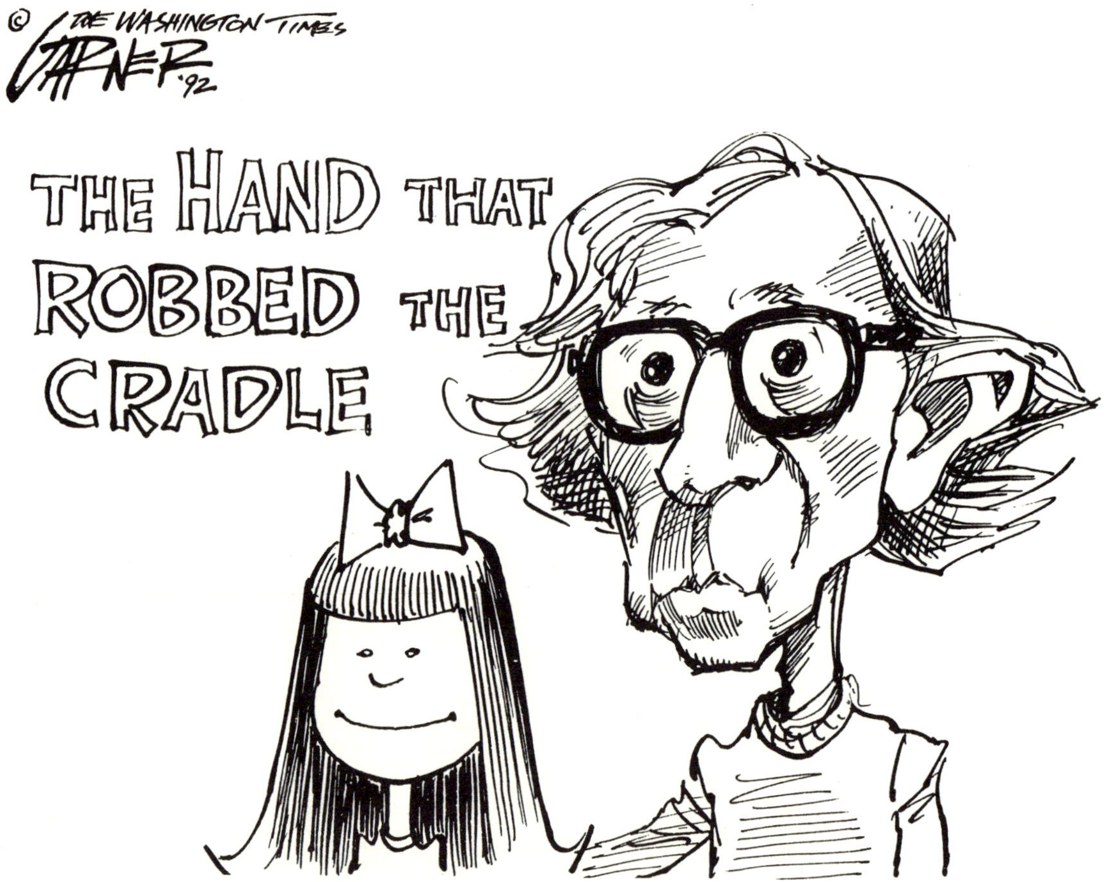
© THE WASHINGTON TIMES
GARNER '92
THE HAND THAT ROBBED THE CRADLE

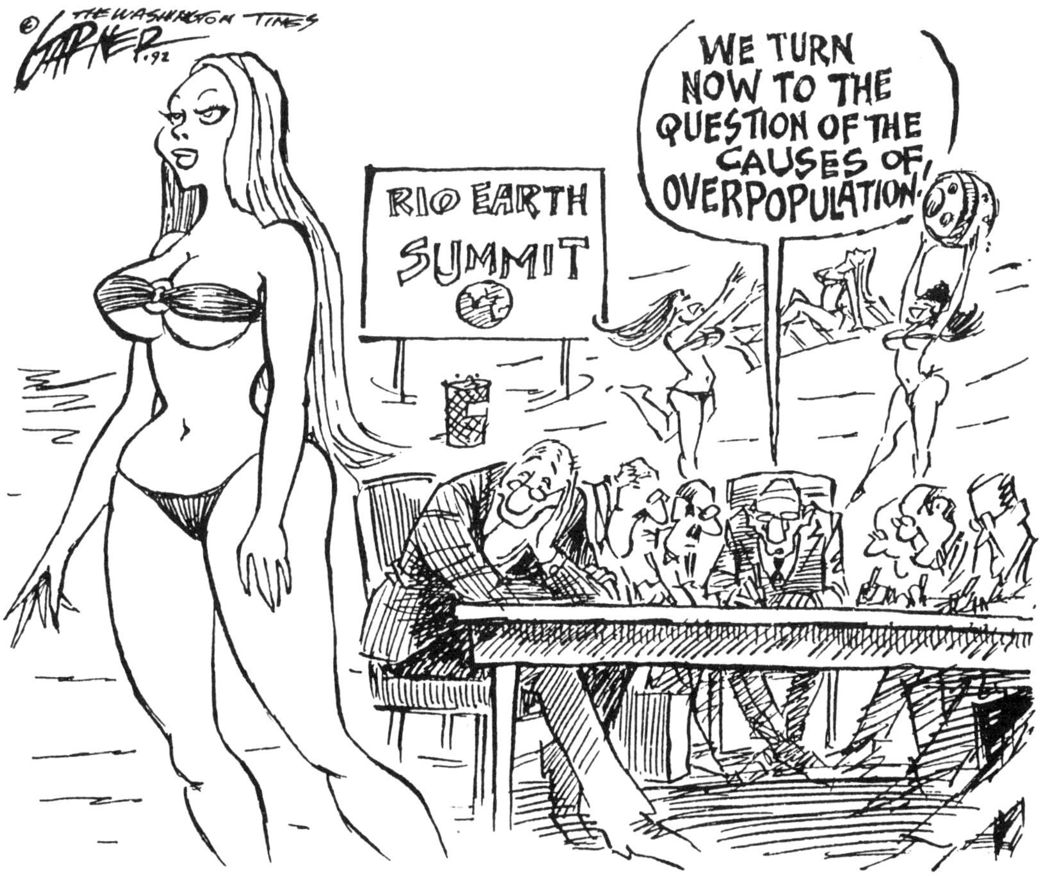
© THE WASHINGTON TIMES
'92
RIO EARTH SUMMIT
WE TURN NOW TO THE QUESTION OF THE CAUSES OF OVERPOPULATION.

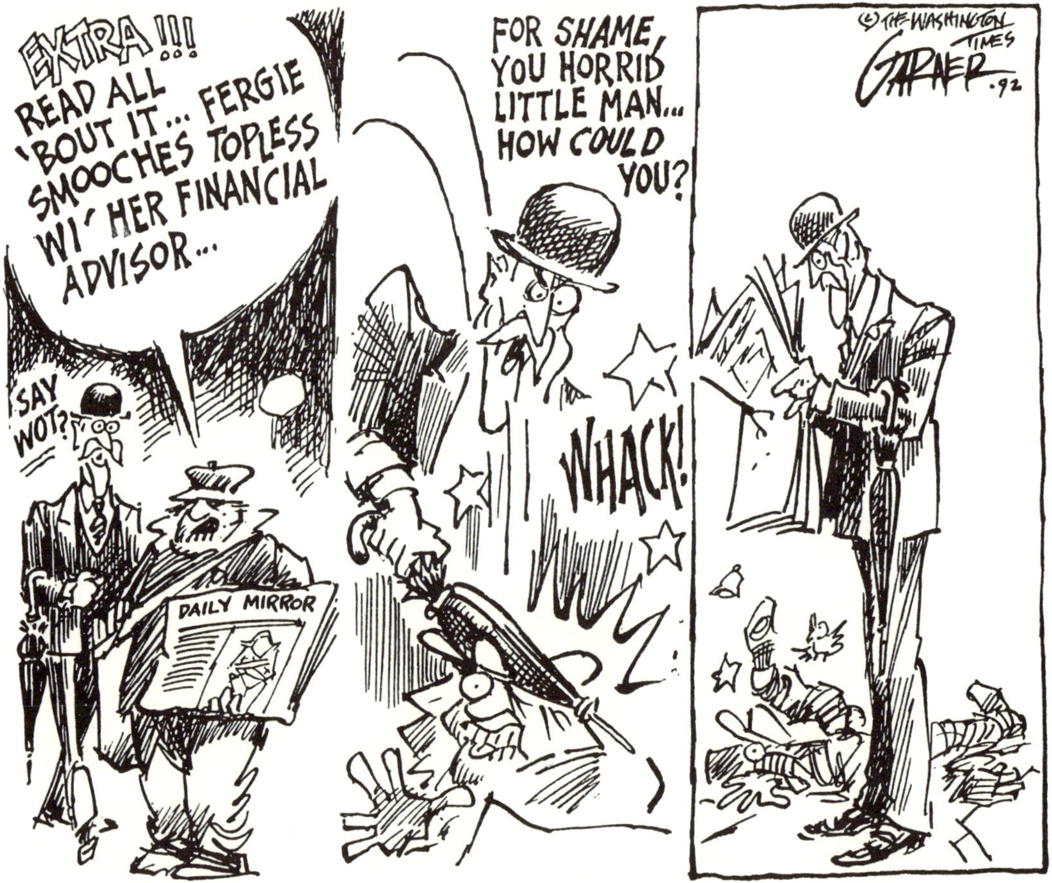
EXTRA!!! READ ALL 'BOUT IT... FERGIE SMOOCHES TOPLESS WI' HER FINANCIAL ADVISOR...
SAY WOT?
DAILY MIRROR
FOR SHAME, YOU HORRID LITTLE MAN... HOW COULD YOU?
WHACK!
© THE WASHINGTON TIMES
GARNER ·92

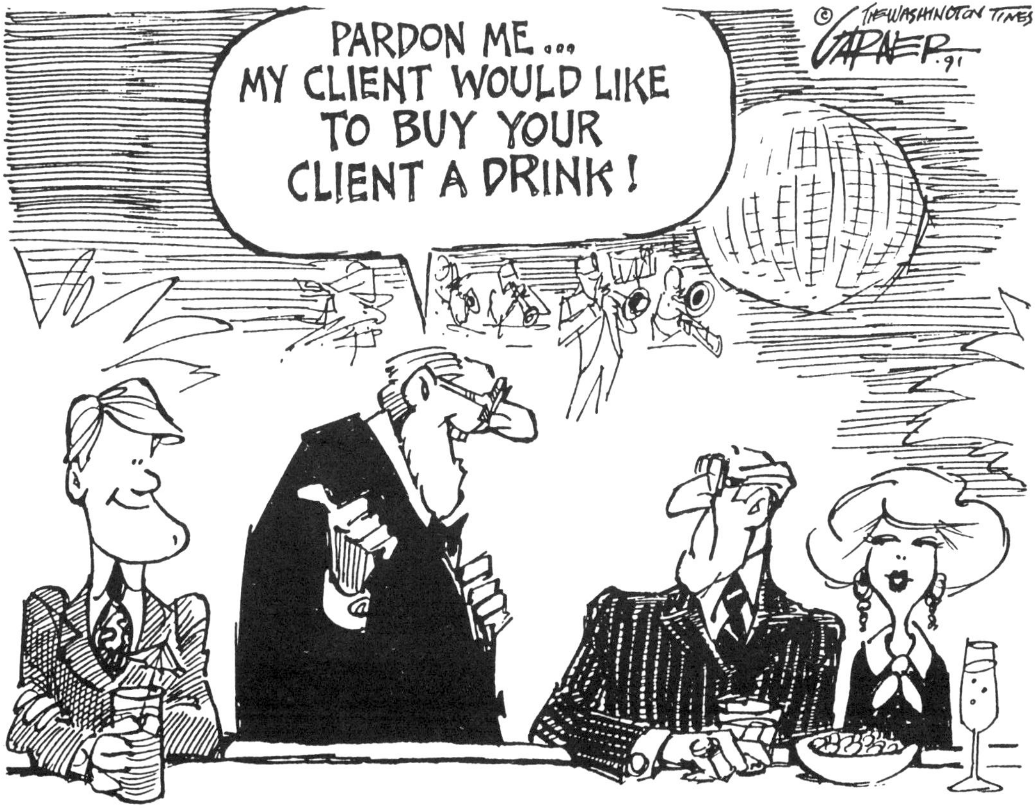

DATING PRACTICES OF FUTURE PUBLIC OFFICIALS

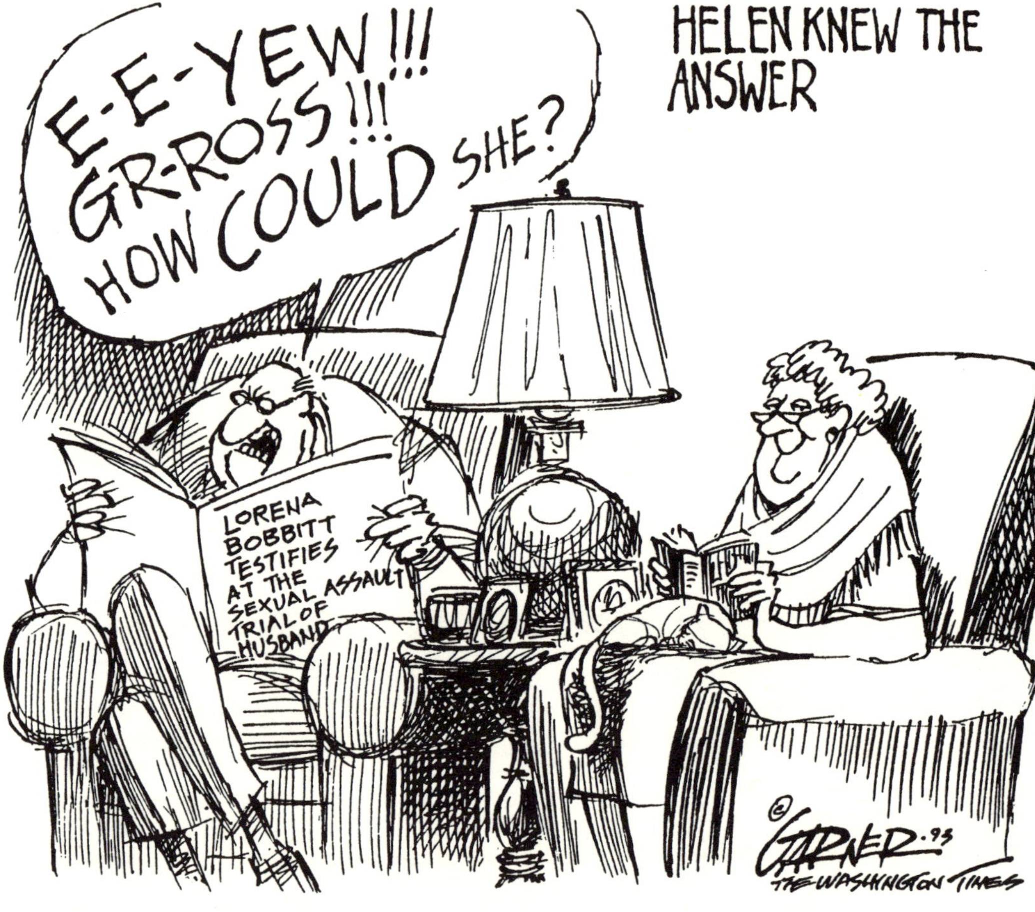

HELEN KNEW THE ANSWER

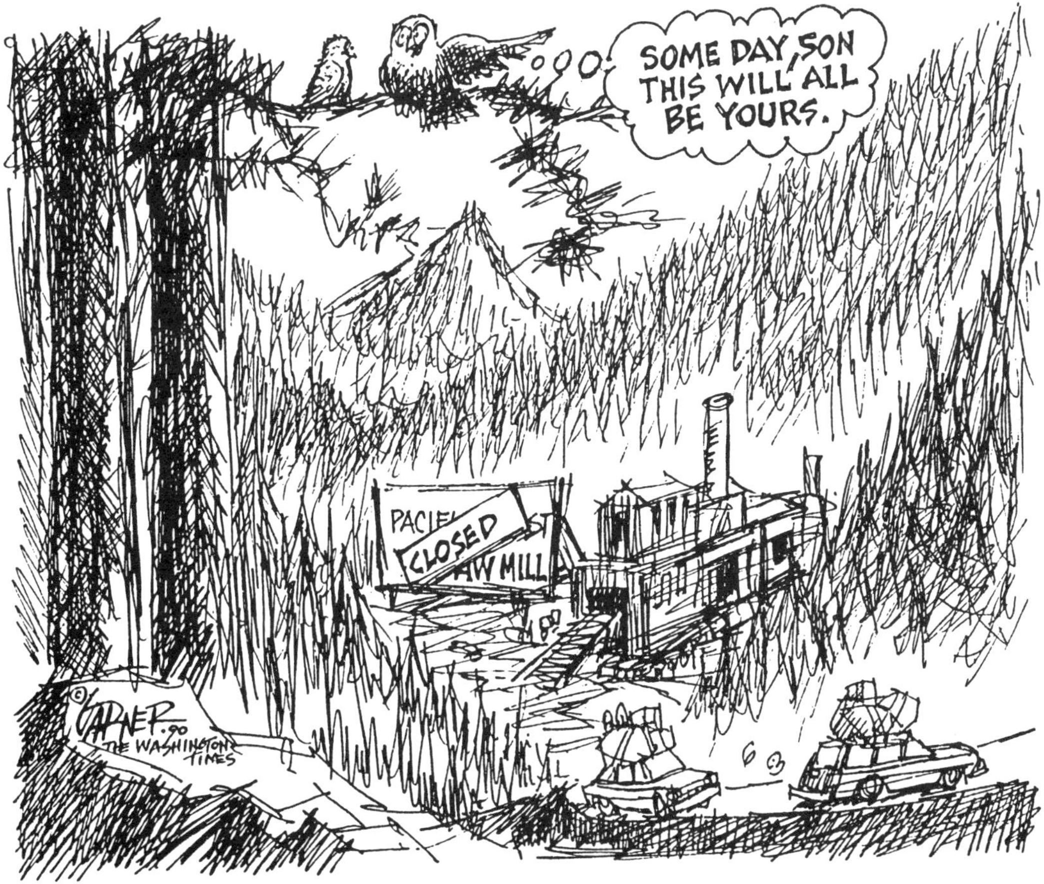
SOME DAY, SON THIS WILL ALL BE YOURS.
CLOSED
AW MILL
THE WASHINGTON TIMES

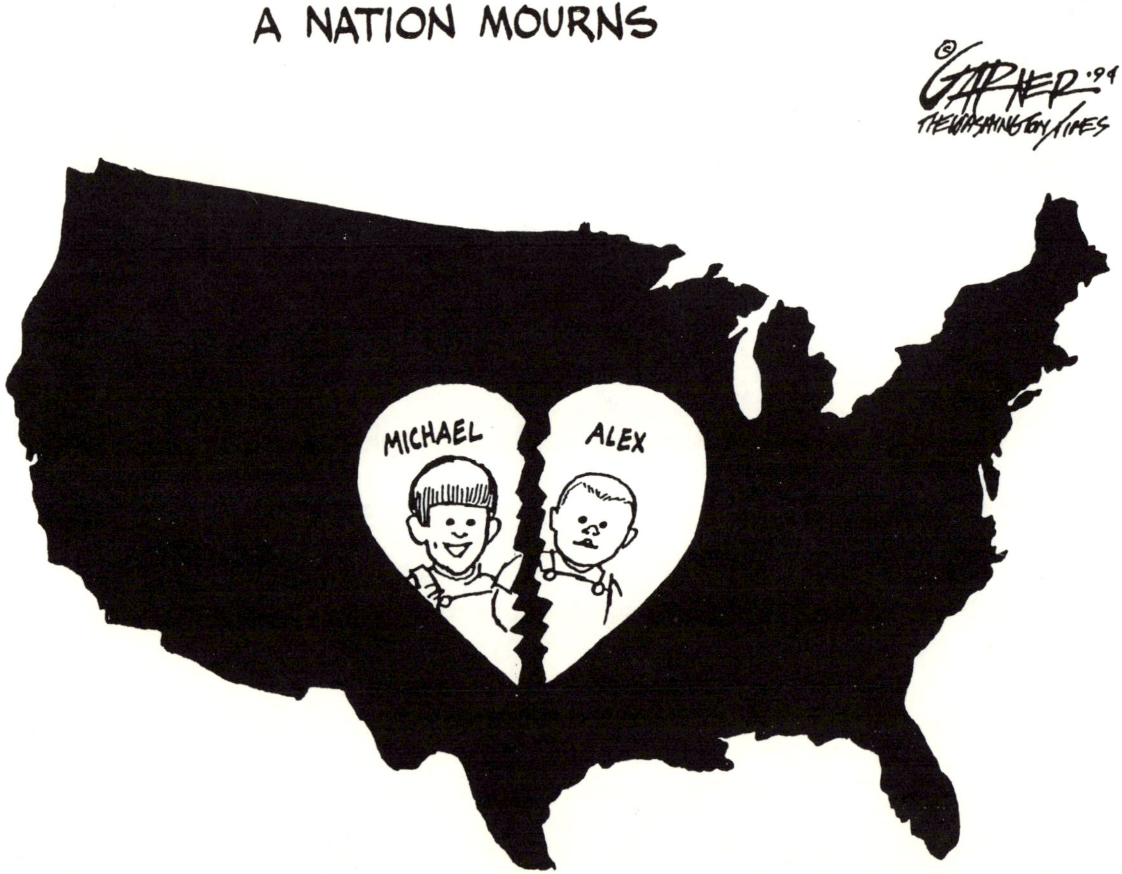
A NATION MOURNS
© GARNER '94
THE WASHINGTON TIMES
MICHAEL
ALEX

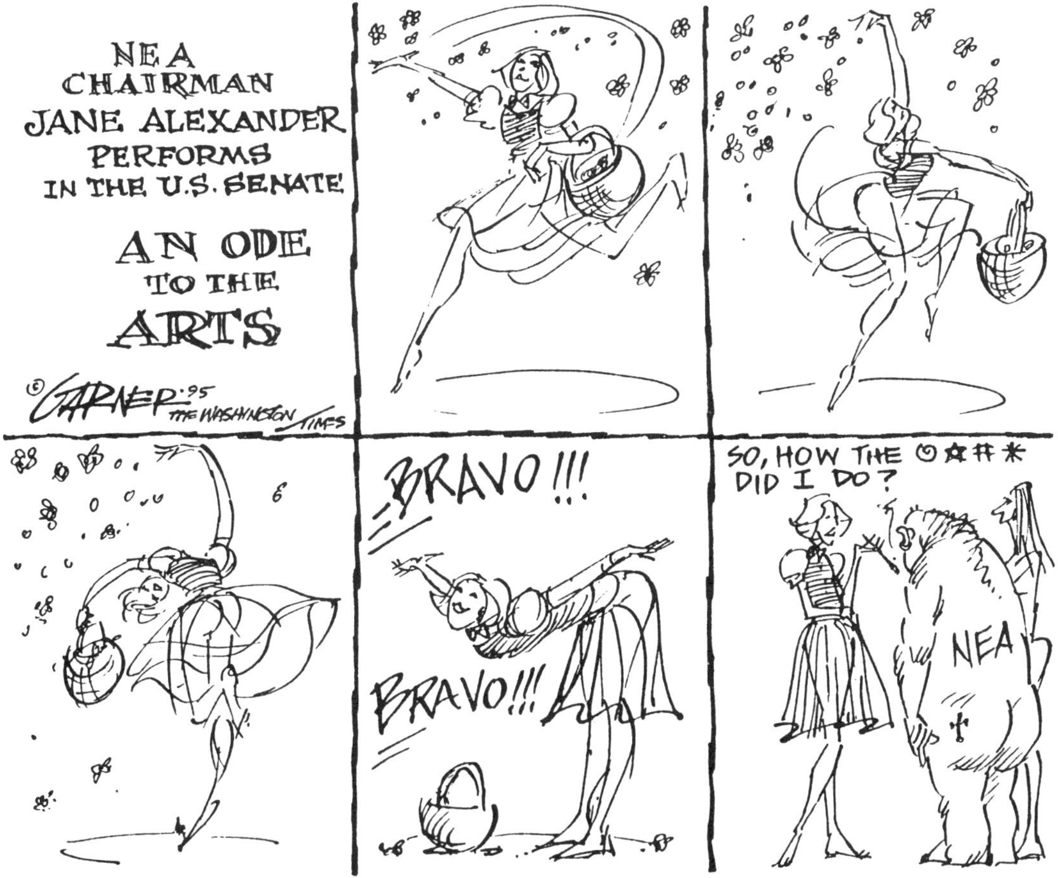
NEA CHAIRMAN JANE ALEXANDER PERFORMS IN THE U.S. SENATE
AN ODE TO THE ARTS
© GARNER '95 THE WASHINGTON TIMES
BRAVO!!!
BRAVO!!!
SO, HOW THE @☆#* DID I DO?
NEA

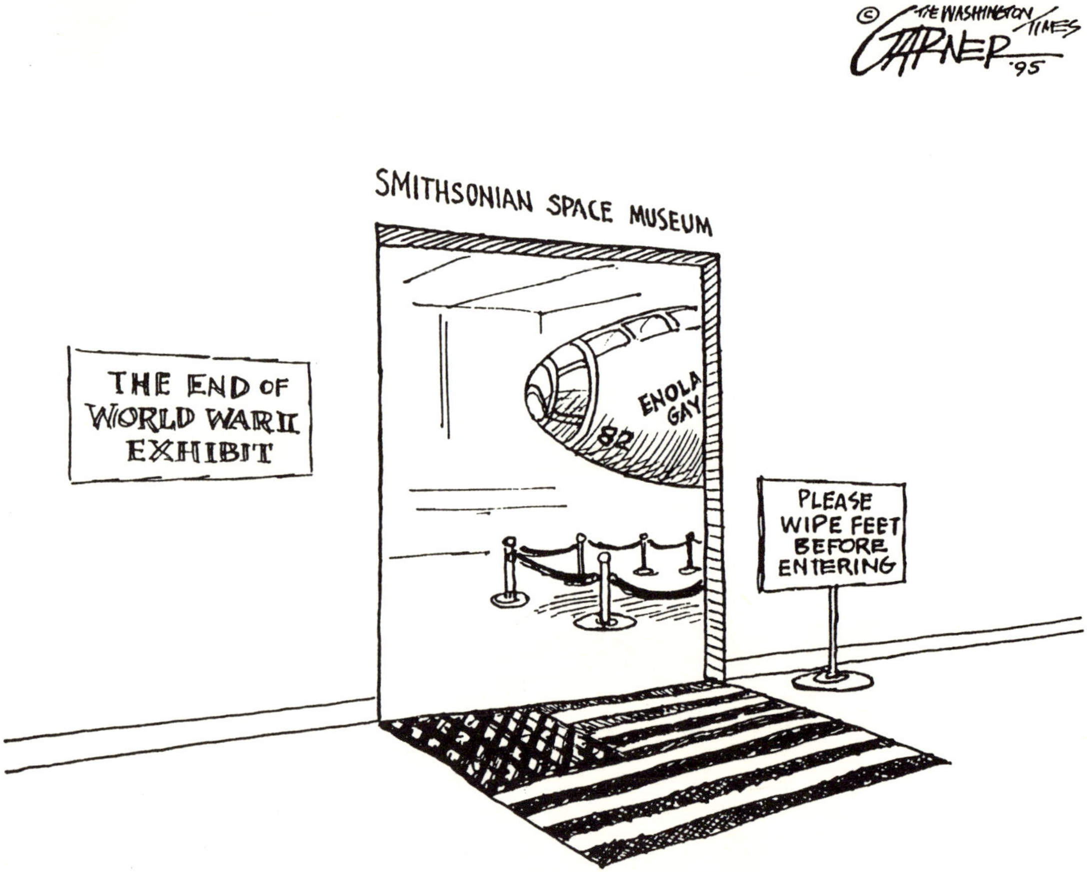
© THE WASHINGTON TIMES GARNER '95
SMITHSONIAN SPACE MUSEUM
THE END OF WORLD WAR II EXHIBIT
ENOLA GAY
82
PLEASE WIPE FEET BEFORE ENTERING

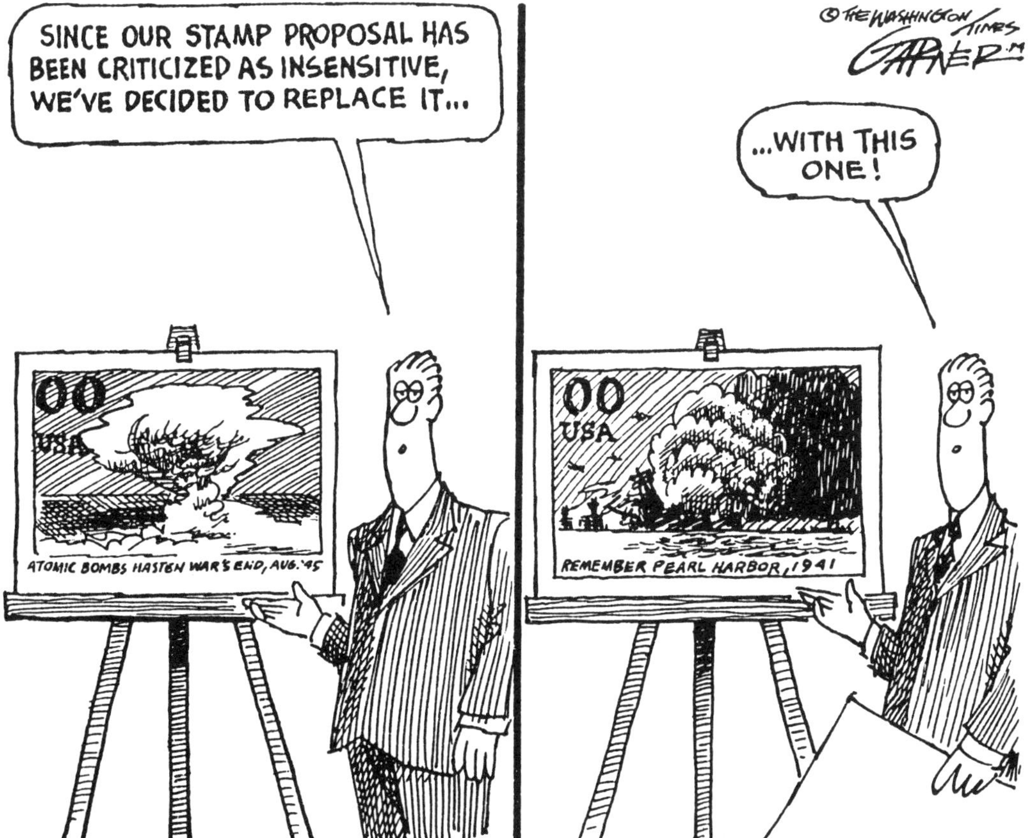
SINCE OUR STAMP PROPOSAL HAS BEEN CRITICIZED AS INSENSITIVE, WE'VE DECIDED TO REPLACE IT...
00 USA
ATOMIC BOMBS HASTEN WAR'S END, AUG. '45
© THE WASHINGTON TIMES
GARNER
...WITH THIS ONE!
00 USA
REMEMBER PEARL HARBOR, 1941

About the Cartoonist

Bill Garner has become, after considerable struggle, a credit to his calling: he is housebroken, pretty well; he handles a knife and fork; only occasionally does he hurl hard objects at those who disagree with him. This is pretty good for an editorial cartoonist—and a Texan.

Though the admissions director refuses to comment, Mr. Garner attended the Texas School of Fine Arts, and then the University of Texas in Austin, working his way through college. He then enlisted in the army and spent seven years in uniform. He was attracted to newspapers when assigned to the *Pacific Stars and Stripes* in Tokyo.

When he left the army, Garner pitched his tent in Washington, D.C., which signifies his basically perverse state of mind. He went to work for *The Washington Star*—which no longer is in business—as a layout artist and part-time editorial cartoonist. From there he signed on with *The Commercial Appeal* in Memphis, where he won a National Headliners Club Award.

He then returned to the nation's capital as editorial cartoonist for *The Washington Times,* where he has won numerous awards, including a National Newspaper Association citation for Best Original Cartoon. He lives in Annapolis, Maryland, with his wife, Patricia, and, so far, has not been asked by the city fathers to seek residence elsewhere.